William R. (William Rathbone) Greg

The Creed of Christendom

Vol. II

William R. (William Rathbone) Greg

The Creed of Christendom
Vol. II

ISBN/EAN: 9783337167578

Printed in Europe, USA, Canada, Australia, Japan

Cover: Foto ©Lupo / pixelio.de

More available books at **www.hansebooks.com**

THE

CREED OF CHRISTENDOM:

ITS FOUNDATIONS CONTRASTED WITH ITS SUPERSTRUCTURE.

BY

WILLIAM RATHBONE GREG.

"The Prayer of Ajax was for Light."

FOURTH EDITION
WITH A NEW INTRODUCTION.

VOL. II.

LONDON:
TRÜBNER & CO., LUDGATE HILL.

MDCCCLXXV.

CONTENTS OF VOLUME II.

CHAPTER XIV.

CHAPTER XV.

CHAPTER XVI.

CHAPTER XVII.

THE CREED OF CHRISTENDOM.

THE
CREED OF CHRISTENDOM.

CHAPTER VIII.

FIDELITY OF THE GOSPEL HISTORY CONTINUED.— MATTHEW.

IN pursuing our inquiry as to the degree of reliance to be placed on Matthew's narrative, we now come to the consideration of those passages in which there is reason to believe that the conversations and discourses of Christ have been incorrectly reported; and that words have been attributed to him which he did not utter, or at least did not utter in the form and context in which they have been transmitted to us. That this should be so, is no more than we ought to expect *à priori*; for, of all things, discourses and remarks are the most likely to be imperfectly heard, inaccurately reported, and materially altered and corrupted in the course of transmission from mouth to mouth. Indeed, as we do not know, and have no reason to believe, that the discourses of Christ were written down

by those who heard them immediately after their
delivery, or indeed much before they reached the
hands of the evangelists, nothing less than a miracle
perpetually renewed for many years could have preserved these traditions perfectly pure and genuine. In
admitting the belief, therefore, that they are in several
points imperfect and inaccurate, we are throwing no
discredit upon the sincerity or capacity, either of the
evangelists or their informants, or the original reporters
of the sayings of Christ ;—we are simply acquiescing
in the alleged operation of natural causes.[1] In some
cases, it is true, we shall find reason to believe that
the published discourses of Christ have been inten-
tionally altered and artificially elaborated by some of
the parties through whose hands they passed ; but in
those days when the very idea of historical criticism
was yet unborn, this might have been done without
any unfairness of purpose. We know that at that
period, historians of far loftier pretensions and more
scientific character, writing in countries of far greater

---

[1] This seems to be admitted even by orthodox writers. Thus
Mr Trench says :—" The most earnest oral tradition will in a little
while lose its distinctness, undergo essential though insensible
modifications.   Apart from all desire to vitiate the committed
word, yet, little by little, the subjective condition of those to
whom it is entrusted, through whom it passes, will infallibly make
itself felt ; and in such treacherous keeping is all which remains
merely in the memories of men, *after a very little while*, rival schools
of disciples will begin to contend not merely how their Master's
words were to be accepted, but *what those very words were.*" —
Trench's Hulsæan Lectures, p. 15.

literary advancement, seldom scrupled to fill up and round off the harangues of their orators and statesmen with whatever they thought appropriate for them to have said—nay, even to elaborate for them long orations out of the most meagre hearsay fragments.[1]

A general view of Matthew, and still more a comparison of his narrative with that of the other three gospels, brings into clear light his entire indifference to chronological or contextual arrangement in his record of the discourses of Christ.   Thus in ch. v., vi., vii., we have crowded into one sermon the teachings and aphorisms which in the other evangelists are spread over the whole of Christ's ministry.   In ch. xiii. we find collected together no less than six parables of similitudes for the kingdom of heaven.   In ch. x. Matthew compresses into one occasion (the sending of the twelve, where many of them are strikingly out of place) a variety of instructions and reflections which must have belonged to a subsequent part of the career of Jesus, where indeed they are placed by the other evangelists.   In ch. xxiv., in the same manner, all the

---

[1] This in fact was the *custom* of antiquity—the rule, not the exception :—See Thucydides, Livy, Sallust, &c. *passim.* We find also (see Acts v. 34-39), that Luke himself did not scruple to adopt this common practice, for he gives us a verbatim speech of Gamaliel delivered in the Sanhedrim, after the apostles had been expressly excluded, and which therefore he could have known only by hearsay report. Moreover, it is certain that this speech must have been Luke's, and not Gamaliel's, since it represents Gamaliel in the year A.D. 34 or 35, as speaking in the past tense of an agitator, Theudas, who did not appear, as we learn from Josephus, till after the year A.D. 44.

prophecies relating to the destruction of Jerusalem and the end of the world are grouped together ; while, in many instances, remarks of Jesus are introduced in the midst of others with which they have no connection, and where they are obviously out of place; as xi. 28-30, and xiii. 12, which evidently belongs to xxv. 29.

In c. xi. 12 is the following expression : "And *from the days of John the Baptist until now,* the kingdom of Heaven suffereth violence, and the violent take it by storm." Now, though the meaning of the passage is difficult to ascertain with precision, yet the expression "from the days of John the Baptist until now," clearly implies that the speaker lived at a considerable distance of time from John ; and though appropriate enough in a man who wrote in the year A.D. 65, or 30 years after John, could not have been used by one who spoke in the year A.D. 30 or 33, while John was yet alive. This passage, therefore, must be regarded as coming from Matthew, not from Jesus.

In c. xvi. 9, 10, is another remark which we may say with perfect certainty was put unwarrantably into the mouth of Christ either by the evangelist, or the source from which he copied. We have already seen that there could not have been more than *one* miraculous feeding of the multitude ; yet Jesus is here made to refer to *two.* The simple and obvious explanation at once forces itself upon our minds, that the evangelist, or his authority, having, in his uncritical and confused conceptions, related two feed-

ings, and finding among his materials a discourse of
Jesus having reference to a miraculous occurrence of
that nature, perceived the inconsistency of narrating
two such events, and yet making Jesus refer to only
one, and therefore added verse 10, by way of correct-
ing the incongruity. The same remark will apply to
Mark also.

The passage at c. xvi. 18, 19, bears obvious marks
of being either an addition to the words of Christ, or
a corruption of them. " He saith unto them, But
whom say ye that I am ? And Simon Peter answered
and said, Thou art the Christ, the Son of the living
God. And Jesus answered and said unto him, Blessed
art thou, Simon Bar-jona : for flesh and blood hath
not revealed it unto thee, but my father which is in
Heaven. And I say also unto thee, That thou art
Peter, and upon this rock I will build my Church ;
and the gates of hell shall not prevail against it. And
I will give unto thee the keys of the kingdom of
Heaven ; and whatsoever thou shalt bind on earth
shall be bound in heaven ; and whatsoever thou shalt
loose on earth shall be loosed in heaven."

The confession by Simon Peter of his belief in the
Messiahship of Jesus is given by all the four evangelists, and there is no reason to question the accuracy
of this part of the narrative. Mark and John, as well
as Matthew, relate that Jesus bestowed on Simon the
surname of Peter, and this part, therefore, may also
be admitted. The remainder of the narrative cor-
responds almost exactly with the equivalent passages

6 THE CREED OF CHRISTENDOM.

in the other evangelists; but the 18th verse has no
parallel in any of them. Moreover, the word "Church"
betrays its later origin. The word ἐκκλησία was used
by the disciples to signify those assemblies and
organizations into which they formed themselves after
the death of Jesus, and is met with frequently in the
epistles, but nowhere in the gospels, except in the
passage under consideration, and one other, which is
equally, or even more, contestable[1]. It was in use
when the gospel was written, but not when the discourse of Jesus was delivered. It must be taken as
belonging, therefore, to Matthew, not to Jesus.

The following verse, conferring spiritual authority,
or, as it is commonly called, "the power of the keys,"
upon Peter, is repeated by Matthew in connection with
another discourse (in c. xviii. 18); and a similar
passage is found in John (c. xx. 23), who, however,
places the promise after the resurrection, and represents it as made to the apostles generally, subsequent
to the descent of the Holy Spirit. But there are considerations which effectually forbid our receiving this
promise, at least as given by Matthew, as having
really emanated from Christ. In the *first* place, in
both passages it occurs in connection with the sus-
picious word " Church," and indicates an ecclesiastical
as opposed to a Christian origin. *Secondly,* Mark,

---

[1] C. xviii. 17. " If he shall neglect to hear them, tell it unto the
Church; but if he neglect to hear the Church, let him be unto
thee as a heathen man and a publican." The whole passage, with
its context, betokens an ecclesiastical, not a Christian spirit.

who narrates the previous conversation, omits this promise so honourable and distinguishing to Peter, which it is impossible for those who consider him as Peter's mouthpiece, or amanuensis, to believe he would have done, had any such promise been actually made.[1] Luke, the companion and intimate of Paul and other apostles, equally omits all mention of this singular conversation. *Thirdly*, not only do we know Peter's utter unfitness to be the depositary of such a fearful power, from his impetuosity and instability of character, and Christ's thorough perception of this unfitness, but we find that immediately after it is said to have been conferred upon him, his Lord addresses him indignantly by the epithet of Satan, and rebukes him for his presumption and unspirituality ; and shortly afterwards this very man thrice denied his master. Can any one maintain it to be conceivable that Jesus should have conferred the awful power of deciding the salvation or damnation of his fellowmen upon one so frail, so faulty, and so fallible ? *Does any one believe that he did ?* We cannot, therefore, regard the 19th verse otherwise than as an unwarranted addition to the words of Jesus, and painfully indicative of the growing pretensions of the Church at the time the gospel was compiled.

In xxiii. 35, we have the following passage purporting to be uttered by Jesus in the course of his denunciations against the Scribes and Pharisees :

---

[1] See Thirlwall, cvii., Introd. to Schleiermacher.

"That upon you may come all the righteous blood shed upon the earth, from the blood of righteous Abel, unto the blood of Zacharias, son of Barachias, whom ye slew between the temple and the altar." Now, two Zachariases are recorded in history as having been thus slain : Zacharias, son of Jehoiada, 850 years before Christ (2 Chron. xxiv. 20), and Zacharias, son of Baruch, 35 years after Christ (Joseph. Bell. Jud. iv. 4).[1] But when we reflect that Jesus could scarcely have intended to refer to a murder committed 850 years before his time as terminating the long series of Jewish crimes; and moreover, that at the period the evangelist wrote, the assassination of the son of Baruch was a recent event, and one likely to have made a deep impression, and that the circumstances of the murder (between the Temple and the Altar) apply much more closely to the second than to the first Zacharias, we cannot hesitate to admit the conclusion of Hug, Eichhorn, and other critics,[2] that the Zacharias mentioned by Josephus was the one intended by Matthew.   Hug says—

"There cannot be a doubt, if we attend to the name, the fact and its circumstances, and the object of Jesus in citing it, that it was the same Ζαχαρίας

It is true that there was a third Zacharias, the Prophet, also son of a Barachias, who lived about 500 years before Christ ; but this man could not have been the one intended by Matthew, for no record exists, or appears to have existed, of the manner of his death, and in his time the Temple was in ruins.—See Hennell, p. 81, note.

[2] Hug, p. 314. Thirlwall, p. xcix., note.

Βαρούχου, who, according to Josephus, a short time before the destruction of Jerusalem, was unjustly slain in the temple. The name is the same, the murder, and the remarkable circumstances which distinguished it, correspond, as well as the character of the man. Moreover, when Jesus says that all the innocent blood which had been shed, from Abel to Zacharias, should be avenged upon 'this generation,' the ἀπὸ and ἕω; denote the beginning and the end of a period. This period ends with Zacharias; he was to be the last before the vengeance should be executed. The threatened vengeance, however, was the ruin of Jerusalem, which immediately followed his death. Must it not, then, have been the same Zacharias whose death is distinguished in history, among so many murdered, as the only righteous man between Ananias and the destruction of the Holy City? The Zacharias mentioned in the Chronicles is not the one here intended. He was a son of Jehoiada, and was put to death, not between the temple and the altar, or ἐν μέσῳ τῷ νάῳ, but in the court; nor was he the last of those unjustly slain, or one with whom an epoch in the Jewish annals terminates."

Here, then, we have an anachronism strikingly illustrative of that confusion of mind which characterises this evangelist, and which betrays at the same time that an unwarrantable liberty has been taken by some one with the language of Jesus. He is here represented as speaking in the past tense of an event which did not occur till 35 years after his death, and which, consequently, though fresh and present to the mind of the *writer*, could not have been in the mind of the *speaker*, unless prophetically; in which case it would have been expressed in the future, not in the past tense[1]; and would, moreover, have been wholly unintelligible to his hearers. If, therefore, as there seems no reason to doubt, the evangelist intended to specify the Zacharias mentioned by Josephus, he was guilty of putting into the mouth of Jesus words which Jesus never uttered.

In ch. xxviii. 19, is another passage which we may say with almost certainty never came from the mouth of Christ: "Go ye therefore and teach all nations, baptising them in the name of the Father, and of the Son, and of the Holy Ghost." That this definite form of baptism proceeded from Jesus, is opposed by the fact that such an allocation of the Father, Son, and Spirit, does not elsewhere appear, except as a form of salutation in the epistles; while as a definite form of baptism it is nowhere met with throughout the New Testament. Moreover, it was not the form *used*, and could scarcely therefore have been the form *commanded;* for in the apostolic epistles, and even in the Acts, the form always is " baptizing into Christ Jesus,"

---

[1] " Hug imagines," says Bishop Thirlwall, loc. cit., that Christ *predicted* the death of this Zacharias, son of Barachias, but that St Matthew, who saw the prediction accomplished, expressed his knowledge of the fact by using the past tense." *But should this then have been the aorist ἐφονεύσατε?*

or, "into the name of the Lord Jesus;"[1] while the threefold reference to God, Jesus, and the Holy Ghost, is only found in ecclesiastical writers, as Justin. Indeed, the formula in Matthew sounds so exactly as if it had been borrowed from the ecclesiastical ritual, that it is difficult to avoid the supposition that it was transferred thence into the mouth of Jesus. Many critics, in consequence, regard it as a subsequent interpolation.

There are two other classes of discourses attributed to Jesus both in this and in the other gospels, over the character of which much obscurity hangs—those in which he is said to have foretold his own death and resurrection; and those in which he is represented as speaking of his second advent. The instances of the first are in Matthew *five* in number, in Mark *four*, in Luke *four*, and in John *three.*[2]

Now we will at once concede that it is extremely probable that Christ might easily have foreseen that a career and conduct like his could, in such a time and country, terminate only in a violent and cruel death; and that indications of such an impending fate thickened fast around him as his ministry drew nearer to a close. It is even possible, though in the highest

---

[1] Rom. vi. 3. Gal. iii. 27. Acts ii. 38; viii. 16; x. 48; xix. 5.
[2] Matth. xii. 40; xvi. 21; xvii. 9, 22, 23; xx. 17-19; xxvi. 3. Mark viii. 31; ix. 10, 31; x. 33; xiv. 28. Luke ix. 22, 44; xviii. 32, 33; xxii. 15. John ii. 20-22; iii. 14; xii. 32, 33; all very questionable.

degree unlikely,[1] that his study of the prophets might have led him to the conclusion that the expected Messiah, whose functions he believed himself sent to fulfil, was to be a suffering and dying Prince. We will not even dispute that he might have been so amply endowed with the spirit of prophecy as distinctly to foresee his approaching crucifixion and resurrection. But we find in the evangelists themselves insuperable difficulties in the way of admitting the belief that he actually did predict these events, in the language, or with anything of the precision, which is there ascribed to him.

In the fourth gospel, these predictions are three in number,[2] and in all the language is doubtful, mysterious, and obscure, and the interpretation commonly put upon them is not that suggested by the words themselves, nor that which suggested itself to those who heard them ; but is one affixed to them by the evangelist after the event supposed to be referred to ; it is an *interpretatio ex eventu.*[3] In the three synoptical

---

[1] It was in the highest degree unlikely, because this was neither the interpretation put upon the prophecies among the Jews of that time, nor their natural signification, but it was an interpretation of the disciples *ex eventu.*

[2] We pass over those touching intimations of approaching separation contained in the parting discourses of Jesus during and immediately preceding the last supper, as there can be little doubt that at that time his fate was so imminent as to have become evident to any acute observer, without the supposition of supernatural information.

[3] In the case of the first of these predictions—" Destroy this temple, and in three days I will raise it up,"—we can scarcely

gospels, however, the predictions are numerous, precise, and conveyed in language which it was impossible to mistake. Thus (in Matt. xx. 18, 19, and parallel passages), " Behold we go up to Jerusalem, and the Son of Man shall be betrayed unto the chief priests, and unto the Scribes, and they shall condemn him to death, and shall deliver him to the Gentiles to mock, and to scourge, and to crucify him : and the third day he shall rise again." Language such as this, definite, positive, explicit, and circumstantial, if really uttered, could not have been misunderstood, but must have made a deep and ineradicable impression on all who heard it, especially when repeated, as it is stated to. have been, on several distinct occasions. Yet we find ample proof that *no such impression was made ;*— that the disciples had no conception of their Lord's approaching death—still less of his resurrection ;— and that so far from their expecting either of these events, both, when they occurred, took them entirely by surprise ;—they were utterly confounded by the one, and could not believe the other.

admit that the words were used by Jesus (if uttered by him at all) in the sense ascribed to them by John ; since the words were spoken *in the temple*, and in answer to the demand for a sign, and could therefore only have conveyed, and have been intended to convey, the meaning which we know they actually did convey to the inquiring Jews. In the two other cases (or three, if we reckon viii. 28 as one), the language of Jesus is too indefinite for us to know what meaning he intended it to convey. The expression " to be lifted up," is thrice used, and may mean exaltation, glorification (its natural signification), or, artificially and figuratively, *might* be intended to refer to his crucifixion.

We find them shortly after (nay, in one instance instantly after) these predictions were uttered, disputing which among them should be greatest in their coming dominion (Matt. xx. 24 ; Mark ix. 35 ; Luke xxii. 25) ;—glorying in the idea of thrones, and asking for seats on his right hand and on his left, in his Messianic kingdom (Matt. xix. 28, xx. 21 ; Mark x. 37 ; Luke xxii. 30) ; which, when he approached Jerusalem, they thought " would immediately appear" (Luke xix. 11, xxiv. 21). When Jesus was arrested in the garden of Gethsemane, they first attempted resistance, and then " forsook him and fled ;" and so completely were they scattered, that it was left for one of the Sanhedrim, Joseph of Arimathea, to provide even ·for his decent burial ;—while the women who " watched afar off," and were still faithful to his memory, brought spices to embalm the body—a sure sign, were any needed, that the idea of his resurrection had never entered into their minds. Further, when the women reported his resurrection to the disciples, " their words seemed to them as idle tales, and they believed them not " (Luke xxiv. 11). The conversation, moreover, of the two disciples on the road to Emmaus is sufficient proof that the resurrection of their Lord was a conception which had never crossed their thoughts ; — and, finally, according to John, when Mary found the body gone, her only notion was that it must have been removed by the gardener (xx. 15).

All this shows, beyond, we think, the possibility

of question, that the crucifixion and resurrection of Jesus were wholly unexpected by his disciples. If further proof were wanted, we find it in the words of the evangelists, who repeatedly intimate (as if struck by the incongruity we have pointed out) that they " knew not," or " understood not," these sayings. (Mark ix. 31 ; Luke ix. 45, xviii. 34 ; John xx. 9.)

Here, then, we have two distinct statements, which mutually exclude and contradict each other. If Jesus really foretold his death and resurrection in the terms recorded in the gospels, it is inconceivable that the disciples should have *misunderstood* him ; for no words could be more positive, precise, or intelligible, than those which he is said to have repeatedly addressed to them. Neither could they have *forgotten* what had been so strongly urged upon their memory by their Master, as completely as it is evident from their subsequent conduct they actually did.[1] They might, indeed, have *disbelieved* his prediction (as Peter appears in the first instance to have done), but in that case, his crucifixion would have led them to expect his resurrection, or, at all events, to think of it :—which it did not. The fulfilment of one prophecy would necessarily have recalled the other to their minds.

The conclusion, therefore, is inevitable—that the predictions were ascribed to Jesus after the event, not

---

[1] Moreover, if they had so completely forgotten these predictions, whence did the evangelists derive them ?

really uttered by him. It is, indeed, very probable that, as gloomy anticipations of his own death pressed upon his mind, and became stronger and more confirmed as the danger came nearer, he endeavoured to communicate these apprehensions to his followers, in order to prepare them for an event so fatal to their worldly hopes. That he did so, we think the conversations during, and previous to, the last supper afford ample proof. These vague intimations of coming evil —*intermingled and relieved, doubtless, by strongly expressed convictions of a future existence of reunion and reward*, disbelieved or disregarded by the disciples at the time—recurred to their minds after all was over ; and gathering strength, and expanding in definiteness and fulness during constant repetition for nearly forty years, had, at the period when the evangelists wrote, become consolidated into the fixed prophetic form in which they have been transmitted to us.

Another argument may be adduced, strongly confirmatory of this view. Jesus is repeatedly represented as affirming that his expected sufferings and their glorious termination must take place, *in order that the prophecies might be fulfilled*. (Matt. xxvi. 24, 54 ; Mark ix. 12, xiv. 49 ; Luke xiii. 33, xviii. 31, xxii. 37, xxiv. 27.) Now, the passion of the disciples for representing everything connected with Jesus as the fulfilment of prophecy, explains why they should have sought, after his death, for passages which might be supposed to prefigure it,[1]—and why these accommodations of prophecy should, in process of time, and of transmission, have been attributed to Jesus himself. But if we assume, as is commonly done, that these references to prophecy really proceeded from Christ in the first instance, we are landed in the inadmissible, or at least the embarrassing and unorthodox conclusion, that he interpreted the prophets erroneously. To confine ourselves to the principal passages only, a profound grammatical and historical exposition has convincingly shown, to all who are in a condition to liberate themselves from dogmatic presuppositions, that in none of these is there any allusion to the sufferings of Christ.[2]

One of these references to prophecy in Matthew has evident marks of being an addition to the traditional words of Christ by the evangelist himself. In Matt.

---

[1] "There were sufficient motives for the Christian legend thus to put into the mouth of Jesus, after the event, a prediction of the particular features of his passion, especially of the ignominious crucifixion.' The more a Christ crucified became "to the Jews a stumbling-block, and to the Greeks foolishness" (1 Cor. i. 23), the more need was there to remove the offence by every possible means; and as among the subsequent events, the resurrection especially served as a *retrospective* cancelling of that shameful death, so it must have been earnestly desired to take the sting from that offensive catastrophe *beforehand* also ; and this could not be done more effectually than by such a minute prediction."—Strauss, iii. 54, where this idea is fully developed.

[2] Even Dr Arnold admitted this fully. (Sermons on Interpretations of Prophecy, Preface.)

xvi. 4, we have the following : " A wicked and adul-
terous generation seeketh after a sign ; and there
shall no sign be given to it but the sign of the
Prophet Jonas." The same expression precisely is
recorded by Luke (xi. 29), with this addition, showing
what the reference to Jonas really meant : " For as
Jonas was a sign to the Ninevites, so also shall the
Son of Man be to this generation. The men of
Nineveh shall rise up in judgment against this generation, and shall condemn it ; *for they repented at
the preaching of Jonas ; and, behold, a greater than
Jonas is here.*" But when Matthew *repeats* the same
answer of Jesus in answer to the same demand for a
sign (xii. 40), he adds the explanation of the reference, " for as Jonas was three days and three nights
in the whale's belly, so shall the Son of Man be three
days and three nights [which Jesus was *not*, but only
one day and two nights[1]] in the heart of the earth ;"
—and he then proceeds with the same context as
Luke.

The prophecies of the second coming of Christ
(Matt. xxiv. Mark xiii. Luke xvii. 22-37 ; xxi.
5-36) are mixed up with those of the destruction of
Jerusalem by Titus in a manner which has long been
the perplexity and despair of orthodox commentators.
The obvious meaning of the passages which contain
these predictions—the sense in which they were
evidently understood by the evangelists who wrote
them down—the sense which we know from many

Nay : possibly only a few hours.

sources[1] they conveyed to the minds of the early
Christians—clearly is, that the coming of Christ to
judge the world should follow *immediately*[2] ("immediately," "in those days,") the destruction of the Holy
City, and should take place during the lifetime of the
then existing generation. "Verily I say unto you,
This generation shall not pass away till all these
things be fulfilled." (Matt. xxiv. 34; Mark xiii. 30;
Luke xxi. 32.) "There be some standing here that
shall not taste of death till they see the son of Man
coming in his kingdom" (Matth. xvi. 28). "Verily
I say unto you, Ye shall not have gone over the cities
of Israel, till the Son of Man be come" (Matth. x. 23).
"If I will that he tarry till I come, what is that to
thee?" (John xxi. 23).

Now if these predictions really proceeded from
Jesus, he was entirely in error on the subject, and the
prophetic spirit was not in him; for not only did his
advent not follow close on the destruction of Jerusalem,
but 1800 years have since elapsed, and neither he nor
the preliminary signs which were to announce him,
have yet appeared. If these predictions did *not* proceed from him, then the evangelist has taken the

---

[1] See 1 Cor. x. 11; xv. 51. Phil. iv. 5. 1 Thess. iv. 15. James
v. 8. 1 Peter iv. 7. 1 John ii. 18. Rev. i. 1, 3; xxii. 7, 10, 12, 20

[2] An apparent contradiction to this is presented by Matth. xxiv.
14; Matth. xiii. 10, where we are told that "the gospel must be
first preached to all nations." It appears, however, from Col. i. 5,
6, 23 (see also Romans x. 18), that St Paul considered this to have
been already accomplished in his time.

liberty of putting into the mouth of Christ words and announcements which Christ never uttered.

Much desperate ingenuity has been exerted to separate the predictions relating to Jerusalem from those relating to the Advent; but these exertions have been neither creditable nor successful ; and they have already been examined and refuted at great length. Moreover, they are rendered necessary only by two previous *assumptions :* first, that Jesus cannot have been mistaken as to the future ; and, secondly, that he really uttered these predictions. Now, neither of these assumptions is capable of proof. The first we shall not dispute, because we have no adequate means of coming to a conclusion on the subject. But as to the second assumption, we think there are several indications that, though the predictions in question were current among the Christians when the gospels were composed, yet that they did not, at least as handed down to us, proceed from the lips of Christ; but were, as far as related to the second advent, the unauthorised anticipations of the disciples ; and, as far as related to the destruction of the city, partly gathered from the denunciations of Old Testament prophecy, and partly from actual knowledge of the events which passed under their eyes.

In the *first* place, it is not admissible that Jesus could have been so true a prophet as to one part of the prediction, and so entirely in error as to the other, both parts referring equally to future events. *Secondly*, the three gospels in which these predictions occur, are allowed to have been written between the years 65 and 72 A.D., or during the war which ended in the destruction of Jerusalem[1]; that is, they were written during and after the events which they predict. They may, therefore, either have been entirely drawn from the events, or have been vaguely in existence before, but have derived their definiteness and precision from the events. And we have already seen in the case of the first evangelist, that he, at least, did not scruple to eke out and modify the predictions he recorded, from his own experience of their fulfilment. *Thirdly*, the parallel passages, both in Matthew and Mark, contain an expression twice repeated—"the elect"—which we can say almost with certainty was unknown in the time of Christ, though frequently found in the epistles, and used, at the time the gospels were composed, to designate the members of the Christian Church.

---

[1] The war began by Vespasian's entering Galilee in the beginning of the year A.D. 67, and the city was taken in the autumn of A.D. 70.

CHAPTER IX.

MANY of the criticisms contained in the two last chapters—tending to prove that Matthew's Gospel contains several statements not strictly accurate, and attributes to Jesus several expressions and discourses which were not really uttered by him—are equally applicable both to Mark and Luke. The similarity —not to say identity—of the greater portion of Mark's narrative with that of Matthew, leaves no room for doubt either that one evangelist copied from the other, or that both employed the same documents, or oral narratives, in the compilation of their histories. Our own clear conviction is that Mark was the earliest in time, and far the most correct in fact.

As we have already stated, we attach little weight to the tradition of the second century, that the second gospel was written by Mark, the companion of Peter. It originated with Papias, whose works are now lost, but who was stated to be a "weak man" by Eusebius, who records a few fragments of his writings. But if the tradition be correct, the omissions in this gospel, as compared with the first, are significant enough. It

omits entirely the genealogies, the miraculous conception, several matters relating to Peter (especially his
walking on the water, and the commission of the
keys),[1] and everything miraculous or improbable relating to the resurrection[2]—everything, in fact, but the
simple statement that the body was missing, and that
a " young man" assured the visitors that Christ was
risen.

In addition to these, there are two or three peculiarities in the discourses of Jesus, as recorded by Mark,
which indicate that the evangelist thought it necessary
and allowable slightly to modify the language of them,'
in order to suit them to the ideas or the feelings of the
Gentile converts; if, as is commonly supposed, it was
principally designed for them. We copy a few
instances of these, though resting little upon them.

Matthew, who wrote for the Jews, has the following passage, in the injunctions pronounced by Jesus
on the sending forth of the twelve apostles : " Go not
into the way of the Gentiles, and into any city of the
Samaritans enter ye not. But go rather to the lost
sheep of the house of Israel." (x. 5.) Mark, who
wrote for the Gentiles, *omits entirely this unpalatable
charge.* (vi. 7-13.)

Matthew (xv. 24), in the story of the Canaanitish
woman, makes Jesus say, " I am not sent but to the

---

[1] See Thirlwall's remarks on this subject. Introd. cvii.
[2] We must not forget that the real genuine Gospel of Mark
terminates with the 8th verse of the 16th chapter.

lost sheep of the house of Israel." Mark (vii. 26) *omits this expression entirely,* and modifies the subsequent remark. In Matthew it is thus :—" It is not meet to take the children's bread and cast it unto the dogs." In Mark it is softened by the preliminary, " *Let the children first be filled,*" &c.

Matthew (xxiv. 20), "But pray ye that your flight be not in the winter, *neither on the Sabbath day.*" Mark omits the last clause, which would have had no meaning for any but the Jews, whose Sabbath day's journey was by law restricted to a small distance.

In the promise given to the disciples, in answer to Peter's question, " Behold we have forsaken all, and followed thee ; what shall we have therefore ?" The following verse, given by Matthew (xix. 28), *is omitted by Mark* (x. 28) :—" Verily I say unto you, " That ye which have followed me, in the regeneration, when the Son of Man shall sit in the throne of his glory, ye also shall sit upon twelve thrones, judging the twelve tribes of Israel."[1]

The Gospel of Luke, which is a work in some respects of more pretension, and unquestionably of more literary merit, than the two first, will require a few additional observations. The remarks we have made on the prophecies of his own sufferings and resurrection, alleged by Matthew and Mark to have

[1] [It is, however, almost impossible to resist the inference that we have here one of the evangelist's unwarranted ascriptions to Jesus of words which he never uttered, when we compare the subsequent contradiction—**xx**. 21-26.]

been uttered by Jesus, apply equally to Luke's narrative, in which similar passages occur ; and in these, therefore, we must admit that the third evangelist, like the other two, ascribed to Jesus discourses which never really proceeded from him.[1] But besides these, there are several passages in Luke which bear an equally apocryphal character, some of which it will be interesting to notice.

The first chapter, from verse 5-80, contains the account of the annunciation and birth of John the Baptist, with all the marvellous circumstances attending it, and also the annunciation to Mary, and the miraculous conception of Jesus—an account exhibiting many remarkable discrepancies with the corresponding narrative in Matthew. We are spared the necessity of a detailed investigation of this chapter by the agreement of the most learned critics, both of the orthodox and sceptical schools, in considering the narrative as poetical and legendary. It is examined at great length by Strauss, who is at the head of the most daring class of the Biblical Commentators of Germany, and by Schleiermacher, who ranks first among the learned divines of that country. The latter (in the work translated by one of our most erudite and liberal

---

[1] The remark will perhaps occur to some, that the circumstance of *three* evangelists ascribing the same language to Jesus, is a strong proof that he really uttered it. But the fallacy of this argument will be apparent when we remember that there is ample evidence that they all drew from the same sources, namely, the extant current tradition.

Prelates, and already often referred to), writes thus, pp. 25-7 :—

"Thus, then, we begin by detaching the first chapter as an originally independent composition. If we consider it in this light somewhat more closely, we cannot resist the impression that it was originally rather a little poetical work than a properly-historical narrative. The latter supposition, in its strictest sense at all events, no one will adopt, or contend that the angel Gabriel announced the advent of the Messiah in figures so purely Jewish, and in expressions taken mostly from the Old Testament ; or that the alternate song between Elizabeth and Mary actually took place in the manner described ; or that Zacharias, at the instant of recovering his speech, made use of it to utter the hymn, without being disturbed by the joy and surprise of the company, by which the narrator himself allows his description to be interrupted. At all events we should then be obliged to suppose that the author made additions of his own, and enriched the historical narrative by the lyrical effusions of his own genius." . . . "If we consider the whole grouping of the narrative, there naturally presents itself to us a pleasing little composition, completely in the style and manner of several Jewish poems, still extant among our apocryphal writings, written in all probability originally in Aramaic by a Christian of the more liberal Judaising school." . . . "There are many other statements which I should not venture to pronounce historical, but would rather explain by the occasion the poet had for them. To these belongs, in the first place, John's being a late-born child, which is evidently only imagined for the sake of analogy with several heroes of Hebrew antiquity ; and, in the next place, the relation between the ages of John and Christ, and likewise the consanguinity of Mary and Elizabeth, which besides, it is difficult to reconcile with the assertion of John (John i. 33), that he did not know Christ before his baptism." .

Strauss's analysis of the chapter is in the highest degree masterly and convincing, and we think cannot fail to satisfy all whose minds have been trained in habits of logical investigation. After showing at great length the unsatisfactoriness and inadmissibility of both the supernatural and rationalistic interpretations, he shows, by a comparison of similar legends in the Old Testament—the birth of Ishmael, Isaac, Samuel, and Samson, in particular—how exactly the narrative in Luke is framed in accordance with the established ideas and rules of Hebrew poetry.[1]

---

[1] We cannot agree with one of Strauss's critics (see Prospective Review, Nov. 1846), that the evident poetical character of the first chapters of Matthew and Luke, their similarity with parts of the apocryphal gospels and early Christian writings, and their dissimilarity in tone with the rest of the gospels with which they are incorporated, are sufficient to decide the question against their genuineness. If this argument were valid, we must pronounce against the genuineness of other passages of our gospels on the same ground—e. g. the miracle of Cana—the miraculous draught of fishes—and the piece of money in the fish's mouth—and others. The genuineness of these initial chapters has often been denied, but without sufficient warrant from external evidence.

"The scattered traits," said he,[1] "respecting the late birth of different distinguished men, as recorded in the Old Testament, blended themselves into a compound image in the mind of the author, whence he selected the features most appropriate to his present subject. Of the children born of aged parents, Isaac is the most ancient prototype. As it is said of Zacharias and Elizabeth, 'they were both advanced in days,' so Abraham and Sarah 'were advanced in days,'[2] when they were promised a son. It is likewise from this history that the incredulity of the father on account of the advanced age of both parents, and the demand of a sign, are borrowed. As Abraham, when Jehovah promised him a numerous posterity through Isaac, who should inherit the land of Canaan, doubtingly inquires, 'Whereby shall I know that I shall inherit it?'—so Zacharias, 'Whereby shall I know this?' The incident of the angel announcing the birth of the Baptist is taken from the history of another late-born son, Samson. The command which before his birth predestined the Baptist—whose later ascetic mode of life was known—to be a Nazarite, is taken from the same source. Both were to be consecrated to God from the womb, and the same diet was prescribed for both.[3] . . . The lyrical effusions in Luke are from the history of Samuel. As Samuel's

---

[1] Leben Jesu, i. 118, et seq.
[2] The original words are the same in both instances.
[3] Compare Luke i. 15, with Judges xiii. 4, 5, and Numbers vi. 3.

mother, when consigning him to the care of the High
Priest, breaks forth into a hymn, so does the father of
John at the circumcision; though the particular expressions in the canticle uttered by Mary, in the same chapter,
have a closer resemblance to Hannah's song of praise,
than that of Zacharias. The only supernatural incident
of the narrative, of which the Old Testament offers no
precise analogy, is the dumbness. But if it be borne
in mind that the asking and receiving a sign from
heaven in confirmation of a promise or prophecy was
common among the Hebrews (Isaiah vii. 11); that
the temporary loss of one of the senses was the peculiar punishment inflicted after a heavenly vision (Acts
ix. 8, 17); that Daniel became dumb while the angel
was speaking with him, and did not recover his speech
till the angel had touched his lips and opened his
mouth (Dan. x. 15); the origin of this incident also
will be found in legend, and not in historical fact. So
that here we stand upon purely mythico-poetical
ground ; the only historical reality which we can hold
fast as positive matter of fact being this :—the impression made by John the Baptist, in virtue of his
ministry, and his relation to Jesus, was so powerful
as to lead to the subsequent glorification of his birth
in connection with the Christian legend of the birth of
the Messiah."

In the second chapter we have the account of the
birth of Jesus, and the accompanying apparition of a
multitude of angels to shepherds in the fields near
Bethlehem—as to the historical foundation of which

Strauss and Schleiermacher are at variance; the
former regarding it as wholly mythical, and the latter
as based upon an actual occurrence, imperfectly
remembered in after times, when the celebrity of Jesus
caused every contribution to the history of his birth
and infancy to be eagerly sought for. All that we
can say on the subject with any certainty is, that the
tone of the narrative is legendary. The poetical
rhapsody of Simeon when Jesus was presented in the
temple may be passed over with the same remark ;—
but the 33rd verse, where we are told that " Joseph
and his mother marvelled at those things which were
spoken of him," proves clearly one of two things :—
either the unhistorical character of the Song of Simeon,
and of the consequent astonishment of the parents of
Jesus—or the unreality of the miraculous annunciation
and conception. It is impossible, if an angel had
actually announced to Mary the birth of the divine
child in the language, or in anything resembling the
language, recorded in Luke i. 31-35 ; and if, in
accordance with that announcement, Mary had found
herself with child before she had any *natural* possibility of being so—that she should have felt any
astonishment whatever at the prophetic announcement
of Simeon, so consonant with the angelic promise,
especially when occurring after the miraculous vision
of the Shepherds, which, we are told, "she pondered
in her heart." Schleiermacher has felt this difficulty,
and endeavours to evade it by considering the first and
second chapters to be two monographs originally by

different hands, which Luke incorporated into his gospel. This was very probably the case ; but it does not avoid the difficulty, as it involves giving up ii. 33 as an unauthorised and incorrect statement.

The genealogy of Jesus, as given in the third chapter, may be in the main correct, though there are some perplexities in one portion of it ; but if the previous narrative be correct, it is not the genealogy of Jesus at all, but only of Joseph, who was no relation to him whatever, but simply his guardian. On the other hand, if the preparer of the genealogy, or the evangelist who records it, knew or believed the story of the miraculous conception, we can conceive no reason for his admitting a pedigree which · is either wholly meaningless, or destructive of his previous statements. The insertion in verse 23, "as was supposed," whether by the evangelist or a subsequent copyist, merely shows that whoever made it perceived the incongruity, but preferred neutralizing the genealogy to omitting it.[1]

The account given by Luke (iii. 21) of the visible and audible signs from heaven at the Baptism of Jesus, has been very generally felt and allowed to be incompatible with the inquiry subsequently made by John the Baptist (vii. 19) as to whether Jesus were the Messiah or not ; and the incongruity is considered

---

[1] The whole story of the Incarnation, however, is effectually discredited by the fact that none of the Apostles or sacred Historians make any subsequent reference to it, or indicate any knowledge of it.

to indicate inaccuracy or interpolation in one of the two narratives. It is justly held impossible that if John had seen the Holy Spirit descending upon Jesus, and had heard a heavenly voice declaring him to be the beloved Son of God, he could ever have entertained a doubt that he was the Messiah, whose coming he himself had just announced [1] (ver. 16). According to Luke, as he now stands, John expected the Messiah—described himself as his forerunner—saw at the moment of the Baptism a supernatural shape, and heard a supernatural voice announcing Jesus to be that Messiah;—and yet, shortly after—on hearing, too, of miracles which should have confirmed his belief, had it ever wavered—he sends a message implying doubt (or rather ignorance), and asking the question which Heaven itself had already answered in his hearing. Some commentators have endeavoured to escape from the difficulty by pleading that the appearances at Baptism might have been perceptible to Jesus alone ; and they have adduced the use of the second

---

[1] Neander conceives that doubt may have assailed the mind of John in his dismal prison, and led to a transient questioning of his earlier conviction, and that it was in this state of feeling that he sent his disciples to Jesus. But, in the first place, the language of the message is less that of *doubt* than of *inquiry*, and would appear to intimate that the idea of Jesus' character and mission had been then first suggested to him by the miracles of which reports had reached him in his prison. And, in the next place, doubt assails men who have *formed an opinion* from observation or induction, not men who have received positive and divine communication of a fact.

person by the divine voice ("*Thou art* my beloved Son") in Mark and Luke, and the peculiar language of Matthew, in confirmation of this view. But (not to urge that, if the vision and the voice were imperceptible to the spectators, they could not have given that public and conclusive attestation to the Messiahship of Jesus which was their obvious object and intention) a comparison of the four accounts clearly shows that the evangelists *meant* to state that the dove was visible and the voice audible to John and to all the spectators, who, according to Luke, must have been numerous. In Matthew the grammatical construction of iii. 16, would intimate that it was Jesus who saw the heavens open and the dove descend, but that the expression "alighting upon him," ἐρχόμενον ἐπ' αὐτόν, should in this case have been ἐφ'αὐτόν, "upon himself." However, it is very possible that Matthew may have written inaccurate, as he certainly wrote unclassical, Greek. But the voice in the next verse, speaking in the third person, "This is my beloved Son," must have been addressed to the spectators, not to Jesus. Mark has the same unharmonizing expression, ἐπ'αὐτόν. Luke describes the scene as passing before numbers, "when all the people are baptized, it came to pass that Jesus also being baptized;"—and then adds to the account of the other evangelists that the dove descended "in a bodily shape," ἐν σωματικῷ εἴδει, as if to contradict the idea that it was a subjective, not an objective fact,—a vision, not a phenomenon; he can only mean that it was an appearance visible to all

II.   C

present. The version given in the fourth evangelist shows still more clearly that such was the meaning generally attached to the tradition current among the Christians at the time it was embodied in the gospels. The Baptist is there represented as affirming that he himself saw the Spirit descending like a dove upon Jesus, and that it was this appearance which convinced him of the Messiahship of Jesus.

Considering all this, then, we must admit that, while the naturalness of John's message to Christ, and the exact accordance of the two accounts given of it, render the historical accuracy of that relation highly probable, the discrepancies in the four narratives of the baptism strongly indicate, either that the original tradition came from different sources, or that it has undergone considerable modification in the course of transmission ; and also that the narratives themselves are discredited by the subsequent message. We think with Schleiermacher, the great defender and eulogist of Luke, that the words ἐν σωματικῷ εἴδει are an interpolation which our evangelist thought himself at liberty to make by way of rendering the picture more graphic, without perceiving their inconsistency with a subsequent portion of his narrative.

In all the synoptical gospels we find instances of the cure of demoniacs by Jesus early in his career, in which the demons, promptly, spontaneously, and loudly, bear testimony to his Messiahship. These statements occur once in Matthew (viii. 29 ;)—four times in Mark (i. 24, 34 ; iii. 11 ; v. 7) ; and three

times in Luke (iv. 33, 41 ; viii. 28).[1] Now, two
points are evident to common sense, and are fully
admitted by honest criticism :—*first*, that these
demoniacs were lunatic and epileptic patients ; and,
secondly, that Jesus (or the narrators who framed the
language of Jesus throughout the synoptical gospels)
shared the common belief that these maladies were
caused by evil spirits inhabiting the bodies of the
sufferers. We are then landed in this conclusion—
certainly not a probable one, nor the one intended to
be conveyed by the narrators—that the idea of Jesus
being the Messiah was adopted by madmen before it
had found entrance into the public mind, apparently
even before it was received by his immediate disciples
—was in fact first suggested by madmen ;—in other
words, that it was an idea which originated with insane
brains—which presented itself to, and found acceptance
with, insane brains more readily than sane ones. The
conception of the evangelists clearly was that Jesus
derived honour (and his mission confirmation) from
this early recognition of his Messianic character by
hostile spirits of a superior order of Intelligences ; but
to us, who know that these supposed superior Intelligences were really unhappy men whose natural

---

[1] It is worthy of remark that no narrative of the healing of
demoniacs, stated as such, occurs in the fourth gospel. This would
intimate it to be the work of a man who had outgrown, or had
never entertained, the idea of maladies arising from possession.
It is one of many indications in this evangelist of a Greek rather
than a Jewish mind.

intellect had been perverted or impaired, the effect of the narratives becomes absolutely reversed ;—and if they are to be accepted as historical, they lead inevitably to the conclusion that the idea of the Messiahship of Jesus was originally formed in disordered brains, and spread thence among the mass of the disciples. The only rescue from this conclusion lies in the admission, that these narratives are not historical, but mythic, and belong to that class of additions which early grew up in the Christian Church, out of the desire to honour and aggrandise the memory of its Founder, and which our uncritical evangelists embodied as they found them.

Passing over a few minor passages of doubtful authenticity or accuracy,[1] we come to one near the close of the gospel, which we have no scruple in pronouncing to be an unwarranted interpolation. In xxii. 36-38, Jesus is reported, after the last Supper, to have said to his disciples, "He that hath no sword, let him sell his garment and buy one. And they said, Lord, behold, here are two swords. And he said, It is enough." Christ never could have uttered such a command, nor, we should imagine, anything which could have been mistaken for it. The very

---

[1] Compare Luke ix. 50 with xi. 23, where we probably have the same original expression differently reported. Schleiermacher, with all his reverence for Luke, decides (p. 94) that Luke vi. 24-26 is an addition to Christ's words by the evangelist himself — an "innocent interpolation" he calls it. For the anachronism in xi. 51, see our remarks on the corresponding passage in Matthew.

idea is contradicted by his whole character, and utterly precluded by the narratives of the other evangelists ; —for when Peter did use the sword, he met with a severe rebuke from his Master :—" Put up thy sword into the sheath : the cup which my Father hath given me shall I not drink it,"—according to John. " Put up again thy sword into its place ; for all they that take the sword shall perish by the sword,"—according to Matthew. The passage we conceive to be a clumsy invention of some early narrator, to account for the remarkable fact of Peter having a sword at the time of Christ's apprehension ; and it is inconceivable to us how a sensible compiler like Luke could have admitted into his history such an apocryphal and unharmonising fragment.

In conclusion, then, it appears certain that in all the synoptical gospels we have events related which did not really occur, and words ascribed to Jesus which Jesus did not utter ; and that many of these words and events are of great significance. In the great majority of these instances, however, this incorrectness does not imply any want of honesty on the part of the evangelists, but merely indicates that they adopted and embodied, without much scrutiny or critical acumen, whatever probable and honourable narratives they found current in the Christian community.

CHAPTER X.

IN the examination of the fourth Gospel a different mode of criticism from that hitherto pursued is required. Here we do not find, so frequently as in the other evangelists, particular passages which pronounce their own condemnation, by anachronisms, peculiarity of language, or incompatibility with others more obviously historical; but the whole tone of the delineations, the tenour of the discourses, and the general course of the narrative, are utterly different from those contained in the synoptical gospels, and also from what we should expect from a Jew speaking to Jews, writing of Jews, imbued with the spirit, and living in the land, of Judaism.

By the common admission of all recent critics, this gospel is rather to be regarded as a polemic, than an historic composition.[1] It was written less with the intention of giving a complete and continuous view of Christ's character and career, than to meet and con-

---

[1] See Hug, Strauss. Hennell. De Wette Also Dr Tait's "Sug gestions."

fute certain heresies which had sprung up in the
Christian church near the close of the first century,
by selecting, from the memory of the author, or the
traditions then current among believers, such narratives and discourses as were conceived to be most
opposed to the heresies in question. Now these
heresies related almost exclusively to the person and
nature of Jesus ; on which points we have many
indications that great difference of opinion existed,
even during the apostolic period. The obnoxious
doctrines especially pointed at in the gospel appear,
both from internal evidence and external testimony,[1]
to be those held by Cerinthus and the Nicolaitans,
which, according to Hug, were as follows :—The one
Eternal God is too pure, perfect, and pervading an
essence to be able to operate on matter ; but from
him emanated a number of inferior and gradually
degenerating spiritual natures, one of whom was the
Creator of the world, hence its imperfections. Jesus
was simply and truly a man, though an eminently
great and virtuous one; but one of the above spiritual
natures—the Christ, the Son of God—united itself to
Jesus at his baptism, and thus conferred upon him
superhuman power. " This Christ, as an immaterial
Being of exalted origin, one of the purer kinds of
spirits, was from his nature unsusceptible of material

---

[1] Irenæus, Jerome, Epiphanius. See Hug, § 51. See also a very
detailed account of the Gnostics in Norton's Genuineness of the
Gospels, ii. c. 1, 2.

affections of suffering and pain. He, therefore, at the commencement of the passion, resumed his separate existence, abandoned Jesus to pain and death, and soared upwards to his native heaven. Cerinthus distinguished *Jesus* and *Christ, Jesus* and the *Son of God*, as beings of different nature and dignity.[1] The Nicolaitans held similar doctrines in regard to the Supreme Deity and his relation to mankind, and an inferior spirit who was the Creator of the world. Among the subaltern orders of spirits they considered the most distinguished to be the only-begotten, the μονογενὴς (whose existence, however, had a beginning), and the λόγος, the Word, who was an immediate descendant of the only-begotten."[2]

These, then, were the opinions which the author of the fourth gospel wrote to controvert ; in confirmation of which being his object we have his own statement (xx. 31): "These are written" (not that ye may know the life and understand the character of our great Teacher, but that ye may believe his nature to be what I affirm) "that ye might believe that Jesus is the Christ, the Son of God ; and that believing, ye might have life through his name." Now, a narrative written with a controversial aim—a narrative, more especially, consisting of recollected or selected circumstances and discourses—carries within it, as everyone

---

[1] Several critics contend that the original reading of 1 John iv. 3, was ." Every spirit that *separateth* Jesus (from the Christ) is not of God."—See Hug, p. 423.

[2] Hug, § 51.

will admit, from the very nature of fallible humanity,
an obvious element of inaccuracy.   A man who *writes
a history to prove a doctrine* must be something more
than a man, if he writes that history with a scrupulous fidelity of fact and colouring.   Accordingly, we
find that the public discourses of Jesus in this gospel
turn almost exclusively upon the dignity of his own
person, which topic is brought forward in a manner .
and with a frequency which it is impossible to regard
as historical.   The prominent feature in the character
of Jesus, as here depicted, is an overweening tendency
to self-glorification.   We see no longer, as in the other
gospels, a prophet eager to bring men to God, and to
instruct them in righteousness, but one whose whole
mind seems occupied with the grandeur of his own
nature and mission.   In the three first gospels we have
the message ; in the fourth we have comparatively little
but the messenger.   If any of our readers will peruse
the gospel with this observation in their minds, we
are persuaded the result will be a very strong and
probably painful impression that they cannot here be
dealing with the genuine language of Jesus, but
simply with a composition arising out of deep conviction of his superior nature, left in the mind of the
writer by the contemplation of his splendid genius and
his noble and lovely character.

The difference of style and subject between the discourses of Jesus in the fourth gospel and in the
synoptical ones, has been much dwelt upon, and we
think by no means too much, as proving the greater

or less unauthenticity of the former. This objection
has been met by the supposition that the finer intellect and more spiritual character of John induced him
to select, and enabled him to record, the more subtle
and speculative discourses of his Master, which were
unacceptable or unintelligible to the more practical
and homely minds of the other disciples ; and reference is made to the parallel case of Xenophon and
Plato, whose reports of the conversations of Socrates
are so different in tone and matter as to render it
very difficult to believe that both sat at the feet of
the same master, and listened to the same teaching.
But the citation is an unfortunate one ; for in this
case, also, it is more than suspected that the more
simple recorder was the more correct one, and that
the sublimer and subtler peculiarities in the discourses
reported by Plato, belong rather to the disciple than
to the teacher. Had John merely *superadded* some
more refined and mystical discourses omitted by his
predecessors, the supposition in question might have
been admitted ; but it is impossible not to perceive
that here the *whole tone* of the mind delineated is
new and discrepant, though often eminently beautiful.

Another argument, which may be considered as
conclusive against the historical fidelity of the discourses of Jesus in the fourth gospel is, that not only
they, but the discourses of John the Baptist likewise,
are entirely in the style of the evangelist himself,
where he introduces his own remarks, both in the
gospel and in the first epistle. He makes both Jesus

and the Baptist speak exactly as he himself speaks. Compare the following passages :—

John iii. 31-36. (Baptist loquitur). He that cometh from above is above all : he that is of the earth is earthly, and speaketh of the earth : he that cometh from heaven is above all. And what he hath seen and heard, that he testifieth ; and no man receiveth his testimony.

He that receiveth his testimony hath set to his seal that God is true. For he whom God hath sent speaketh the words of God ; for God giveth not the spirit by measure. The Father loveth the Son, and hath given all things into his hand.

John viii. 23. (Jesus loq.). Ye are from beneath ; I am from above ; ye are of this world ; I am not of this world. iii. 11. (Jesus loq.). We speak that we do know, and testify that we have seen ; and ye receive not our testimony.

viii. 26. (Jesus loq.). I speak to the world those things which I have heard of him.—(See also vii. 16-18 : xiv. 24.) v. 20. (Jesus loq.). The Father loveth the Son, and showeth him all things that himself doeth. xiii. 3. (Evangelist loq.). Jesus knowing that the Father had given all things into his hands.

He that believeth on the Son hath everlasting life, and he that believeth not the Son shall not see life ; but the wrath of God abideth on him.

vi. 47 (Jesus loq.). He that believeth on me hath everlasting life. —(See also 1 Epistle v. 10-13, and Gospel iii. 18, where the evangelist or Jesus speaks). vi. 40 (Jesus loq.). And this is the will of Him that sent me, that every one which seeth the Son and believeth on him, may have everlasting life.

1 Epistle iii. 14. We know that we have passed from death unto life.

v. 24 (Jesus loq.). He that heareth my word . . . hath passed from death unto life.

1 Epistle iv. 6. We are of God : he that knoweth God heareth us : he that is not of God heareth not us.

viii. 47 (Jesus loq.). He that is of God heareth God's words : ye therefore hear them not, because ye are not of God.

1 Epistle v. 9. If we receive the witness of men, the witness of God is greater : for this is the witness of

v. 34 etc. (Jesus loq.). I receive not testimony from man. . . . . I have greater witness than that of

God which he hath witnessed of his Son.

xix. 35 (John loq.). And his record is true ; and he knoweth that he saith true.

xxi. 24. This is the disciple which testifieth of these things ; . . . and we know that his witness is true.

John . . . the Father himself which hath sent me, hath borne witness of me.

v. 32. There is another that beareth witness of me ; and I know that the witness which he witnesseth of me is true.

Another indication that in a great part of the fourth gospel we have not the genuine discourses of Jesus, is found in the mystical and enigmatical nature of the language. This peculiarity, of which we have scarcely a trace in the other evangelists, beyond the few parables which they did not at first understand, but which Jesus immediately explained to them, pervades the fourth gospel. The great Teacher is here represented as absolutely labouring to be unintelligible, to soar out of the reach of his hearers, and at once perplex and disgust them. " It is the constant method of this evangelist, in detailing the conversations of Jesus, to form the knot and progress of the discussions, by making the 'interlocutors understand literally what Jesus intended figuratively. The type of the dialogue is that in which language intended spiritually is understood carnally." The instances of this are inconceivably frequent and unnatural. We have the conversation with the Jews about " the temple of his body " (ii. 21) ; the mystification of Nicodemus on the subject of regeneration (iii. 3-10) ; the conversation with the Samaritan woman (iv. 10-15) ; with his disciples about " the food which

ye know not of" (iv. 32) ; with the people about the
" bread from heaven " (vi. 31-35) ; with the Jews
about giving them his flesh to eat (vi. 48-66) ; with
the Pharisees about his disappearance (vii. 33-39,
and viii. 21, 22) ; again about his heavenly origin
and pre-existence (viii. 37, 34, and 56-58) ; and with
his disciples about the sleep of Lazarus (xi. 11-14).
Now, in the first place, it is very improbable that
Jesus, who came to preach the gospel to the poor,
should so constantly have spoken in a style which his
hearers could not understand ; and in the next place,
it is equally improbable that an Oriental people, so
accustomed to figurative language,[1] and whose literature was so eminently metaphorical, should have mis-
apprehended the words of Jesus so stupidly and
so incessantly as the evangelist represents them to
have done.

But perhaps the most conclusive argument against
the historical character of the discourses in the fourth
gospel, is to be found in the fact that, whether
dialogues or monologues, they are complete and continuous, resembling compositions rather than recollec-
tions, and of a length which it is next to impossible
could have been accurately retained — even if we
adopt Bertholdt's improbable hypothesis, that the

---

[1] See the remarks of Strauss on the conversation with Nicodemus, from which it appears that the image of a new birth was a
current one among the Jews, and could not have been so misunderstood by a master in Israel, and in fact that the whole conversation
is almost certainly fictitious.—ii. 153.

apostle took notes of Jesus' discourses at the time of their delivery. Notwithstanding all that has been said as to the possible extent to which the powers of memory may go, it is difficult for an unprepossessed mind to believe that discourses such as that contained in the 14th, 15th, and 16th chapters, could have been accurately retained and reported unless by a shorthand writer, or by one favoured with super-natural assistance. "We hold it therefore to be established" (says Strauss,[1] and in the main we agree with him), "that the discourses of Jesus in the fourth gospel are mainly free compositions of the evangelist ; but we have admitted that he has culled several sayings of Jesus from an authentic tradition, and hence we do not extend this proposition to those passages which are countenanced by parallels in the synoptical gospels. In these latter compilations we have an example of the vicissitudes which befall discourses that are preserved only in the memory of a second party. Severed from their original connection, and broken up into smaller and smaller fragments, they present, when reassembled, the appearance of a mosaic, in which the connection of the parts is a purely ex-ternal one, and every transition an artificial juncture. The discourses in John present just the opposite appear-ance. Their gradual transitions, only occasionally ren-dered obscure by the mystical depths of meaning in which they lie—transitions in which one thought

---

[1] Leben Jesu, ii. 187.

develops itself out of another, and a succeeding proposition is frequently but an explanatory amplification
of the preceding one—are indicative of a pliable, unre-
sisting mass, such as is never presented to a writer by
the traditional sayings of another, but by such only as
proceeds from the stores of his own thought, which he
moulds according to his will. For this reason the
contributions of tradition to these stores of thought
were not so likely to have been *particular independent sayings of Jesus, as rather certain ideas which
formed the basis of many of his discourses,* and
which were modified and developed according to the
bent of a mind of Greek or Alexandrian culture." [1]

Another peculiarity of this gospel—arising, probably,
out of its controversial origin—is its exaltation of
dogma over morality—of belief over spiritual affection.
In the other gospels, piety, charity, forgiveness of
injuries, purity of life, are preached by Christ as the
titles to his kingdom and his Father's favour. Whereas,
in John's gospel, as in his epistles, belief in Jesus as
the Son of God, the Messiah, the Logos—belief, in
fact, in the evangelist's view of his nature—is constantly represented as the one thing needful. The

---

[1] See also Hennell, p. 200. "The picture of Jesus bequeathing
his parting benedictions to the disciples, seems fully to warrant
the idea that the author was one whose imagination and affections
had received an impress from real scenes and real attachments.
The few relics of the words, looks, and acts of Jesus, which friendship itself could at that time preserve unmixed, he expands into a
complete record of his own and the disciples' sentiments; what
they felt, he makes Jesus speak."

whole tone of the history bears token of a time when the message was beginning to be forgotten in the Messenger; when metaphysical and fruitless discussions as to the nature of Christ had superseded devotion to his spirit, and attention to the sublime piety and simple self-sacrificing holiness which formed the essence of his own teaching. The discourses are often touchingly eloquent and tender; the narrative is full of beauty, pathos, and nature; but we miss the simple and intelligible truth, the noble, yet practical, morality of the other histories; we find in it more of Christ than of Christianity, and more of John than of Jesus. If the work of an apostle at all, it was of an apostle who had caught but a fragment of his Master's mantle, or in whom the good original seed had been choked by the long bad habit of subtle and scholastic controversies. We cannot but regard this gospel as decidedly inferior in moral sublimity and purity to the other representations of Christ's teaching which have come down to us; its religion is more of a dogmatic creed, and its very philanthropy has a narrower and more restricted character. We will give a few parallels to make our meaning clearer.

John xiii. 1. Now when Jesus knew that his hour was come, that he should depart out of this world unto the Father, having *loved his own* which were in the world, he loved them unto the end.

John xiii. 35. By this shall all' men know that ye are my disciples, if ye have love *one to another*.

Matth. v. 43. Ye have heard that it hath been said, Thou shalt love thy neighbour, and hate thine enemy. But I say unto you, *Love your enemies*, bless them that curse you, *do good to them that hate you*, pray for them which despitefully use you, and persecute you; .. for *if ye love them which love you, what reward have*

John xv. 12. This is my commandment, that *ye love one another, as I have loved you.*

you? do not even the Publicans the same?

Luke x. 27. Thou shalt love thy neighbour as thyself.—(Definition of a neighbour, as any one whom we can serve.)

John x. vii. 9. I pray for them : *I pray not for the world, but for those whom thou hast given me* out of the world (v. 20). Neither pray I for these alone, *but for them also which shall believe on me* through their word.[1]

Luke vi. 28. Pray for them which despitefully use you; bless them which persecute you.

Luke xxiii. 34. Father, forgive them, for they know not what they do.

John iii. 14. And as Moses lifted up the serpent in the wilderness, even so must the Son of Man be lifted up; That *whosoever believeth on him* should not perish, but have eternal life.

Matth. v. 3, 8. Blessed are the poor in spirit, *for theirs is the kingdom of heaven.* Blessed are the pure in heart, *for they shall see God.*

John vi. 40. And this is the will of him that sent me, that every one which seeth the Son, *and believeth on him, may have everlasting life.*

Matth. vii. 21. *Not every one that saith unto me, Lord, Lord,* shall enter into the kingdom of heaven ; *but he that doeth the will of my Father which is in Heaven.* Many will say to me in that day, Lord, Lord, have we not prophesied in thy name? and in thy name have cast out devils? and in thy name done many wonderful works? *And then will I profess unto them, I never knew you : depart from me ye that work iniquity.*

John xvii. 3. And *this is life eternal,* that they might know thee, the only true God, and Jesus Christ whom thou hast sent.

John vi. 29. This is the work of

Matth. xix. 16, et seq. And, be-

---

[1] I venture here to insert a note written by a friend to whom the MS. of this work was submitted for correction. "These passages are the growth of an age in which Christians were already suffering persecution. In such times a special and peculiar love to 'the brethren' is natural and desirable ; without it they could not be animated to risk all that is needed for one another. I could not call it, at that time, a 'narrow philanthropy,' but it certainly does not belong to the same moral state, nor come forth from the same heart, at the same time, as that of the other Gospels. In the present day, however, the results are intensely evil : for this Gospel defines those who are to love another by an intellectual creed ; and however this be enlarged or contracted, we have here the essence of Bigotry.

II.   D

God, *that ye believe on him* whom he hath sent.

John iii. 36. *He that believeth on the Son hath everlasting life* : and *he that believeth not on the Son shall not see life ;* but the wrath of God abideth on him.

hold, one came and said unto him, Good Master, what good thing shall I do that I may have eternal life ? And he said unto him, Why callest thou me good, &c., &c. ; but if *thou wilt enter into life, keep the commandments,* &o. Matth. xxv. 31-46.—(Definition of Christ's reception of the wicked and the righteous.)—And these shall go away into everlasting punishment, but the *righteous into life eternal.*

Mark xii. 28-34. And the Scribe answered, Well, Master, thou hast said the truth : for there is one God, and there is none other but he ; &o. &o. . . . And when Jesus saw that he answered discreetly, he said unto him, *Thou art not far from the Kingdom of God.*

Luke ix. 51-56. And when James and John saw this (that the Samaritans would not receive Jesus), they said, Lord, wilt thou that we command fire to come down from heaven, and consume them, even as Elias did ? But he turned and rebuked them, and said, Ye know not what manner of spirit ye are of, &c.

Luke x. 25-28. And, behold, a certain lawyer stood up, and tempted him, saying, Master, what shall I do to inherit eternal life ? He said unto him, What is written in the law ? How readest thou ? And he answering said, Thou shalt love the Lord thy God with all thy heart, and with all thy soul, and with all thy strength, and with all thy mind ; and thy neighbour as thyself. And Jesus said unto him, Thou hast answered rightly : *this do, and thou shalt live.*

There are several minor peculiarities which distinguish this gospel from the preceding ones, which we can do no more than indicate. We find here little

about the Kingdom of Heaven—nothing about Christ's
mission being confined to the Israelites—nothing about
the casting out of devils—nothing about the destruction of Jerusalem—nothing about the struggle between
the law and gospel—topics which occupy so large a
space in the picture of Christ's ministry given in the
synoptical gospels ; and the omission of which seems
to refer the composition of this narrative to a later
period, when the Gentiles were admitted into the
Church—when the idea of demoniacal possession had
given way before a higher culture—when Jerusalem
had been long destroyed—and when Judaism had
quite retired before Christianity, at least within the
pale of the Church.[1]

---

[1] Modern criticism has detected several slight errors and inaccu-
racies in the fourth gospel, such as Sychar for Sichem, Siloam
erroneously interpreted *sent*, &c., &c., from which it has been
argued that the writer could not have been a native of Palestine,
and by consequence not the Apostle John.

[These, however, are insignificant in comparison with the discrepancy as to the date of the Last Supper in the different Evangelists, the Synoptists fixing it *on* the Feast of the Passover, and
the fourth Gospel on the previous day. This discrepancy gave rise
to the famous "Quarto-deciman Controversy" as it is called, which
so long agitated the early Church, and was at last only quelled by
an authoritative decree of the Emperor Constantine. Those who
wish to understand the question, and the light which its details
throw upon the probable authorship of the fourth Gospel, will find
an exhaustive account in Section ix. of Mr. Tayler's learned inquiry
already referred to.—The remarkable points are that the early con-
troversialists, who took the view and held to the practice of the
Synoptists, appealed to *the Apostle John* as their strongest authority
on their side ;—while it was not till very late in the discussion
that their adversaries seem to have thought of quoting the fourth

Though we have seen ample reason to conclude that nearly all the discourses of Jesus in the fourth gospel are mainly the composition of the evangelist from memory or tradition, rather than the genuine utterances of our great Teacher, it may be satisfactory, as further confirmation, to select a few single passages and expressions, as to the unauthentic character of which there can be no question. Thus at ch. iii. 11, Jesus is represented as saying to Nicodemus, in the

---

Gospel in *their* favour ;—that this Gospel entirely ignores the institution of the Eucharist in its account of the last days of Jesus, though apparently alluding to it in some earlier chapters ;—and that the object of the Author appears to have been to represent, by implication at least, Christ as *being* himself the Paschal Lamb, not as partaking of it.

If the fourth gospel were really the work of the Apostle John, it would seem impossible to avoid the inference that the institution of " the Sacrament" of bread and wine as recorded by the other Evangelists is entirely unhistorical, and then all the stupendous ecclesiastical corollaries flowing from it fall to the ground. It is impossible that John could have *forgotten* such commands or assertions as are supposed to be involved in the words, " Take eat ; this is my body," &c.—It is equally impossible that, if they were ever spoken, and signified what Christians in general believe to be their significance, the disciple who leaned on the bosom of Jesus while they were uttered, could have so undervalued their meaning as to have omitted to record them. The dilemma, then, seems to be inescapable :—*Either* John did not write the fourth Gospel—in which case we have the direct testimony of no eye-witness to the facts and sayings of Christ's ministry ;—*Or* the Sacrament of the Lord's Supper, as deduced from the Synoptical accounts, with the special doctrines of Sacramental grace to partakers of it, and of the Atonement (as far as it is warranted or originally was suggested by those words of Christ,) becomes " the baseless fabric of a vision."]

midst of his discourse about regeneration, "We speak
that we do know, and testify that which we have seen ;
and ye receive not our witness,"—expressions wholly
unmeaning and out of place in the mouth of Jesus on
an occasion where he is testifying nothing at all, but
merely propounding a mystical dogma to an auditor
dull of comprehension—but expressions which are
the evangelist's habitual form of asseveration and
complaint.

It is not clear whether the writer intended verses
16-21 to form part of the discourse of Jesus, or merely
a commentary of his own. If the former, they are
clearly unwarrantable ; their point of view is that of
a period when the teaching of Christ had been known
and rejected, and they could not have been uttered
with any justice or appropriateness at the very commencement of his ministry.

Ch. xi. 8. "His disciples say unto him, Master, the
Jews of late sought to stone thee : and goest thou
thither again ?" *The Jews* is an expression which
would be natural to Ephesians or other foreigners when
speaking of the inhabitants of Palestine, but could not
have been used by Jews speaking of their own countrymen. They would have said, the People, or, the
Pharisees. The same observation applies to xiii. 33,
and also probably to xviii. 36.

Ch. xvii. 3. "And this is life eternal, that they
might know Thee the only true God, and *Jesus Christ*
whom Thou hast sent." This would be a natural

expression for the evangelist, but scarcely for his Master.

As before observed, great doubt hangs over the whole story of the testimony borne by the Baptist to Jesus at his baptism. In the fourth evangelist, this testimony is represented as most emphatic, public, and repeated—so that it could have left no doubt in the minds of any of his followers, either as to the grandeur of the mission of Jesus, or as to his own subordinate character and position (i. 29-36 ; iii. 26-36). Yet we find, from Acts xviii. 25, and again xix. 3, circles of John the Baptist's disciples, who appear never even to have heard of Jesus—a statement which we think is justly held irreconcilable with the statements above referred to in the fourth gospel.

The question of miracles will be considered in a future chapter, and several of those related in this Gospel—significantly *seven* in number, and in culminating order—have special characteristics of their own ; but there is one miracle, peculiar to John, of so singular and apocryphal a character as to call for notice here. The turning of water into wine at the marriage feast in Cana of Galilee has long formed the opprobrium and perplexity of theologians, and must continue to do so as long as they persist in regarding it as an accurate historical relation. None of the numberless attempts to give anything like a probable explanation of the narrative has been attended with the least success. They are for the most part melancholy specimens of ingenuity misapplied, and plain honesty perverted by an originally false assumption. No portion of the gospel history, scarcely any portion of Old Testament, or even of apocryphal, narratives, bears such unmistakable marks of fiction.   It is a story which, if found in any other volume, would at once have been dismissed as a clumsy and manifest invention. In the first place, it is a miracle wrought to supply more wine to men who had already drunk much—a deed which has no suitability to the character of Jesus, and no analogy to any other of his miracles. *Secondly,* though it was, as we are told, the first of his miracles, his mother is represented as expecting him to work a miracle, and to commence his public career with so unfit and improbable a one. *Thirdly,* Jesus is said to have spoken harshly[1] to his mother, asking her what they had in common, and telling her that " his hour (for working miracles) was not yet come," when he knew that it *was* come. *Fourthly,* in spite of this rebuff, Mary is represented as still expecting a miracle, and *this particular one,* and as making preparation for it : " She saith to the servants, Whatsoever he saith unto you, do it ;" and accordingly Jesus immediately began to give orders to them. *Fifthly,* the superior quality of the wine, and the enormous quantity produced (135 gallons, or in our language, above 43 dozen[2]) are obviously fabulous. And those who are

---

[1] All attempts at explanation have failed to remove this character from the expression—γύναι τί ἐμοὶ καὶ σοί.
[2] See the calculation in Hennell, and in Strauss, ii. 432. The

familiar with the apocryphal gospels will have no difficulty in recognising the close consanguinity between the whole narrative and the stories of miracles with which they abound. It is perfectly hopeless, as well as mischievous, to endeavour to retain it as a portion of authentic history.

μιτρητὴς is supposed to correspond to the Hebrew *bath*, which was equal to 1½ Roman amphora, or 8·7 gallons; the whole quantity would therefore be from 104 to 156 gallons.

CHAPTER XI.

THE conclusion at which we have arrived in the foregoing chapters is of vital moment, and deserves to be
fully developed. When duly wrought out, it will be
found the means of extricating Religion from Orthodoxy—of rescuing Christianity from Calvinism. We
have seen that the Gospels, while they give a fair and
faithful *outline* of Christ's character and teaching
(the Synoptical gospels at least) fill up that outline
with much that is not authentic ; that many of the
statements therein related are not historical, but
mystical or legendary ; and that portions at least of
the language ascribed to Jesus were never uttered by
him, but originated either with the Evangelists themselves, or more frequently in the traditional stores
from which they drew their materials. We cannot,
indeed, say in all cases, nor even in most cases, *with
certainty*—in many we cannot even pronounce with
any very strong *probability*—that such and such
particular expressions or discourses are, or are not, the
genuine utterances of Christ. With respect to some,
we can say with confidence, that they are *not* from

him ; with respect to others, we can say with almost
equal confidence that they are his actual words ; but
with regard to the majority of passages, this certainty
is not attainable. But as we *know* that much did not
proceed from Jesus—that much is unhistorical and
ungenuine—we are entitled to conclude—we are even
forced, by the very instinct of our reasoning faculty,
to conclude that the unhistorical and ungenuine
passages are those in which Jesus is represented as
speaking and acting in a manner unconformable to his
character as otherwise delineated, irreconcilable with
the tenour of his teaching as elsewhere described, and
at variance with those grand moral and spiritual truths
which have commanded the assent of all disciplined
and comprehensive minds, and which could scarcely
have escaped an intellect so just, wide, penetrating,
and profound, as that of our great Teacher.

Most reflecting minds rise from a perusal of the
gospel history with a clear, broad, vivid conception of
the character and mission of Christ, notwithstanding
the many passages at which they have stumbled, and
which they have felt—perhaps with needless alarm
and self-reproach—to be incongruous and unharmonizing with the great whole. The question naturally
arises, Did these incongruities and inconsistencies
really exist in Christ himself ? or, are they the result
of the imperfect and unhistorical condition in which
his biography has been transmitted to us ? The
answer, it seems to us, ought to be this :—We cannot
prove, it is true, that some of these unsuitabilities did

not exist in Christ himself, but we have shown that
many of them belong to the history, not to the subject
of the history, and it is only fair, therefore, in the
absence of contrary evidence, to conclude that the
others also are due to the same origin.

Now the peculiar, startling, perplexing, revolting,
and contradictory doctrines of modern orthodoxy—so
far as they have originated from or are justified by
the Gospels at all—have originated from, or are
justified by, not the general tenour of Christ's character and preaching, *but those single, unharmonizing,
discrepant, texts of which we have been speaking.*
Doctrines, which unsophisticated men feel to be inadmissible and repellant, and which those who hold them
most devotedly, secretly admit to be fearful and perplexing, are founded on particular passages which
contradict the *generality* of Christ's teaching, but
which, being attributed to him by the evangelists,
have been regarded as endowed with an authority
which it would be profane and dangerous to resist. In
showing, therefore, that several of these passages did
not emanate from Christ, and that in all probability
none of them did, we conceive that we shall have
rendered a vast service to the cause of true religion,
and to those numerous individuals in whose tortured
minds sense and conscience have long struggled for the
mastery. We will elucidate this matter by a few
specifications.[1]

---

[1] It is true that many of the doctrines in question had not a
scriptural origin at all, but an ecclesiastical one ; and, when origi-

One of the most untenable, unphilosophical, un-
charitable doctrines of the orthodox creed—one most
peculiarly stamped with the impress of the bad passions
of humanity—is, that *belief* (by which is generally
signified belief in Jesus as the Son of God, the promised Messiah, a Teacher sent down from Heaven on
a special mission to redeem mankind) *is essential, and
the one thing essential, to Salvation.* The source of
this doctrine must doubtless be sought for in that
intolerance of opposition unhappily so common
among men, and in that tendency to ascribe bad
motives to those who arrive at different conclusions
from themselves, which prevails so generally among
unchastened minds. But it cannot be denied that the
gospels contain many texts which clearly affirm or
fully imply a doctrine so untenable and harsh. Let
us turn to a few of these, and inquire into the degree
of authenticity to which they are probably entitled.

The most specific assertion of the tenet in question,
couched in that positive, terse, sententious, damnatory
language so dear to orthodox divines, is *found in the
spurious portion of the gospel of Mark* (c. xvi. 16),[1]
and is there by the writer, whoever he was, unscrupu-

---

nated, were defended by texts from the *epistles*, rather than the
gospels. The authority of the epistles we shall consider in a subsequent chapter, but if in the meantime we can show that those
doctrines have no foundation in the language of Christ, the *chief*
obstacle to the renunciation of them is removed.

[1] " He that believeth and is baptized shall be saved ; but he that
believeth not shall be damned," a passage which, were it not happily
spurious, would suffice to " damn " the book which contains it.

lously put into the mouth of Jesus after his resurrection. In the synoptical gospels may be found a few texts which may be wrested to *support* the doctrine, but there are none which teach it. But when we come to the fourth gospel we find several passages similar to that in Mark,[1] proclaiming Salvation to believers, *but all in the peculiar style and spirit of the Author of the first Epistle of John*, which abounds in denunciations precisely similar[2] (but directed, it is remarkable, apparently against heretics, not against infidels, against those who believe amiss, not against those who do not believe at all)—all, too, redolent of the temper of that Apostle who wished to call down fire from heaven on an unbelieving village, and *who was rebuked by Jesus for the savage and presumptuous suggestion.*

In the last chapter we have shown that the *style* of these passages is of a nature to point to John, and not to Jesus, as their author, and that the *spirit* of them is entirely hostile and incompatible with the language of Jesus in other parts more obviously faithful. It appears, therefore, that the passages confirmatory of the doctrine in question are found exclusively in a portion of the synoptists which is certainly spurious, and in portions of the fourth gospel which are almost certainly unhistorical; and that they are contradicted by other passages in all the gospels.

---

[1] John iii. 16, 18, 36; v. 24; vi. 29, 40, 47; xi. 25, 26; xx, 31.
[2] 1 John ii. 19, 22, 23; iv. 2, 3, 6, 15; v. 1, 5, 10, 12, 13.

It only remains to show that as the doctrine is at
variance with the spirit of the mild and benevolent
Jesus, so it is too obviously unsound not to have been
recognised as such by one whose clear and grand
intelligence was informed and enlightened by so pure
a heart.

In the first place, Christ must have known that the
same doctrine will be presented in a very different
manner, and with very different degrees of evidence
for its truth, by different preachers ; so much so that
to *resist* the arguments of one preacher would imply
either dulness of comprehension or obstinate and
wilful blindness, while to *yield* to the arguments of his
colleague would imply weakness of understanding or
instability of purpose. The same doctrine may be
presented and defended by one preacher so clearly,
rationally, and forcibly that all sensible men (idiosyn-
cracies apart) must accept it, and by another preacher
so feebly, corruptly, and confusedly, that all sensible
men must reject it. The rejection of the Christianity
preached by Luther, and of the Christianity preached
by Tetzel, of the Christianity preached by Loyola and
Dunstan, and of the Christianity preached by Oberlin
and Pascal, cannot be worthy of the same condemnation. Few Protestants, and no Catholics, will deny
that Christianity *has been* so presented to men as to
make it a simple affair both of sense and virtue to
reject it. To represent, therefore, the reception of a
doctrine as a matter of merit, or its rejection as a
matter of blame, *without reference to the consideration*

RESULTS OF THE FOREGOING CRITICISM.   63

how and by whom it is preached, is to leave out the main element of judgment—an error which could not have been committed by the just and wise Jesus.

Further. · The doctrine and the passages in question ascribe to " belief" the highest degree of merit, and the sublimest conceivable reward—" eternal life ;" and to " disbelief," the deepest wickedness, and the most fearful penalty, " damnation," and " the wrath of God." Now, here we have a logical error, betraying a confusion of intellect which we may well scruple to ascribe to Jesus. Belief is an effect produced by a cause. It is a condition of the mind induced by the operation of evidence presented. Being, therefore, an *effect*, and not an *act*, it cannot be, or have, a merit. The moment it becomes a distinctly voluntary act (*and therefore a thing of which merit can be predicated*) it ceases to be genuine—it is then brought about (if it be not an abuse of language to name this state " belief ") by the will of the individual, not by the *bonâ fide* operation of evidence upon his mind— which brings us to the *reductio ad absurdum*, that belief can only become meritorious by ceasing to be honest.

In sane and competent minds, if the evidence presented is sufficient, belief will follow as a necessary consequence—if it does not follow, this can only arise from the evidence adduced being insufficient—and in such case to pretend belief, or to attempt belief, would be a forfeiture of mental integrity ; and cannot therefore be meritorious, but the reverse. To disbelieve

in spite of adequate proof is impossible—to believe
without adequate proof, is weak or dishonest.   Belief,
therefore, can only become meritorious by becoming
sinful—can only become a fit subject for reward by
becoming a fit subject for punishment.   Such is the
sophism involved in the dogma which theologians have
dared to put into Christ's mouth, and to announce on
his authority.

But, it will be urged, the disbelief which Christ
blamed and menaced with punishment was (as appears
from John iii. 19) the disbelief implied in a wilful
rejection of his claims, or a refusal to examine them
—a love of darkness in preference to light.   If so,
the language employed is incorrect and deceptive, and
the blame is predicated of an effect instead of a cause
—it is *meant* of a voluntary action, but it is *predicated*
of a specified and denounced consequence which is no
natural or logical indication of that voluntary action,
but may arise from independent causes.   The moralist
who should denounce gout as a sin, meaning the sinfulness to apply to the excesses of which gout is
often, but by no means always, a consequence and an
indication, would be held to be a very confused
teacher and inaccurate logician.   Moreover, this is
not the sense attached to the doctrine by orthodox
divines in common parlance.   And the fact still
remains that Christ is represented as rewarding by
eternal felicity a state of mind which, *if honestly
attained*, is inevitable, involuntary, and therefore in
no way a fitting subject for reward, and which, if not

RESULTS OF THE FOREGOING CRITICISM. 65

honestly attained, is hollow, fallacious, and deserving
of punishment rather than of recompense.

We are aware that the orthodox seek to escape
from the dilemma, by asserting that belief results from
the state of the heart, and that if this be right belief
will inevitably follow. This is simply false in fact.
How many excellent, virtuous, and humble minds, in
all ages, have been *anxious*, but unable to believe—
have prayed earnestly for belief, and suffered bitterly
for disbelief—in vain !

The dogma of the Divinity, or, as it is called in the
technical language of polemics, *the proper Deity*, of
Christ, though historically proveable to have had an
ecclesiastical, not an evangelical, origin [1]—though
clearly negatived by the whole tenour of the synoptical
gospels, and even by some passages in the fourth
gospel [and though it is difficult to read the narrative
of his career with an unforestalled mind without being
clear that Jesus had no notion of such a belief himself,
and would have repudiated it with horror]—can yet
appeal to several isolated portions and texts, as
suggesting and confirming, if not asserting it. On
close examination, however, it will be seen that all
these passages are to be found either in the fourth
gospel—which we have already shown reason to conclude is throughout an unscrupulous and most inexact

---

[1] " The Unscriptural Origin and Ecclesiastical History of the
Doctrine of the Trinity," by *the Rev. J. Hamilton Thom.*

II.   E

paraphrase of Christ's teaching—or in those portions
of the three first gospels which, on other accounts and
from independent trains of argument, have been
selected as at least of questionable authenticity.   It is
true that the doctrine in question is now chiefly
defended by reference to the Epistles ; but at the
same time it would scarcely be held so tenaciously by
the orthodox if it were found to be wholly destitute of
evangelical support.   Now, the passages which appear
most confirmatory of Christ's Deity, or Divine Nature,
are, in the first place, the narratives of the Incarnation, or the miraculous Conception, as given by
Matthew and Luke.   We have already entered pretty
fully into the consideration of the authenticity of these
portions of Scripture, and have seen that we may
almost with certainty pronounce them to be fabulous,
or mythical.   The two narratives do not harmonize
with each other ; they neutralize and negative the
genealogies on which depended so large a portion of
the proof of Jesus being the Messiah ;[1]—the marvellous statement they contain is not referred to in any
subsequent portion of the two gospels, and is tacitly
but positively negatived by several passages—it is
never mentioned in the Acts or in the Epistles, and
was evidently unknown to all the Apostles—and,

---

[1] The Messiah must, according to Jewish prophecy, be a lineal
descendant of David : this Christ was, according to the genealogies :
this he was not, if the miraculous conception be a fact.   If, therefore, Jesus came into being as Matthew and Luke affirm, we do
not see how he could have been the Messiah.

finally, the tone of the narrative, especially in Luke, is poetical and legendary, and bears a marked similarity to the stories contained in the apocryphal gospels.

The only other expressions in the three first gospels which lend the slightest countenance to the doctrine in question, are the acknowledgements of the disciples, the centurion, and the demoniacs, that Jesus was the Son of God,[1]—some of which we have already shown to be of very questionable genuineness,—and the voice from heaven said to have been heard at the baptism and the transfiguration, saying, "This is my beloved Son," &c. But, besides that, as shown in chapter vii., considerable doubt rests on the accuracy of the first of these relations : the testimony borne by the heavenly voice to Jesus can in no sense mean that he was *physically* the Son of God, or a partaker of the divine nature, inasmuch as the very same expression was frequently applied to others, and as indeed a " Son of God " was, in the common parlance of the Jews, simply a prophet, a man whom God had sent, or to whom he had spoken.[2]

But when we come to the fourth gospel, especially

---

[1] An expression here merely signifying a Prophet or the Messiah.

[2] " The Lord hath said unto me (David), Thou art my Son ; this day have I begotten thee."—(Ps. ii. 7.) Jehovah says of Solomon, " I will be his father, and he shall be my son."—(2 Sam. vii. 14.) The same expression is applied to Israel (Exod. iv. 22, Hos. xi. 1), and to David (Ps. lxxxix. 27). " I have said, Ye are gods, and all of you are children of the Most High."—(Ps. lxxxii. 6). " If he called them gods, unto whom the word of God

to those portions of it whose peculiar style betrays
that they came from John, and not from Jesus,
the case is very different. We find here many
passages evidently intended to convey the impression
that Jesus was endowed with a superhuman nature,
but nearly all expressed in language savouring less of
Christian simplicity than of Alexandrian philosophy.
The evangelist commences his gospel with a confused
statement of the Platonic doctrine as modified in
Alexandria, and that the Logos was a partaker of the
Divine Nature, and was the Creator of the world ; on
which he proceeds to engraft his own notion, that
Jesus was this Logos—that the Logos or the divine
wisdom, the second person in Plato's Trinity, became
flesh in the person of the prophet of Nazareth. Now,
can any one read the epistles, or the three first gospels
—or even the whole of the fourth—and not at
once repudiate the notion that Jesus was, and knew
himself to be, the Creator of the World ?—which John
affirms him to have been. Throughout this gospel
we find constant repetitions of the same endeavour to
make out a superhuman nature for Christ; but the
ungenuineness of these passages has already been fully
considered.

---

came," &c.—(John x. 35.) " Behold what manner of love the
Father hath bestowed upon us, that we should be called the Sons
of God. . . . Beloved, now are we the Sons of God."—(1 John
iii. 1, 2.) (See also Gal. iii. 26 ; iv. 5, 6.) " As many as are led
by the spirit of God, they are the Sons of God."—(Rom. viii. 14.)
" But to as many as received him, he gave power to become the
Sons of God."—(John i. 12.

[Take, again, the doctrine of the Eternity of future punishments—the most *impossible* of the tenets included in the popular creed. It rests upon and is affirmed by one single Gospel text, Matt. xxv. 46;—for, though "hell fire," "everlasting fire "—*i.e.*, the fire that was kept perpetually burning in the adjacent valley of Gehenna for the consumption of the city refuse—is often spoken of as typifying the fate of the wicked, yet the expression distinctly implies, not everlasting *life* in fire, *but the precise opposite*,—namely *death*, annihilation, total destruction, in a fire ever at hand and never extinguished. The doctrine is not only in diametric antagonism to all that we can conceive or accept of the attributes of the God of Jesus, but to the whole spirit and teaching of our Great Master. It is at variance with other texts and with the general view [1] gathered from authentic Scripture, which teaches the "perishing," the "death," of the wicked, not their everlasting life in torment. And finally, the isolated text in question occurs in one only of the gospels,— and occurs there (as will be seen by comparing Matt. xxv. 31, with xxiv. 30) in immediate connection with the prophecy as to the coming of the end of the world within the life-time of the then existing generation,— a prophecy, the erroneousness of which is now demonstrated, and which there is (to say the least) no

---

[1] See countless arguments from the pens, not of unbelievers, but of qualified divines—among later ones, "Harmony of Scripture on future Punishments," by the Rev. S. Minton, and a paper by "Anglicanus," in the *Contemporary Review*, for May 1872.

need for believing ever to have come out of the mouth of Christ. What are called the "eschatological" discourses are notoriously among the passages in the gospels of most questionable genuineness.

Yet it is on the authority of a single verse so suspiciously located, so repeatedly contradicted elsewhere either distinctly or by implication, and so flagrantly out of harmony with the spirit both of Theism and of Christianity, that we are summoned to accept a dogma revolting alike to our purer instincts and our saner reason !]

Once more : the doctrine of the Atonement, of Christ's death having been a sacrifice in expiation of the sins of mankind, is the keystone of the common form of modern orthodoxy. It takes its origin from the epistles, and we believe can only appeal to *three* texts in the evangelists, for even partial confirmation. In Matth. xx. 28, it is said, "The Son of Man came, not to be ministered unto, but to minister, and to give his life *a ransom for many,*" an expression which may *countenance* the doctrine, but assuredly does not contain it. Again in Matth. xxvi. 28, we find, "This is my blood of the New Testament, which is shed for many *for the remission of sins.*" Mark (xiv. 24) and Luke (xxi. 20), however, who gave the same sentence, *both omit the significant expression;* while John omits, not only the expression, but the entire narrative of the institution of the Eucharist, which is said elsewhere to have been the occasion of it. In the fourth gospel, John the Baptist is represented as saying of Jesus (i. 29), " Behold the Lamb of God, which taketh away the sin of the world," an expression which may possibly be intended to convey the doctrine, but which occurs in what we have already shown to be about the most apocryphal portion of the whole gospel.

In fine, then, we arrive at this irresistible conclusion ; that—knowing several passages in the evangelists to be unauthentic, and having reason to suspect the authenticity of many others, and scarcely being able with absolute certainty to point to any which are perfectly and indubitably authentic—the probability *in favour* of the fidelity of any of the texts relied on to prove the peculiar and perplexing doctrines of modern orthodoxy, is far inferior to the probability *against* the truth of those doctrines. A doctrine perplexing to our reason and painful to our feelings *may* be from God ; but in this case the proof of its being from God must be proportionally clear and irrefragable ; the assertion of it in a narrative which does not scruple to attribute to God's Messenger words which he never uttered, is not only no proof, but scarcely even amounts to a presumption. There is no text in the evangelists, the divine (or Christian) origin of which is sufficiently unquestionable to enable it to serve as the foundation of doctrines repugnant to natural feeling or to common sense.

But, it will be objected, if these conclusions are sound, absolute uncertainty is thrown over the whole gospel history, and over all Christ's teaching. To this we reply, *in limine*, in the language of Algernon Sydney, " No consequence can destroy any truth ; " the sole matter for consideration is, Are our arguments correct ? not, Do they lead to a result which is embarrassing and unwelcome ?

But the inference is excessive ; the premises do not reach so far. The uncertainty thrown is not over the main points of Christ's history, which, after all its retrenchments, still stands out an intelligible though a skeleton account—not over the grand features, the pervading tone, of his doctrines or his character, which still present to us a clear, consistent, and splendid delineation ; but over those individual statements, passages, and discourses, which mar this delineation, which break its unity, which destroy its consistency, which cloud its clearness, which tarnish its beauty. The gain to us seems immense. It is true, we have no longer *absolute* certainty with regard to any one especial text or scene : such is neither necessary nor attainable ; it is true that, instead of passively accepting the whole heterogeneous and indigestible mass, we must, by the careful and conscientious exercise of those faculties with which we are endowed, by ratiocination and moral tact, separate what Christ did, from what he did not teach, as best we may. But the task will be difficult to those only who look in the gospels for a minute, dogmatic, and sententious creed —not to those who seek only to learn Christ's spirit,

that they may imbibe it, and to comprehend his
views of virtue and of God, that they may draw
strength and consolation from those fountains of living
water.[1]

---

[1] " The character of the record is such that I see not how any
great stress can be laid on particular actions attributed to Jesus.
That he lived a divine life, suffered a violent death, taught and
lived a most beautiful religion—this seems the great fact about
which a mass of truth and error has been collected."—Theodore
Parker, Discourse, p. 188.

CHAPTER XII.

WE now come to the very important question—as to the amount of authority which belongs to the teaching of the apostles. Are they to be implicitly relied on as having fully imbibed Christ's spirit ? and as faithful, competent, infallible expounders of his doctrine ? May we, in a word, regard their teaching as the teaching of Jesus himself ?

What their teaching was we know with perfect certainty, though not with all the fulness that might be desired. We have the teaching itself in the epistles, and a record of it in the Acts.

The latter work is not perfectly to be relied on. It conveys a vivid, and on the whole, in all probability, a faithful, picture of the formation of the early Christian churches, their sufferings, their struggles, their proceedings, and the spirit which animated them ; and, being written by a participator in those events, and a companion of Paul[1] through a portion

---

[1] Luke is generally considered to be the same as Silas. It is remarked that when Silas is represented in the narrative as being with Paul, the narrator speaks in the first person plural. "We came to Samothrace," &c. &c., xvi. 11; Rom. xvi. 21; Col. iv. 14; 2 Thes. i. 1; 2 Tim. iv. 11; Philem. 24.

of his missionary wanderings, must be regarded as
mainly historical; and we shall, therefore, make use
of the narrative with considerable confidence.   But,
as a source for discovering the special doctrines
preached by the apostles, it is of questionable safety,
inasmuch as the writer evidently allowed himself the
freedom indulged in by all historians of antiquity—
of composing speeches in the names of his actors ;
and thus the discourses, both of Paul and Peter, can
only be regarded as proceeding from Luke himself,
containing, probably, much that *was* said, but much,
also, that was only fitting to have been said, on such
occasions.

We have already adduced one unmistakable
instance of this practice in a previous chapter, where
Luke not only gives the speech of Gamaliel in a secret
Council of the Sanhedrim, from which the apostles
were expressly excluded,[1] but makes him refer, in the
past tense, to an event which did not take place till
some years after the speech was delivered.   In the
same way we have long discourses delivered by
Stephen, Peter, and Paul, at some of which Luke
may have been present, but which it is impossible
he should have remembered verbatim ; we have the
same invalid argument and erroneous reference to
prophecy regarding the resurrection of Christ put into
the mouths of two such opposite characters as Peter
and Paul (ii. 27, xiii. 35) ; we have another account

---

[1] Acts v. 34.

of a conversation in a *secret* council of the Jews (iv. 15-17) ; we have the beautiful oration of Paul at Athens, when we know that he was quite alone (xvii. 14, 15) ; we have the *private* conversation of the Ephesian craftsmen, when conspiring against the apostles (xix. 25, 27) ; we have the *private* letter of the Chief Captain Lysias to Felix (xxiii. 26); we have two *private* conversations between Festus and Agrippa about Paul (xxv. 14-22, and xxvi. 31, 32) ; and all these are given in precisely the style and manner of an ear-witness. We cannot, therefore, feel certain that any particular discourses or expressions attributed by Luke to the apostles were really, genuinely, and *unalteredly,* theirs. In the epistles, however, they speak for themselves, and so far there can be no mistake as to the doctrines they believed and taught.

Before proceeding further we wish to premise one remark. The epistles contained in our canon are *twenty-one* in number, viz. fourteen of Paul (including the Hebrews), three of John, two of Peter, one of James, and one of Jude. But the authorship of the Epistle to the Hebrews is more than doubtful ; the second of Peter, the second and third of John, and even those of James and Jude, were at a very early period reckoned among the spurious or doubtful writings.[1] The epistles of certain or *acknowledged*

---

[1] De Wette, i. 69-83. See also Hug, 583-650. The Epistle of James we are still disposed to consider genuine ; that of Jude is unimportant ; the second of Peter, and the third of John, are almost certainly spurious.

genuincness are thus reduced to *fifteen*, viz. thirteen of Paul, one of John, and one of Peter.

Thus, of fifteen epistles, of which we can pronounce with tolerable certainty that they are of apostolic origin, two only proceeded from the companions of Jesus, and the remaining thirteen from a man who had never seen him, save in a vision, nor heard his teaching, nor learnt from his disciples ;—a converted persecutor, who boasted that he received his instructions from direct supernatural communications.[1]

We will now proceed to establish the following propositions :—

I. That the Apostles differed from each other in opinion, and disagreed among themselves.

II. That they held and taught some opinions which we know to have been erroneous.

III. That both in their general tone, and in some important particulars, their teaching differed materially from that of Christ as depicted in the synoptical gospels.

I. Infallible expounders of a system of Religion or Philosophy cannot disagree among themselves as to the doctrines which compose that system, nor as to the spirit which should pervade it. Now, the Apostles did disagree among themselves in their exposition of the nature and constituents of their Master's system—

---

[1] Galatians i. 11-19.

and this, too, in matters of no small significance; they are not, therefore, infallible or certain guides.

Putting aside personal and angry contentions, such as those recorded in Acts xv. 39, which, however undignified, are, we fear, natural even to holy men; the first recorded dispute among the Apostles we find to have related to a matter of the most essential importance to the character of Christianity—viz., whether or not the Gospel should be preached to any but Jews—whether the Gentiles were to be admitted into the fold of Christ? We find (c. xi.) that when the Apostles and brethren in Judea heard that Peter had ventured to visit Gentiles, to eat with them, to preach to them, and even to baptize them, they were astonished and scandalised by the innovation, and " contended with him." The account of the discussion which ensued throws light upon two very interesting questions: upon the views entertained by Jesus himself (or at least as to those conveyed by him to his disciples), as to the range and limit of his mission; and upon the manner in which, and the grounds on which controversies were decided in the early Church.

We have been taught to regard Jesus as a prophet who announced himself as sent from God on a mission to preach repentance, and to teach the way of life to all mankind, and who left behind him the Apostles to complete the work which he was compelled to leave unfinished. The mission of Moses was to separate and educate a peculiar people, apart from the rest of the

world, for the knowledge and worship of the one true
God :—The mission of Christ was to bring all nations
to that knowledge and worship—to extend to all
mankind that salvation which, in his time, was considered to belong to the Jews alone, as well as to
point to a better and a wider way of life. Such is the
popular and established notion. But when we look
into the New Testament we find little to confirm this
view, and much to negative it. Putting aside our own
prepossessions, and inferences drawn from the character
of Christ, and the comprehensive grandeur of his
doctrine, nothing can well be clearer from the evidence
presented to us in the Scriptures, than that Jesus considered himself sent, not so much to the world at
large as to the Jews exclusively, to bring back his
countrymen to the true essence and spirit of that
religion whose purity had in his days been so
grievously corrupted ; and to elevate and enlarge their
views from the stores of his own rich and comprehensive mind.

It will be allowed by all that the Apostles, at the
commencement of their ministry after the crucifixion of
their Lord, had not the least idea that their mission
extended to any but the Jews, or that their Master
was anything but a Jewish Messiah and Deliverer.
Their first impatient question to him when assembled
together after the resurrection, is said to have been,
" Lord, wilt thou at this time restore the kingdom to
Israel ?"[1]   The whole of the account we are now con-

---

[1] Acts i. 6.

sidering, brings out in strong relief their notions as to
the narrow limits of their ministry. When Peter is
sent for by Cornelius, and hears the relation of his
vision, he exclaims, as if a perfectly new idea had
struck him, " Of a truth I perceive that God is no
respecter of persons ; but in every nation he that
feareth him and worketh righteousness is accepted of
him" (Acts x. 34) ; and he goes on to expound " the
word which God sent to *the children of Israel*" (v.
3G), and which the Apostles were commanded to
"preach to the people" (v. 42), " the people," as the
context (v. 41) shows, meaning simply the Jews. The
Jewish believers, we are told (v. 45), " as many as
came with Peter were astonished, *because that on the
Gentiles also* was poured out the gift of the Holy
Ghost." When Peter was called to account by the
other Apostles ·for having preached to and baptized
Gentiles (xi. 1)—a proceeding which evidently (xi. 2,
3) shocked and surprised them all—he justified himself, not by reference to any commands of Jesus, not
by quoting precept or example of his Master, but
simply by relating a vision or dream which he supposed to proceed from a divine suggestion. The
defence appeared valid to the brethren, and they
inferred from it, in a manner which shows what a
new and unexpected light had broken in upon them,—
" *Then* hath God also to the Gentiles granted repentance
unto. life" (xi. 18.) Now, could this have been the
case, had Christ given his· disciples any commission to
preach the gospel to the Gentiles, or given them the

slightest reason to suppose that other nations besides the Jews were included in that commission ? (See also for confirmation xi. 19, and xiii. 46.) It is to be observed also that throughout the elaborate arguments contained in the Epistle to the Romans, to show that the gospel *ought* to be preached to the Gentiles—that there is no difference between Greek and Jew, &c.— Paul, though he quotes largely from the Hebrew Prophets, *never appeals to any sayings of Jesus*, in confirmation of his view ; and in the Acts, in two instances, his mission to the Gentiles is represented as arising out of a direct subsequent revelation (in a vision) to himself. (Acts xxii. 21 ; xxvi. 17 ; ix. 15.)

As, therefore, none of the Apostles, either in their writings or in their discussions, appeal to the sayings or deeds of Christ during his lifetime as their warrant for preaching the gospel to the Gentiles, but on the contrary, one and all manifest a total ignorance of any such deeds or sayings—we think it must be concluded that the various texts extant, conveying his commands to " preach the gospel to all nations," could never have proceeded from him, but are to be ranked among the many *ascribed* sayings, embodying the ideas of a later period, which we find both in the Acts and the evangelists.[1] None of these are quoted or referred to

---

[1] These texts are the following (Matth. viii. 11, 12) : " Many shall come from the east and west, and shall sit down with Abraham, and Isaac, and Jacob, in the kingdom of Heaven. But the children of the kingdom shall be cast into outer darkness." This, however, as well as the parable of the vineyard (xxi. 43),

by the Apostles in their justification, and therefore could not have been known to them, and, since unknown, could not be authentic.

On the other hand, there are several passages in the gospels which, if genuine, clearly indicate that it was not from any neglect or misunderstanding of the instructions of their Lord, that the Apostles regarded their mission as confined to the Jews. "Go not into the way of the Gentiles, and into any city of the Samaritans enter ye not: but go rather to the lost sheep of the house of Israel" (Matth. x. 5, 6.) " I am not sent but to the lost sheep of the house of Israel" (Matth. xv. 24.) "Verily I say unto you, that ye which have followed me, in the regeneration when the Son of Man shall sit in the throne of his glory, ye also shall sit upon twelve thrones, judging the twelve tribes of Israel" (Matth. xix. 28).[1] "It is easier for heaven and earth to pass

and that of the supper (Luke xiv. 16), might be merely an indignant denunciation called forth by the obstinacy of the Jews in refusing to listen to his claims. Matth. xxiv. 14, xxviii. 19; Mark xvi. 15, we have already shown reason to believe spurious; and Luke xxiv. 47, with Acts i. 8, bear equal marks of unauthenticity. It is true that Jesus talked with a Samaritan woman, and healed a Samaritan leper; but the Samaritans were not Gentiles, only heretical Jews. We find from Acts viii. 5, 14, that the Apostles early and without scruple preached to and baptized *Samaritans*. Jesus also healed a Gentile centurion's servant: but in the first place, the servant might have been a Jew, though his master was not; and, secondly, a temporal blessing, a simple act of charity, Jesus could not grudge even to strangers.

[1] It is, however, nearly impossible to consider this verse as genuine, especially when read in connection with ch. xx. 20-28.

than one tittle of the law to fail" (Luke xvi. 17.) "Think not I am come to destroy the law and the prophets : I am not come to destroy, but to fulfil" (Matth. v. 17). "This day is salvation come to this house, forasmuch as he also is a son of Abraham" (Luke xix. 9.) "Salvation is of the Jews" (John iv. 22.)

It would appear, then, that neither the historical nor the epistolary Scriptures give us any reason for surmising that Jesus directed, or contemplated, the spread of his gospel beyond the pale of the Jewish nation ; that the apostles at least had no cognizance of any such views on his part; that when the question of the admission of the Gentiles to the knowledge of the gospel, came before them in the natural progress of events, it created considerable difference of opinion among them, and at first the majority were decidedly hostile to any such liberality of view, or such extension of their missionary labours. The mode in which the controversy was conducted, and the grounds on which it was decided, are strongly characteristic of the moral and intellectual condition of the struggling church at that early period. The objectors bring no argument to show why the Gentiles should *not* be admitted to the gospel light, but they put Peter at once on his defence, as having, in preaching to others than to Jews, done a thing which, *primâ facie*, was out of rule, and required justification. And Peter replies to them, not by appeals to the paramount authority of Christ, —not by reference to the tenour of his life and teach-

ing,—not by citing the case of the Centurion's servant,
or the Canaanitish woman, or the parables of the
vineyard and the supper,—not by showing from the
nature and fitness of things that so splendid a plan
of moral elevation, of instruction—such a comprehensive scheme of redemption, according to the orthodox
view—ought to be as widely preached as possible,
— not by arguing that Christ had come into the
world to spread the healing knowledge of Jehovah,
of our God and Father, to all nations, to save all
sinners and all believers ; but simply by relating a
vision, or rather a dream—the most natural one possible to a man as hungry as Peter is represented to
have been—the interpretation of which—*at first a
puzzle to him* — is suggested by the simultaneous
appearance of the messengers of Cornelius, who also
pleads a heavenly vision as a reason for the summons.
This justification would scarcely by itself have been
sufficient, for the dream might have meant nothing at
all, or Peter's interpretation of it—evidently a doubtful and *tentative* one—might have been erroneous ;
so he goes on to argue, that the event showed him to
have been right, inasmuch as, after his preaching, the
Holy Ghost fell upon all the household of Cornelius :
" And as I began to speak, the Holy Ghost fell on
them, as on us at the beginning ; . . . . . forasmuch
then as God gave them the like gift as unto us who
believed on the Lord Jesus Christ ; what was I, that
I could withstand God ? " (Acts xi. 15, 17). This
argument clenched the matter, satisfied the brethren,

and settled, once for all, the question as to the admission of the Gentiles into the church of Christ.

It becomes necessary, therefore, to inquire more closely into the nature of this argument which appeared to the apostles so conclusive and irrefragable. What was this Holy Spirit ? and in what way did it manifest its presence ? so that the apostles recognised it at once as the special and most peculiar gift vouchsafed to believers.

The case, as far as the Acts and the epistles enable us to learn it, appears clearly to have been this :— The indication—or at least the most common, specific, and indubitable indication—of the Holy Spirit having fallen upon any one, was his beginning to "speak with tongues," to utter strange exclamations, unknown words, or words in an unknown tongue. Thus, in the case of the apostles on the day of Pentecost, we are told, " They were all filled with the Holy Ghost, and *began to speak with other tongues*, as the Spirit gave them utterance " (Acts ii. 4). Again, in the case of the household of Cornelius, " And they . . . . were astonished . . . . because that on the Gentiles also was poured out the gift of the Holy Ghost. *For they heard them speak with tongues*, and magnify God " (x. 45, 46). The same indication appeared also in the case of the disciples of the Baptist, whom Paul found at Ephesus : " And when Paul had laid his hands on them, the Holy Ghost came upon them ; *and they spake with tongues*, and prophesied" (xix. 6). The " speaking with tongues " (to which in the last instance is added " prophesying," or preaching) is the only specified external manifestation, cognisable by the senses, by which it was known that such and such individuals had received the Holy Ghost. What, then, was this " speaking with tongues ? "[1] The popular idea is, that it was the power of speaking foreign languages without having learned them— supernaturally, in fact. This interpretation derives countenance, and probably its foundation, from the statement of Luke (Acts ii. 2-8), which is considered to intimate that the apostles preached to each man of their vast and motley audience in his own native language. But there are many difficulties in the way of this interpretation, and much reason to suspect in the whole narrative a large admixture of the mythic element.

1. We have already seen that Luke is not to be implicitly trusted as an historian ; and some remarkable discrepancies between the accounts of the gospels and the Acts will be noted in a subsequent chapter, when we treat of the Resurrection and Ascension.[2]

2. It appears from Matthew (x. 1, 8, 20), that the Holy Spirit had been already imparted to the apostles during the lifetime of Jesus, and a second outpouring

---

[1] See also the passage in the spurious addition to Mark's Gospel (xvi. 17). " And these signs shall follow them that believe : in my name shall they cast out devils ; *they shall speak with new tongues*," &c. The date at which this interpolation was written is unknown, but it serves to show that, at that period, speaking with new tongues was one of the established signs of belief.

[2] See also similar differences between the Acts and the Epistles of Paul in narrating the same events.

therefore could not be required. John, however, tells us (xx. 20), that Jesus expressly and *personally* conferred this gift after his resurrection, but *before his ascension:* " And when he had said this, he *breathed* on them, and saith unto them, *Receive ye the Holy Ghost.*" But in the Acts, the " breathing " had become " a rushing mighty wind," and the outpouring of the Spirit is placed some days *after the ascension,* and the personal interposition is dispensed with. These discrepant accounts cannot all be faithful, and that of Luke is apparently the least authentic.

3. We have no evidence anywhere that the apostles knew, or employed, any language except Hebrew (or Aramaic) and Greek—Greek being (as Hug has clearly proved [1]) the common language in use throughout the eastern provinces of the Roman Empire. Nay, we have *some* reason to believe that they were *not* acquainted with other languages ; for by the general tradition of the early church,[2] Mark is called the " in-

---

[1] Hug, ii. 1, § 10, p. 326.

[2] Papias, Irenæus, and Jerome all call him so. See Eusebius. Another consideration which renders the story still more doubtful is, that it appears very probable that Greek, though not always the native, was the current language, or a current language, among all those nations enumerated (vers. 9-10). Media, Mesopotamia, Asia Minor, Arabia, and Egypt were full of Greek cities, and Greek was generally spoken there. (See the dissertation of Hug, above referred to.) If therefore the apostles had addressed the audience in Greek, as it was probably their habit to do, they would naturally have been intelligible even to that miscellaneous audience. Acts xxii. 2, shows that even in Jerusalem addressing the people in Hebrew was an unusual thing.

terpreter" of Peter. Now, if Peter had been gifted as
we imagine on the day of Pentecost, he would have
needed no interpreter.

4. The language in which the occurrence is related
would seem to imply that the miracle was wrought
upon the hearers, rather than on the speakers—that
whatever the language in which the Apostles *spoke*,
the audience *heard* them each man in his own.
" When the multitude came together they were confounded, because that *every man heard them speak
in his own language."* . . . . " Behold, are not all
these which speak Galileans ? And how *hear we
every man in our own tongue*, wherein we were
born ?" The supposition that the different Apostles
addressed different audiences in different languages,
successively, is inconsistent with the text, which clearly
indicates that the whole was one transaction, and took
place at one time. " Peter standing up . . . said . . .
These are not drunken as ye suppose, seeing *it is but
the third hour of the day.*"

5. The people, we are told, "were in doubt" at the
strange and incomprehensible phenomenon, and said,
" What meaneth this ? " while others thought the
Apostles must be drunk—a natural perplexity and
surmise, if the utterances were incoherent and unintelligible ejaculations—but not so, if they were discourses addressed to each set of foreigners in their
respective languages. Moreover, Peter's defence is
not what it would have been in the latter case. He
does not say, " We have been endowed from on high

with the power of speaking foreign languages which we have never learned : we are, as you say, ignorant Galileans, but God has given us this faculty that we might tell you of his Son ;" but he assures them that those utterances which led them to suppose him and his fellow-disciples to be drunk were the consequences of that outpouring of spiritual emotion which had been prophesied as one of the concomitants of the millennium. "This is that which was spoken by the Prophet Joel ; and it shall come to pass in the last days, saith Jehovah, I will pour out of my Spirit upon all flesh ; and your sons and your daughters shall prophesy, and your young men shall see visions, and your old men shall dream dreams."

6. Luke indicates in several passages, that in the other cases mentioned the Holy Spirit fell upon the recipients *in the same manner, and with the same results*, as on the Apostles on the day of Pentecost (Acts x. 47 ; xi. 15-17 ; xv. 8, 9 [1]). Now, in these cases there is no reason whatever to believe that the "gift of tongues" meant the power of speaking foreign languages. In the first case (that of Cornelius) it could not have been this ; for as all the recipients began to "speak with tongues," and yet were members

---

[1] Peter says, "Can any man forbid water, that these should not be baptized, which have received the Holy Ghost *as well as we ?"* . . . "The Holy Ghost fell on them, *as on us at the beginning.*" . . . . "Forasmuch, then, as God *gave them the like gift as unto us.*" . . . . "And God gave them the Holy Ghost, *even as unto us, and put no difference between us and them.*"

of one household, such an unnecessary display of newly-acquired knowledge of power would have been in the highest degree impertinent and ostentatious.

There can, we think, be no doubt—indeed we are not aware that any doubt has ever been expressed—that the remarks of Paul in the 12th, 13th, and 14th chapters of the first epistle to the Corinthians, respecting the "speaking with tongues,"—the "gift of tongues,"—"the unknown tongue," &c.,—refer to the same faculty, or supposed spiritual endowment, spoken of in the Acts ; which fell on the Apostles at the day of Pentecost, and on the household of Cornelius, and the disciples of Apollos, as already cited. The identity of the gift referred to in all the cases is, we believe, unquestioned. Now the language of Paul clearly shows, that this "speaking with tongues" was not preaching in a *foreign* language, but in an *unknown* language ;—that it consisted of unintelligible, and probably incoherent, utterances.[1] He repeatedly distinguishes the gift of tongues from that of preaching (or, as it is there called, prophesy), and the gift of speaking the unknown tongues from the gift of interpreting the same. " To one is given by the Spirit . . . . . . the working of miracles ; to another prophesy ; to another *divers kinds of tongues ;* to another *the interpretation of tongues.*" . . . . . . " Have all

---

[1] We are glad to corroborate our opinion by a reference to that of Neander, who, in his " History of the Planting of the Early Church," comes to the same conclusion, chap. i.

the gifts of healing ? do all speak with tongues ? do all interpret ? " (1 Cor. xii. 10-30. See also xiii. 1, 2, 8.) "Let him that speaketh in an unknown tongue pray that he may interpret" (xiv. 13.) Again, he classes this power of tongues (so invaluable to missionaries, had it been really a capacity of speaking foreign languages) very low among spiritual endowments. "First Apostles, secondarily prophets, thirdly teachers, *after that* miracles, *then* gifts of healing, helps, governments, *diversities of* tongues" (xii. 28.) "Greater is he that prophesieth than he that speaketh with tongues" (xiv. 5). He further expressly explains this gift to consist in unintelligible utterances, which were useless to, and lost upon, the audience. "He that speaketh in an unknown tongue speaketh not unto man, but unto God, *for no man understandeth him*" (xiv. 2). (See also ver. 6-9, 16.) Finally, he intimates pretty plainly that the practice of speaking these unknown tongues was becoming vexatious, and bringing discredit on the Church ; and he labours hard to discourage it. "I thank my God that I speak with tongues more than ye all : yet in the Church I had rather speak five words with my understanding, that I might teach others also, than ten thousand words in an unknown tongue" (xiv. 18, 19). "If the whole Church be come together into one place, and all speak with tongues, and there come in unlearned men or unbelievers, will they not say ye are mad ? " (ver. 23). "If any man speak in an unknown tongue, let it be by two, or at most by three, and that

by course ; and let one interpret. . . . . For
God is not the author of confusion, but of peace "
(ver. 27-33). (See also ver. 39, 40.)

It is, we think, almost impossible to read the whole
of the three chapters from which the above citations
are made, without coming to the conclusion that in
the early Christian Church there were a number of
weak, mobile, imaginative minds, who, over-excited by
the sublimity of the new doctrine expounded to them,
and by the stirring eloquence of its preachers, passed
the faint and undefinable line which separates
enthusiasm from delirium, and gave vent to their
exaltation in incoherent or inarticulate utterances,
which the compassionate sympathy, or the con-
sanguineous fancies, of those around them, dignified
with the description of speaking, or prophesying, in
an unknown tongue. No one familiar with physiology,
or medical or religious history,[1] can be ignorant how

---

[1] Somewhat similar phenomena have manifested themselves on
several occasions in the course of the last eight hundred years, and
even in our own day, when religious excitement has proved too
strong for weak minds or sensitive frames to bear without giving
way. We find them recorded in the case of the ecstatics of
Cevennes, who underwent severe persecution in France after the
revocation of the Edict of Nantes, and among the *convulsionnaires*
of St. Medard near the close of last century. Both these cases are
examined in considerable detail in a very curious and valuable work
by Bertrand, a French physician, " Sur les Varietés de l'Extase "
(pp. 323, 359.) But our own country has presented us within a
few years with a reproduction of precisely the same results arising
from similar causes. There is extant a very remarkable and
painfully-interesting pamphlet by a Mr. Baxter, who was at one

contagious delusions of this nature always prove, and
when once these incoherences became the recognized
sign of the descent of the Spirit, every one would,
of course, be anxious to experience, and to propagate

---

time a shining light in Mr. Irving's congregation, and a great
"speaker with tongues," in which he gives a detailed account of
all the accompanying phenomena. It was written after he had
recovered; though he never relinquished his belief in the supernatural nature of these utterances, but finally concluded them to be
from Satan, on the ground of some of the speakers uttering what he
thought false doctrine. The description he gives of his own state
and that of others during the visitations indicates in a manner that
no physiologist can mistake, a condition of cerebral excitement
implying hysteria, and verging on madness, and by no means
uncommon. Sometimes, when praying, his shrieks were so loud
that he was compelled to " thrust his handkerchief into his mouth
that he might not alarm the house." Others fell down " convulsed
and foaming like demoniacs." "My whole body was violently
agitated; for the space of ten minutes I was paralyzed under a
shaking of my limbs, and no expression except a convulsive sigh."
His friends " remarked on his excited state of mind." A servant
was taken out of his house deranged, and pronounced by the
tongues to be possessed by a devil. Another "speaker with
tongues" did nothing but mutter inarticulate nonsense with a
" most revolting expression of countenance." Mr. Baxter says
the utterances which were urged upon him by " the power," were
sometimes intelligible, sometimes not; sometimes French, sometimes Latin, and sometimes in languages which he did not know,
but which his wife thought to be Spanish. He says at last, " My
persuasion concerning the unknown tongue is that it is *no language
whatever*, but a mere collection of words and sentences, often a
mere jargon of sounds." One man seldom began to speak without
the contagion seizing upon others, so that numbers spoke at once,
as in Paul's time. It is clear to any one who reads Mr. Baxter's
candid and unpretending narrative, that a skilful physician would
at once have terminated the whole delusion by a liberal exhibition
of phlebotomy and anodynes.

them.   We have seen the same thing precisely in our own day among the Irvingites.   How is it, then, that the same phenomena of mental weakness and excitability which in the one case aroused only pity and contempt, should in the other be regarded with a mysterious reverence and awe ?

The language of Paul in reference to the "unknown tongues" appears to us clearly that of an honest and a puzzled man, whose life in an age of miracles, and whose belief in so many grand religious marvels, has prepared him to have faith in more ;—whose religious humility will not allow him to prescribe in what manner the Spirit of God may, or may not, operate : —but at the same time, whose strong good sense makes him feel that these incomprehensible utterances must be useless, and were most probably nonsensical, morbid, and grotesque.   He seems to have been anxious to repress the unknown tongue, yet unwilling harshly to condemn it as a vain delusion.

That there was a vast amount of delusion and unsound enthusiasm in the Christian Church at the time of the Apostles, not only seems certain, but it could not possibly have been otherwise, without such an interference with the ordinary operations of natural causes as would have amounted to an incessant miracle. Wonders, real or supposed, were of daily occurrence. The subjects habitually brought before the contemplation of Believers were of such exciting and sublime magnificence that even the strongest minds cannot too long dwell upon them without some degree of perilous emotion. The recent events which closed the life of the Founder of their Faith, and above all the glorious truth, or the splendid fiction, of his resurrection and ascension, were depicted with all the stirring grandeur of oriental imagination. The expectation of an almost immediate end of the world, and the reception into glory and power of the living believer,—the hope which each one entertained, of being " caught up " to meet his Redeemer in the clouds—was of itself sufficient to overthrow all but the coldest tempers ; while the constant state of mental tension in which they were kept by the antagonism and persecution of the world without, could not fail to maintain a degree of exaltation very unfavourable to sobriety either of thought or feeling. All these influences, too, were brought to bear upon minds the most ignorant and unprepared, upon the poor and the oppressed, upon women and children ; and to crown the whole, the most prominent doctrine of their faith was that of the immediate, special, and hourly influence of the Holy Spirit—a doctrine of all others the most liable to utter and gross misconception, and the most apt to lead to perilous mental excitement. Hence they were constantly on the lookout for miracles. Their creed did not supply, and indeed scarcely admitted, any criterion of what was or was not of divine origin—for who could venture to pronounce or define how the Spirit might or should manifest itself ?—and thus ignorance and folly too often become the arbiters of wisdom—and the ravings of delirium were listened to as the words of inspiration, and of God. If Jesus could have returned to earth thirty years after his death, and sat in the midst of an assembly of his followers, who were listening in hushed and wondering prostration of mind to a speaker in the "unknown tongue," how would he have wept over the humiliating and disappointing spectacle ! how would he have grieved to think that the incoherent jargon of delirium or hysteria should be mistaken for the promptings of his Father's spirit.

We are driven, then, to the painful, but unavoidable, conclusion, that those mysterious and unintelligible utterances which the Apostles and the early Christians generally looked upon as the effects of the Holy Spirit —the manifestation of its presence, the signs of its operation, the special indication and criterion of its having fallen upon any one—were in fact simply the physiologically natural results of morbid and perilous cerebral exaltation, induced by strong religious excitement acting on uncultivated and susceptible minds ;— results which in all ages and nations have followed in similar circumstances and from similar stimulants ; —and that these "signs," to which Peter appealed, and to which the other brethren succumbed, as proving that God intended the Gospel to be preached to Gentiles as well as to Jews, showed only that Gentiles were susceptible to the same excitements, and manifested that susceptibility in the same manner, as the Jews.

Shortly after the question as to the admission of the Gentiles into the Christian Church had been decided in the singular and inconclusive manner above related, a second subject of dispute arose among the brethren —a corollary almost of the first—the nature of which strongly confirms some of the views we have just put forth.   The dispute was this :—whether it was necessary for those Gentiles who had been baptized and admitted into the Christian Community, to observe the ritual portion of the Jewish law ?—whether, in fact, by becoming Christians, they had, *ipso facto*, become Jews, and liable to Judaic observances ?   The mere broaching of such a question, and the serious schism it threatened in the infant sect, show how little the idea had yet taken root among the disciples, of *the distinctness of the essence*, the superiority of the spirit, the newness of the dispensation, taught by Jesus, and how commonly Christianity was regarded as simply a purification and renewal of Judaism.

It appears from the 15th chapter of the Acts, that when Paul and Barnabas were at Antioch, teaching and baptizing the Gentiles, certain Jewish Christians (Pharisees we are told in verse 5) caused considerable trouble and dissension by asserting that it was necessary for the new converts " to be circumcised, and to keep the law of Moses "—a doctrine which Paul and Barnabas vehemently opposed.   The question was so important, and the dissension became so serious, that a council of the Apostles and Elders was summoned at Jerusalem to discuss and decide the matter.   From

11.   G

the brief account given by Luke of the proceedings
of this conclave it does not appear that there was
any material difference among those assembled—the
speakers among them, at least Peter, Paul, and James,
all arguing on the same side ; but from the account
of the same [1] transaction, given by Paul in the second
chapter of his Epistle to the Galatians, it is clear that
Peter (covertly or subsequently) took the Jewish side
of the discussion, " When Peter was come to Antioch,
I withstood him to the face, because he was to be
blamed.   For before that certain came from James, he
did eat with the Gentiles ; but when they were come
he withdrew and separated himself, fearing them
which were of the circumcision.   And the other Jews
dissembled likewise with him ; insomuch that Barnabas also was carried away with their dissimulation.
But when I saw that they walked not uprightly,
according to the truth of the Gospel, I said unto Peter
before them all, If thou, being a Jew, livest after the
manner of the Gentiles, and not as do the Jews, why
compellest thou the Gentiles to live as do the Jews ? "
This speech, directed *against* Peter, is so like that
which Luke (Acts xv. 10, 11) puts into the mouth of
Peter, that we cannot but suppose some mistake on
the historian's part.[2]   It is certain, however, both
from the narrative in the Acts and from the whole

---

[1] The same, or a similar one.

[2] Unless, as has been suggested, Peter, afterwards overpowered
by the unanimity of the Judaizers, flinched from his principles, and
so incurred Paul's indignation.

tenor of the Pauline Epistles, that the case was argued
without any reference to the intentions of Christ, or to
instructions left by him—but, instead, by inconclusive
quotations from prophecy, and by considerations of
practical good sense. The decision at which they
arrived, on the suggestion of James, seems on the
whole to have been both wise and sound ; viz., that
the Gentile converts should not be burdened with the
observances of the ritual law, but should abstain from
everything which could be considered as countenancing or tolerating idolatry, from fornication, and from
food which, probably from its unwholesomeness, was
considered unlawful in most oriental countries.

The discussion and decision of this Council on a
question of such vital import, both to the success and
to the character of Christianity—a question involving
its spiritual nature and essence as apart from ceremony
—shew strongly and clearly the two points essential
to our present argument : *first*, that difference of
opinion on matters of vital significance existed among
the Apostles ; and, *secondly*, that these matters were
discussed in their Councils on argumentative grounds,
without the least pretension on the part of any of
them to infallibility, supernatural wisdom, or exclusive
or peculiar knowledge of the mind of Christ.

That very different views as to the essentials and
most important elements of Christianity were taken
by the several Apostles, or rather, perhaps, that the
same elements underwent very material modifications
in passing through such different minds—that to some

its essence seemed to consist in the ethical and spiritual, and to others in the speculative and scholastic, ideas which it contained or suggested—can scarcely be doubted by any one who will read simultaneously, and for the purpose of comparison, Paul's Epistle to the Corinthians, the Epistle of James, and the first of John and Peter. But the discrepancy is of a kind that will be perceptible on an attentive perusal, rather than one which can be pointed out by a citation of particular passages. It is a discrepancy of tone and spirit. No one, we think, can fail to perceive that the views of Christ's object, character, and mission, entertained by Paul and by James, were radically different.[1]

There is some evidence also that the Apostles not only differed from each other, but that their own respective views varied materially on important subjects in the course of their ministry. This will appear, more especially, in contrasting the exhortations of Paul on the subject of marriage, for example, contained in 1 Cor. vii., with those given in 1 Timothy iv. 3, v. 14.   .

II. Our second position was, that the Apostles held some opinions which we know to be erroneous. It is

---

[1] Hug (p. 613) says, " In this epistle (that of James) the Apostle Paul is (if I may be allowed to use so harsh an expression for a while) contradicted so flatly, that it would seem to have been written in opposition to some of his doctrines and positions. All that Paul has taught respecting faith, its efficacy in justification, and the inutility of works, is here directly contravened."

essential not to overstate the case. They held several opinions which we *believe* to be erroneous, but only one which, as it related to a matter of fact, we *know* to have been erroneous. They unanimously and unquestioningly believed and taught that the end of the world was at hand, and would arrive in the lifetime of the then existing generation. On this point there appears to have been no hesitation in their individual minds, nor any difference of opinion among them.

The following are the passages of the Apostolic writings which most strongly express, or most clearly imply this conviction.

Paul. (1 Thess. iv. 15, 16, 17.) "This *we say unto you by the word of the Lord*, that *we which are alive and remain unto the coming of the Lord*, shall not prevent them which are asleep. For . . . . the dead in Christ shall rise first ; then *we which are alive and remain* shall be caught up together with them in the clouds to meet the Lord in the air : and so shall we ever be with the Lord." (1 Cor. vii. 29.) "But this I say, brethren, *the time is short :* it remaineth that both they that have wives, be as though they had none ; and they that weep, as though they wept not ; and they that rejoice, as though they rejoiced not ; and they that buy, as though they possessed not ; and they that use this world as not abusing it ; *for the fashion of this world passeth away.*" (1 Cor. xv. 51.) "Behold I shew you a mystery ; *we shall not all sleep*, but we shall all be changed." (See also 1 Tim. iv. 1 ; 2 Tim. iii. 1.)

Peter. (1 Ep. i. 5, 20.) " An inheritance incorruptible, and undefiled, and that fadeth not away, reserved in heaven for you, who are kept by the power of God through faith unto salvation, *ready to be revealed in the last time.*" " Christ . . . who verily was foreordained before the foundation of the world, but was manifest *in these last times* for you." (iv. 7.) " *The end of all things is at hand.*"

John. (1 Ep. ii. 18.) " Little children, *it is the last time :* and as ye have heard that antichrist shall come, even now are there many antichrists ; whereby *we know that it is the last time.*"

James. (v. 8.) " Be ye also patient ; . . . *for the coming of the Lord draweth nigh.*"[1]

We may well conceive that this strong conviction must, in men like the Apostles, have been something far beyond a mere abstract or speculative opinion. In fact, it modified their whole tone of thought and feeling ; and could not fail to do so.[2] The firm and living faith that a few years would bring the second coming of their Lord in his glory, and the fearful termination of all earthly things—when " the heavens should be gathered together as a scroll, and the elements should

---

[1] See also Acts i. 11 ; and 2 Peter iii.

[2] How indisputably this conviction was the current one in the Apostolic age may be perceived from finding that Matthew makes no scruple of putting the announcement into the mouth of Christ himself, " Verily I say unto you, this generation shall not pass away till ye shall see the Son of Man coming in the clouds of heaven," &c., &c.—Matthew xxiv. 30-34.

melt with fervent heat "—and that many among them should be still alive, and should witness these awful occurrences with human eyes, and should join their glorified Master without passing through the portals of the grave—could not exist in their minds without producing not only a profound contempt for all the pomps and distinctions of the world, but an utter carelessness for the future interests of mankind, for posterity, even for kindred—without indeed distorting all the just proportions of those scenes of nature and society, in the midst of which their lot was cast.[1] If the world, and all its mighty and far-stretching interests—if the earth, and its infinite and ever-varying beauties—if the sky, and its myriads of midnight glories—were indeed to be finally swept away in the time and the presence of the existing actors in the busy scene of life, where was the use of forming any new ties of kindred or affection, which must terminate so suddenly and so soon ? Why give a moment's thought to the arts which embellish life, the amenities which adorn it, the sciences which smooth it or prolong it, or the knowledge which enriches and dignifies its course ? Marriage, children, wealth, power, astronomy, philosophy, poetry—what were they to men who knew that ten or twenty years would transplant not only themselves but the whole race of man, to a world where all would be. forgotten, and would leave the earth—the scene of these things—a destroyed and blackened chaos ? To this conviction may be traced St Paul's confused and

---

[1] See Natural History of Enthusiasm, § v., pp. 100, 101.

fluctuating notions on the subject of marriage. And this conviction, teeming with such immense and dangerous consequences, and held by all the Apostles, was, we now know, wholly incorrect and unfounded. Next to the resurrection of Christ, there was probably no doctrine which they held so undoubtingly, or preached so dogmatically as this, with regard to which they were totally in error.

If, then, they were so misinformed, or mistaken, on a point having so immediate and powerful a bearing upon practical life, how is it possible to place absolute confidence in them when they deal with matters of deeper speculation, or enforce obscure and startling dogmas, or lay down conditions of salvation apparently at least at variance with those announced by Christ ?

III. Our third position is, that the teaching of the Apostles in some important particulars, but still more in its general tone, differed from that of their Master, as the latter is recorded in the synoptical gospels.

We know that the Apostles, during the lifetime of their Lord, were very far indeed from imbibing his spirit, or fully apprehending his doctrine. Their misconceptions of his mission and his teaching are represented as constant and obstinate, almost to stupidity. They are narrow, where he was liberal and comprehensive ; they were exclusively Jewish, where he was comparatively cosmopolitan ; they were violent, where he was gentle; impetuous, where he was patient ; vindictive, where he was forgiving ; worldly, where he was spiritual. They had their thoughts too much fixed on " the restoration of the Kingdom to Israel," and the " twelve thrones" on which they hoped to sit ; they could not embrace or endure the sublime conception of a suffering Teacher and Redeemer ; of a victory to be achieved by death ; they were dismayed and confounded by their Master's crucifixion ; they had no expectation of his resurrection ; and when his hour of calamity arrived, " they all forsook him and fled."

Disciples who so little resembled and so imperfectly understood their Lord during his life, could not be adequate representatives or expounders of his religion after his death, unless some new and strange influence had come upon them, of energy sufficient to rectify their notions and to change their characters. The Supernaturalists, who comprise the great body of the Christian World, conceive this influence to have consisted in that Holy Spirit which, according to John, was promised, and, according to Luke, was given, after the Ascension of Christ, and which was to " teach them all things," and to " bring all things to their remembrance" which their Lord had taught them. According to the Rationalists, this metamorphosing influence must be traced to the death of Jesus, which spiritualized the views of the disciples by extinguishing their worldly and ambitious hopes.[1] The first is

---

[1] " The death, resurrection, and ascension of Christ, introduced a necessary change into the conceptions of the Apostles ; these drove out of their Messianic idea the spirit of the world, and introduced into it the spirit of God. They could not retain their

a possible, the second is a reasonable and probable explanation. The death and resurrection of Christ must have worked, and evidently did work, a very great modification in many of the notions of the twelve Apostles, and materially changed their point of view of their Lord's mission. But there are many indications that this change was not a radical one; it affected rather the *accessories* than the *essence* of their Messianic notions; for, though they relinquished their expectation of an immediate restoration of the kingdom, they still, as we have seen, retained the conviction that that restoration would take place, in their own day, in a far more signal and glorious manner.

Jewish ideas of the reign of the Messiah, in connection with the crucified Jesus. . . . His death struck down a principal part of their errors, and his exaltation forced upon them a new idea of his Kingdom. . . . Christ returns to earth to show that God was with him : and| he ascends into heaven to repel the imagination which otherwise might possibly arise, nay, which actually had arisen, that even yet he might raise his standard upon earth, and realise the gigantic illusion of the Jew."—(Sermon on the Comforter, by the Rev. J. H. Thom, Liverpool, p. 28.) There is much reason in these remarks, but they must be taken with large deductions. It is astonishing how much of the " Jewish conceptions of the Messiah" the Apostles *did* contrive to retain "in connection with a crucified and ascended Christ." They still looked for his victorious earthly reappearance in Judæa, in their own times ; an expectation to which the words attributed by Luke (Acts i. 11) to the angels, bear ample testimony, and, if genuine, would have gone far to justify. " Ye men of Galilee, why stand ye gazing up into heaven ? This same Jesus, which is taken up from you into heaven, shall so come in like manner as ye have seen him go into heaven."—See also the view of Paulus on this subject, quoted by Hare (Mission of the Comforter, ii. 480.)

Their views were spiritualized up to a certain point, *but no further*, even as to this great subject ; and on other points the change seems to have been less complete. The Epistle of James, indeed, is a worthy relic of one who had drunk in the spirit, and appreciated the lessons of the meek, practical, and spiritual Jesus. But in the case of the other two Apostles, Peter is Peter still, and John is the John of the Gospel. Peter is the same fine, simple, affectionate, impetuous, daring, energetic, *impulsive* character, who asked to walk on the water, and 'was over-confident in his attachment to his Master, but who has now derived new strength and dignity from his new position, and, from the sad experience of the past, has learned to look with a steady eye on suffering and death. And John, in the Epistles, is precisely the same mixture of warm affectionateness to his friends, and uncharitableness to his enemies, which the few glimpses we have of him in the Gospels would lead us to specify as his characteristics. We meet with several passages in his writings which indicate that the gentle, forbearing, and forgiving spirit of the Master had not yet thoroughly penetrated and chastened the mind of the disciple—several passages which Jesus, had he read them, would have rebuked as before, by reminding his zealous follower that he knew not what manner of spirit he was of.[1]

---

[1] " Who is a liar, but he that denieth that Jesus is the Christ? He is antichrist that denieth the Father and the Son."—(1 Ep. ii.

The case of Paul is peculiar, and must be considered by itself. His writings are more voluminous than those of the other Apostles, in a tenfold proportion, and have a distinctive character of their own ; yet he never saw Christ in the flesh, and was a bitter persecutor of his followers till suddenly converted by a vision. What, then, were his means of becoming acquainted with the spirit and doctrines of his Lord ?

And, first, as to the vision which converted him. We have *four* narratives of this remarkable occurrence —one given by Luke, as an historian, in the 9th chapter of the Acts ; a second, *reported* by Luke (c. xxii.), as having been given by Paul himself in his speech to the people at Jerusalem ; a third, reported also by Luke (c. xxvi.), as having been given by Paul to King Agrippa ; and a fourth, more cursory, from Paul himself, in the first chapter of his Epistle to the Galatians, which omits entirely the external and marvellous part of the conversion, and speaks only of an internal[1] revelation.

22.) We are of God : he that knoweth God heareth us; he that is not of God heareth not us."—(iv. 6.) " There is a sin unto death : I do not say that he shall pray for it."—(v. 16.) " We know that we are of God, and the whole world lieth in wickedness." —(v. 19.) " If there come any unto you, and bring not this doctrine, receive him not into your house; neither bid him God speed."—(2 Ep. verse 10.) " I wrote unto the Church : but Diotrephes, who loveth to have the pre-eminence among them, receiveth us not. Wherefore, if I come, I will remember his deeds which he doeth, prating against us with malicious words."—(3 Ep. ver. 9, 10.)

[1] " But when it pleased God . . . to *reveal his Son in me*, that I might preach him among the Heathen," &c.—Gal. i. 16.

Now there are certain discrepancies in these accounts, which, while they seem to show that the occurrence—either from carelessness, confusion, or defect of memory—has not been related with perfect accuracy, leave us also in doubt as to the precise nature of this vision ; as to whether, in fact, it was mental or external. Luke, in his narrative, omits to state whether the supernatural light was visible to the companions of Paul as well as to himself. Paul, in his speech to the Jews, declares that it was. Paul is said to have heard a voice speaking to him, saying, "Saul, Saul, why persecutest thou me ?" Luke affirms that Paul's companions heard this voice as well as himself ; but this assertion Paul afterwards, in his speech at Jerusalem (Acts xxii. 9), expressly contradicts ; and we are, therefore, left with the impression that the supernatural voice fell rather upon Paul's mental, than on his outward ear—was, in fact, a spiritual suggestion, not an objective fact. Again, in his speech at Jerusalem, Paul represents the heavenly voice as referring him to future conferences, at Damascus (xxii. 10), for particulars of his commission ; in his address to Agrippa (xxvi. 16-18), he represents the same voice as giving him his commission on the spot.

Thus, in the three versions of the story which come, entirely or proximately, from the pen of Luke, we have positive and not reconcilable contradictions ; while in that reference to it, which alone we are *certain* proceeded direct from Paul, the supernatural and external is wholly ignored.

But the important practical question for our consideration is this :—In what manner, and from what
source, did Paul receive instruction in the doctrines of
Christianity ?   Was it from the other Apostles, like
an ordinary convert ? or by special and private revelation from heaven ?   Here, again, we find a discrepancy
between the statements of Luke and Paul.   In Acts
ix. 19, 20 ; xxii. 10 ; and xxvi. 20, it is expressly
stated that immediately after his conversion, and
during his abode with the disciples at Damascus, he
was instructed in the peculiar doctrines of his new
faith, and commenced his missionary career accordingly, *there and then.*   If this statement be correct,
his teaching will have the authority due to that of an
intelligent and able man, *well instructed at second
hand,* but no more.   Paul, however, entirely contradicts this supposition, and on several occasions
distinctly and emphatically declares that he did not
receive his religious teaching from any of the disciples
or apostles (whom he rather avoided than otherwise),
but by direct supernatural communications from the
Lord Jesus Christ.[1]

For example :—" Paul, an apostle, *not of man, neither by men,
but by Jesus Christ.*"   " But I certify unto you, brethren, that the
Gospel which was preached of me is not after man.   For I *neither
received it of man, neither was I taught it, but by the revelation of
Jesus Christ.*"   But when it pleased God to reveal his Son in me,
that I might preach him among the heathen, *immediately I conferred
not with flesh and blood :* neither went I up to Jerusalem to them
which were apostles before me ; but I went into Arabia, and
returned again into Damascus.   Then after three years, I went up

Of course Paul's own account of the mode in which he received his knowledge of Christianity must be taken, in preference to that of a narrator like Luke, whose information could only have been second-hand, though probably derived from Paul himself. Paul intimates, as we have seen, that he rather slighted and avoided all ordinary channels of instruction, and prides himself on the originality, exclusiveness, and directness, of the sources of his knowledge. The decision, therefore, of his fidelity and competence as a representative and teacher of the doctrines of Christ, depends entirely on the conclusion we may form as to the genuineness and *reality* of the visions and revelations with which he claims to have been favoured. If these were actual and positive communications from his risen and glorified Master, the question admits of no further discussion ; Paul was the greatest of the Apostles, and · his writings of paramount authority to any other. If,

---

to Jerusalem to see Peter, and abode with him fifteen days. But *other of the apostles saw I none,* save James the Lord's brother."— (Galatians i. 1, 11, 15-19.) " By revelation he made known unto me the mystery . . . whereby ye may understand my knowledge in the mystery of Christ."—(Eph. iii. 3.) " I will come to visions and revelations of the Lord. I knew a man in Christ about four-teen years ago (whether in the body or out of the body I cannot tell : God knoweth).; such an one caught up to the third heaven. And I knew such a man (whether in the body or out of the body I cannot tell : God knoweth) ; How that he was caught up into Paradise, and heard unspeakable words which it is not lawful for a man to utter. . . . And lest I should be exalted above measure through the abundance of the revelations," &c.—(2 Cor. xii. 1, 2, 3, 4, 7.)

on the other hand, these visions were merely the workings of a powerful and fiery mind in the solitude and seclusion of an Arabian hermitage, such as an ardent and excited temperament, like that of Paul, might easily come to regard as the suggestions of the Divine Spirit, and, perhaps, even could with difficulty distinguish from them ; then all his numerous epistles are the teachings, not of Jesus, but of Paul.

Now, not only have we no evidence—(perhaps we *could* have none)—beyond the bare assertion of Paul himself, that these alleged communications had any other than a subjective existence—were in fact anything beyond a mere mental process ; but among all the passages which refer to this subject, there are none which do not more readily bear this interpretation than any other, with one exception.[1] That exception is the statement of Luke, that the heavenly voice at mid-day was heard by Paul's companions as well as by himself—a statement which, being afterwards contradicted by Paul (or by Luke for him), may at once be put aside as incorrect.   Paul " immediately," as he says, upon his miraculous conversion, went into seclusion to meditate and commune with his own heart upon the marvellous change which had taken place in all his feelings ; and the state into which he more than once describes himself as having fallen, is that of

---

[1] Perhaps the assertion of Paul that he had seen Jesus, "and last of all he was seen by me also" (1 Cor. xv. 8) may be considered as another exception.   The sight of Jesus, however, probably refers to the vision at the moment of his conversion.

trance, a condition of the cerebral system—assuredly not a sound one—which solitude, fasting, and religious excitement combined, produce in all ages and countries, and nowhere so readily as in the East. (Acts xxii. 17 ; 2 Cor. xii. 2, 3, 24.) We cannot, of course, and do not wish, to take upon us to affirm that, while in this state, Paul was *not* favoured with divine communications ; we merely wish to make it clear that we have no reason to believe that he was so favoured, beyond his own assertion—an assertion which has been made with equal sincerity and conviction by hundreds of extatics whom similar causes have brought into a similar physiological condition.

There is much in the tone of the doctrinal writings of Paul which we believe and feel to be at variance, or at least little in harmony, with the views and spirit of Jesus, but nothing perhaps which we can *prove* to be so. We must therefore conclude with the ungracious task of pointing out a few passages of which the moral tone shows that the writer was not adequately imbued with the temper of Him who said, " Do good to those that hate you : Pray for them which despitefully use you, and persecute you." (2 Thess. i. 6-8; ii. 11, 12 ; 1 Tim. i. 20 ; 2 Tim. iv. 14 ; Gal. i. 8, 9.)

II.   H

CHAPTER XIII.

MIRACLES.

THE position which the miracles of the New Testament are made to hold in the Christian economy is of the first importance. In the popular theory they lie at the very foundation of the system. The current and, till recently, scarcely questioned opinion of Protestant christendom respecting them was this :—" The miracles which Jesus wrought constitute the proof of his divine commission, and the guarantee for the truth of the doctrines which he preached. His declarations and his precepts are to be received with unquestioning submission and belief, *because* he wrought miracles in proof of his authority to teach and to command." [1] According to this view (still the prevalent one, though of late largely modified by the more thinking among the orthodox) the truth of Christ's doctrines is made to rest upon the reality of his miracles ; we should not know the doctrines to be divine, had it not been for the attesting wonders

---

[1] See Paley, Evid.

wrought by the teacher ; and whatever doctrines are preached by a worker of miracles, are, *ipso facto*, proved to be of divine authority, and must therefore be received without question.

Now this popular notion appears to us to contain much confusion, and at least two fatal fallacies ; for the more clear disentanglement and exposure of which we shall proceed to show.

I. That miracles wrought by any individual are not, nor can be, a proof of the truth of the doctrines which he preaches ; and,

II. That miracles are not the real basis of Christianity, and cannot be a safe foundation on which to rest its claims, inasmuch as miracles can never be proved by *documentary* evidence—least of all, by such documentary evidence as we possess.

Before proceeding further, we will define the precise theological meaning affixed to the word miracle in the popular mind (as far as the popular mind can be said to attach a precise meaning to any word). This is the more necessary, as a writer of great eminence and ability, in his attempt to show that miracles may be not a violation, but a fulfilment, of the order of nature, appears to us to have confounded a *miracle* with a *prodigy*.

In common parlance—which alone we profess to use—a miracle is a suspension or violation of the ordinary course of nature, *at the will of an individual* indicating, therefore, the possession by that individual of superhuman power. A similar suspension or violation, *unconnected with the command or prediction of any individual*, is simply a *prodigy*, not a *miracle*. A prodigy is merely a marvellous and abnormal occurrence, of the cause and meaning of which we are wholly ignorant; a miracle is a marvellous and supernatural occurrence, the cause of which lies open to us in the expressed volition of an agent. Lazarus rising out of a four days' grave, without any discoverable cause or antecedent, would merely present to us a prodigy; Lazarus coming forth at the command of Christ was a manifest miracle.

Mr Babbage, in that ingenious chapter, in his "Ninth Bridgewater Treatise," wherein he endeavours to show that miracles may be merely natural, but exceptional occurrences—*the exceptional expressions of a natural law* expressly provided for beforehand— seems to have altogether lost sight of this distinction. We might not have deemed it necessary to controvert this theory, had it not been recently adopted and promulgated in a popular work of fiction ("Alton Locke"), by a clergyman of the Church of England. But when so sanctioned it becomes incumbent upon us to unmask the fallacy. "The object of the present chapter (says Mr Babbage) is to show that miracles are not deviations from the laws assigned by the Almighty for the government of matter and of mind ; but that they are the exact fulfilment of much more extensive laws than those we suppose to exist." His conception is that, in the final arrangement of all things the Deity provided for the occurrence of those deviations from the established course of nature which we call miracles, at certain periods, and under certain circumstances ; and he contends that such an arrangement suggests grander views of creative power and foresight than either casual interpositions or a uniform and undisturbed order of proceeding would do. We may concede both points ; we merely contend that such prearranged occurrences would not be *miracles* in the ordinary sense of the word, on which ordinary sense all theological arguments are based. If Lazarus rose from the dead in obedience to, and in consequence of, "an exceptional law" impressed upon matter in primeval times (which is Mr Babbage's conception of the case, and which *may* be a correct one), then he was not raised from the dead by an action upon the laws of nature, emanating from the will of Christ ; and all arguments based upon this (the prevalent) view of the event fall to the ground. On Mr Babbage's supposition, the connection between the command of Christ, " Lazarus, come forth ! " and the resurrection of the dead man, was not that of cause and effect, but merely that of coincidence or simultaneity ; or, at the utmost, the command was uttered, because Jesus, of his superhuman knowledge, knew that the moment was arrived when one of these " exceptional laws" was about to operate, in fact the *command* was a *prediction,*—a supposition contradicted by the whole language of the narrative, and unavailing for the popular argument ; which is, that

Christ had the power of countermanding nature—not merely that of foreseeing events hidden from ordinary knowledge.

Mr Babbage's conception, therefore, though it may make miracles more admissible by scientific minds, does so by depriving them of their theological utility. It makes the fact credible by annulling the argument drawn from it. Or, to speak more correctly, it renders prodigies credible, by *making them cease to be miracles*.[1]

I. We now proceed to illustrate the first of our two positions. A miracle, we say, cannot authenticate a doctrine. A miracle, if genuine, proves the possession, by him who works it, of superhuman power—but it is a strained and illogical inference to assume that it proves anything beyond this. This inference, so long and so universally made—and allowed—arises from a confusion in the popular mind between *power* and *wisdom*—between the divine nature as a whole, and *one* of the divine attributes. It involves the immense and inadmissible assumption that the possession of superhuman power necessarily implies the possession of superhuman knowledge also, and the will truly to impart that knowledge ; that the power to heal diseases, or to

---

[1] If Mr Babbage means, as an expression at page 97 seems to intimate, that the Creator had provided for these exceptional occurrences taking place *whenever Christ performed a certain operation* which He gave him power to perform, and told him when to perform — then we are at a loss to discover in what way the conception varies from, or is superior to, the vulgar view.

still the waves, implies and includes a knowledge of the mind of God. The thoughts of ordinary men, undistinguishing and crude, jump rapidly to a conclusion in such matters ; and on recognizing (or conceiving that they recognize) supernatural power in any individual, at once and without ratiocination endow him with all other divine attributes, and bow before him in trembling and supine prostration.

Yet at other times, and in most countries, men have, by happy inconsistency, admitted the falseness of this logic. Wherever there is found a belief in one evil angel, or in many (and such is the current nominal belief of Christendom), the distinction between the attributes of Deity is made, and power is divorced from wisdom, truth, and goodness, and in a great degree from knowledge also. If there be such existences as Satan, Arimanes, or inferior agencies of evil—(and who can say that there are not ? What orthodox Christian but believes there are ?)—then superhuman power exists apart from divine wisdom, and in antagonism to it ;—then the power to work miracles involves no knowledge of divine truth, or at least no mission to teach it—nay, may imply the very opposite, and can therefore authenticate no doctrine enunciated by the worker.

The common feeling no doubt is, that as all supernatural power is the special gift of God, He would not have bestowed it upon any but the good, nor for any purpose but that of conferring blessings and spreading truth. But this inference is wholly at variance with the analogies of the divine economy. _All_ power is the gift of God—the power of intellect, the power of rank, the power of wealth, as well as the power of working physical marvels,—yet are these given to the good alone, or chiefly ?—are these bestowed on those who employ them exclusively, or mainly, in the service of mercy and truth ? Would not the reverse of the statement be nearer to the fact ?

So strongly has the force of our position been felt by reasoners—so plain does it appear that it is the doctrine which must authenticate the miracle, not the miracle which can authenticate the doctrine,—that few could be found at the present day who would not admit that no miracle worked by a preacher would induce them to receive from him a doctrine manifestly dishonouring to God. Many of our modern divines,— Dr. Arnold, Archdeacon Hare, Mr. Locke, Mr. Trench, and others,—express this feeling in the strongest language. Dr. Arnold says (" Christian Course and Character," notes, pp. 462-3) :

" Faith, without reason, is not properly faith, but mere power-worship ; and power-worship may be devil-worship ; for it is reason which entertains the idea of God—an idea essentially made up of truth and goodness, no less than of power. A sign of power, exhibited to the senses, might, through them, dispose the whole man to acknowledge it as divine ; yet power in itself is not divine, it may be devilish. . . . . How can we distinguish God's voice from the voice of evil ? . . . . We distinguish it (and can distinguish it no otherwise), by comparing it with that idea of God which reason intuitively enjoys, the gift of reason being God's original revelation of himself to man. Now, if the voice which comes to us from the unseen world agree not with this idea, *we have no choice but to pronounce it not to be God's voice: for no signs of power, in confirmation of it, can alone prove it to be from God.*"

Locke says:—" I do not deny in the least that God can do, or hath done, miracles for the confirmation of truth ; I only say that we cannot think He should do them to enforce doctrines or notions of. himself, or any worship of Him, not conformable to reason, or that we can receive such as truth *for the miracles' sake* ; and even in those books which have the greatest proof of revelation from God, and the attestation of miracles to confirm their being so, the miracles are to be judged by the doctrine, and not the doctrine by the miracles." [1]

---

[1] See also Lord King's Life of Locke, i. 231 et seq. Trench's Hulsean Lectures for 1845, pp. 8, 9.—" After all is done, men will feel in the deepest centre of their being, that it is the moral which must prove the historic, *not the historic which can ever prove the moral;* that evidences drawn from without may be accepted as the welcome *buttresses,* but that we can know no other *foundations,* of our Faith, than those which itself supplies. Revelation, like the sun, must be seen by its own light." Hare's Mission of the Comforter, ii. p. 553.—The notion that miracles have an augmentative and demonstrative efficacy, and that the faith of Christians is to be grounded upon them, belongs to a much later age, and is in fact the theological parallel to the materialist hypothesis, that all our knowledge is derived from the senses."

Further. The idea that a miracle can authenticate a doctrine, or is needed to do so, involves an additional fallacy. It implies that our understanding is competent to decide whether *an act* be divine, but not whether *a doctrine* be divine;—that the power displayed in a prodigy may be sufficient to justify us in confidently assuming it to be from God,—but that the beauty, the sublimity, the innate light of a doctrine or a precept cannot be sufficient to warrant us in pronouncing it to be from Him;—that God can impress his stamp unmistakably on his physical, but not on his moral emanations;—that His handwriting is legible on the sea, or the sky, on the flower, or on the insect, but not on the soul and intellect of man. It involves the coarse and monstrous conception that God's presence in His chosen temple can only be made manifest by a loud appeal to those external senses which perish with the flesh;—that He pervades the earthquake and the whirlwind, but *not* ' the still small voice;'—that, in fine, the eye or the ear is a truer and quicker percipient of Deity than the Spirit which came forth from Him ;—*that God is more cognizable by the senses than by the soul,*—by the material philosopher than by the pure-hearted but unlearned worshipper.

The power to work miracles, then, does not, in the eye of reason, imply any other supernatural endowment. Neither does it in the eye of Scripture. We have many indications, in both the Old and the New Testament, that neither miracles, nor the cognate gift of prophecy, were considered to qualify a Teacher, or to authenticate his teaching. The possession of mira- culous and prophetic power is distinctly recognized in individuals who not only were not divinely authorized agents or teachers, but were enemies of God and of his people. Passing over the remarkable but inconclusive narratives relative to the Egyptian magicians, and to Balaam,—we find in Deut. xiii. 1-5, an express warn- ing to the children of Israel against being led astray by those who shall employ *real* miraculous or prophetic gifts to entice them away from the worship of Jehovah, a warning couched in language which distinctly ex- presses that the miracle must be judged of by the doctrine of the thaumaturgist,—not be considered to authenticate it. "If there arise among you a prophet, or a dreamer of dreams, and giveth thee a sign or a wonder, *and the sign or the wonder come to pass,* whereof he spake unto thee, saying, Let us go after other Gods, which thou hast not known, and let us serve them ; thou shalt not hearken to the words of that prophet, or that dreamer of dreams : *and that prophet, or that dreamer of dreams shall be put to death."*

The same proposition is affirmed with almost equal distinctness in Matth. vii. 22, 23. "Many will say to me in that day, Lord, Lord, have we not prophesied in thy name ? and in thy name have cast out devils ? and in thy name done many wonderful works ? And then will I profess unto them, I never knew you : depart from me, ye that work iniquity." Again,

Matth. xxiv. 24, " For there shall arise false Christs, and false prophets, and *shall shew great signs and wonders ;* insomuch that, if it were possible, they shall deceive the very elect." In Matth. xii. 27, and Mark ix. 38, Christ clearly admits the power to work miracles in both his enemies and his ignorers.

If anything further were wanted to show the view taken by Jesus of this matter, we should find it in his steady refusal to authenticate his mission by a miracle, when, in strict conformity to Jewish ideas (and to divine prescription, if the Mosaic books may be at all trusted), the rulers of the synagogue, in the plain performance of their official duty, called upon him to work one. (See Matth. xii. 39 ; xvi. 4, and the parallel passages, as Mark viii. 11.) He reproaches the deputation for their demands—grieves over it, according to Mark,—and says positively, " There shall no sign be given to this generation." In another conversation with the Pharisees, the same idea is still more clearly enunciated. He there (John vi. 30-33) distinctly tells them that though Moses may have been accredited by miracles, *he* will be judged of by his doctrine only. " They said therefore unto him, What sign shewest thou then, that we may see, and believe thee ? what dost thou work ? Our fathers did eat manna in the desert ; as it is written, He gave them bread from heaven to eat. Then Jesus said unto them, Verily, verily, I say unto you, Moses gave you not that bread from heaven ; but my Father giveth you the true bread from heaven. . . . I am the bread of life," &c. The low estimation in which miracles were held by the Apostle Paul (2 Cor. xii. 28), clearly shows that he did not regard them as *the* credentials of his mission; and several passages in the Acts seem to intimate that, by the early Christians, the possession of the miraculous or prophetic gift was not considered inconsistent both with false doctrine and enmity to Christ's Church. (Acts viii. 9-11; xiii. 6-10; xvi. 16; 2 Cor. xi. 13.) Finally, we have the conclusive fact that, according to the Gospel narrative, the power to work miracles had been expressly conferred upon all the apostles, who "forsook Jesus and fled" in his day of trial,—upon Judas who betrayed him,—upon Peter, who thrice denied him.

It is said, however, by some, that miraculous power is bestowed upon Prophets, as their *credentials*; not as proving their doctrines, but as proving them to be sent from God. But, is it not clear, that these credentials, if they mean anything at all, must mean that men are to listen to the Prophets who present them, as God's mouthpieces? What is the object of proving them to be sent from God, except for the sake of the inference that *therefore* what they teach must be God's truth?

II. Having now proved our first position,—that miracles cannot authenticate either the doctrines or the divine commission of the thaumaturgist—we proceed to the establishment of our second thesis, viz.,—

that miracles cannot be the basis of Christianity, or of any historical or transmitted religion.

We fully admit at the outset of our argument that a miracle, as well as any other occurrence, is capable of proof by testimony—provided only the testimony be adequate in kind and in quantity. The testimony must be of the same kind as that on which we should accept any of the more rare and marvellous among natural phenomena, and must be clear, direct, and ample, in proportion to the marvellousness, anomalousness, and rarity of the occurrence. This, it appears to us, is all that philosophy authorizes us to demand for the authentication of the *fact-part* of a miracle.

Miracles, we say, are not, and never can be, a sure foundation for a revealed religion—an historic creed. A true Revelation, addressed to all mankind, and destined for all ages, must be attested by evidence adequate and accessible to all men and to all ages. It must carry with it its own permanent and unfading credentials. Now, miracles are evidence only to those who see them, or can sift the testimony which affirms them. Occurrences so anomalous and rare, which violate the known and regular course of nature, can, at the utmost, only be admitted on the evidence of our own senses, or on the carefully-sifted testimony of eye-witnesses. Therefore, a revelation, whose credentials· are miracles, *can be a revelation only to the age in which it appears.* The superhuman powers of its Preacher can authenticate it only to those who witness the exertion of them, and—more faintly and feebly—to those who have received and scrutinized *their* direct testimony :—the superhuman excellence of its doctrines may authenticate it through all time, and must constitute, therefore, its only adequate and abiding proof.

Now, the essence of the whole question lies in this: —that *we have not the Apostles and Evangelists to cross-examine;* we do not know that they ever were cross-examined ; we do not know what was the nature of the evidence or testimony which satisfied their minds ; and we have ample indications that they, like most imperfectly-educated men, were satisfied with a nature and amount of proof which would never satisfy us.

We have stated that we are far from denying the adequacy of positive and direct testimony to prove a miracle, if its amount and quality be suitable. What would be the amount and quality required ? It will be allowed on all hands that the testimony of *one* witness, however competent and honest, would not suffice. We must have the *concurring* testimony of *several competent* and *independent* witnesses. Mr Babbage has made a calculation (which many will think puerile, but which assuredly does not overstate the case), that, to prove some of the chief miracles, such as the raising of the dead, the *concurring* testimony of *six independent, competent, veracious* witnesses will suffice, *but not less.*

Now, let us ask, Have we, for any of the gospel

miracles, evidence—we do not say as strong as this, but—approaching to it ? in the slightest degree similar to it ?   Have we the concurring testimony of six independent and competent witnesses ? or of five ? or of three ? or of two ?   Do we *know* that we have the testimony even of *one* witness ?   Do we know anything at all about the competency, or the independence of any of the witnesses ?   Have we any reason to believe that the Evangelists sifted the testimony they received ?   Have we, in fine, the distinct statement of any one individual that he saw or wrought such or such a specific miracle ?   No ; but what we have instead is this :—We have four documents, written *we have to guess* when—proceeding from we know not whom—transmitted to us we know not how purely ; —three of them evidently compositions from oral testimony or tradition, and clearly *not* from *independent* testimony ; and all four, not *concurring*, but often singularly discrepant ;—which documents relate that such miracles were wrought by a certain individual in a certain place and time.   It is obvious that we have not here even *an approach* to personal testimony.[1] We do not know with the least certainty who any of these four narrators were ;—not one of them says, "*I* witnessed this miracle ;"—we do not, therefore, know that they were witnesses at all ;—and we do know that their testimony was not *independent* nor always

---

[1] We assume here, *not* that the fourth Gospel was *not* written by the Apostle John, but simply that *we do not know that it was.*

concurring. At the best, therefore, we have only documents of unknown date and uncertain authorship, stating, with many discrepancies and contradictions, that certain miraculous occurrences were witnessed *by others,* at least thirty years before the record was composed;—evidence which, in an honest court of justice, would not suffice to affect person or property to the slightest possible extent;—evidence, nevertheless, on which we are peremptorily summoned to accept the most astounding dogmas, and to bow to the heaviest yoke.

Since, then, for the miracles recorded in the synoptical gospels we have not even that degree of evidence which would be required to establish any remarkable or questionable occurrence; and since the only superior authority for those of the fourth Gospel rests on the supposition of its being the production of the Apostle John—a supposition doubtful and unproven, to say no more; we might be dispensed from entering into any more close examination of the narratives themselves— as in a court of justice the jury frequently decide against the plaintiff on his own showing—pronounce that the appellant *has no case,* without requiring to hear the objections of the respondent. But it is important to call attention to a few considerations which should long since have warned divines of the perilous position they had taken up, when they resolved to base Christianity upon the miraculous narratives of the Gospel.

1. The whole tenor of the Old Testament, and

II.   I ⁺

many passages in the New, plainly indicate either
that the power of working miracles was so common
in those days as to argue nothing very remarkable in
its possessor, or that a belief in miracles was so general
and so easily yielded as to render the testimony of
such facile believers inadequate to prove them.   On
the first supposition, they will not warrant the inference drawn from them ; on the second, they are
themselves questionable.

Now, it is certain that the miracles recorded in the
New Testament do not appear to have produced on
the beholders or the hearers the same effect as they
would do at the present day, nor to have been regarded
in the same light even by the workers of them.
When Jesus was told by his disciples (Mark ix. 38)
that they had found some unauthorized person casting
out devils in his name, he expresses no amazement—
*intimates no doubt as to the genuineness of the
miracle*—but rebukes his disciples for interfering
with the thaumaturgist, saying, "Forbid him not ;
for there is no man which shall *do a miracle* in my
name that can lightly speak evil of me." The casting
out of devils—*i.e.*, the healing of the more furious
epileptic and maniacal disorders—was the most. frequent and among the most striking and the oftenest
appealed to of the miracles of Jesus ; yet in the conversation already referred to between himself and the
Pharisees (Matth. xii. 24-27) he speaks of it as one
that was constantly and habitually performed by their
own exorcists ; and, so far from insinuating any differ-

ence between the two cases, *expressly puts them on a level.*[1] Paul, though himself gifted with miraculous power, and claiming (Rom. xv. 19 ; 2 Cor. xii. 11) to be equally so gifted with any of the other Apostles (2 Cor. xi. 5), yet *places this power very low in the rank of spiritual* endowments (1 Cor. xii. 8, 9, 10, 28)[2]—*distinguishing in both passages miracles or thaumaturgic signs from gifts of healing;* and speaks of them in a somewhat slighting tone, which is wholly irreconcilable with the supposition that the miracles of which he speaks were real and indisputable ones after the modern signification of the word, *i.e.,* unquestionable deviations from the observed order of nature at the command of man.

2. Though the miracles of Christ are frequently referred to in the Gospels as his credentials, as proofs of his divine mission ; yet there are not wanting many significant indications that they were wrought rather as a consequence and reward of belief than as means to produce it. For example, we have the repeated refusal of Jesus to satisfy the Jewish chiefs by a display of his miraculous gifts, though we can perceive nothing unreasonable or unsuitable to pure Judaism

---

[1] Matth. vii. 22 ; xxiv. 24 ; Gal. iii. 5, and many other passages, show how *ccmmon* miracles then were, or were esteemed.

[2] " For to one is given by the Spirit the word of wisdom ; to another the word of knowledge ; to another faith ; to another the gifts of healing ; to another *the working of miracles;* to another prophecy," &c. "And God hath set some in the Church, first apostles, secondarily prophets, thirdly teachers ; *after that* miracles, then gifts of healings, helps, governments, diversities of tongues."

in the demand (John vi. 30). We have the remarkable fact that Jesus here not only declines to work a
new miracle in attestation of his mission, but does not
even refer his questioners to his former miracles. We
have the reproach of Jesus to the people of Galilee—
"Except ye see signs and wonders, ye will not believe" (John iv. 48), clearly intimating that these
were not the criterions by which he intended his
mission to be judged. On several occasions, *before*
working a miracle, he ascertains the faith of the
applicant, and speaks of the miracle as if it were to
be the reward, not the provocative, of their faith
(Matthew ix. 27, 29; ix. 2; viii. 10; ix. 22; xv.
28; Mark i. 40). And, finally, the Evangelists
twice assign the want of faith of the people—the
very reason, according to the orthodox view, why
miracles *should* be worked before them—as the reason
why Jesus *would not* work them. "And he did not
many mighty works there *because of their unbelief*"
(Matt. xiii. 58). "And he could there do no mighty
work, save that he laid his hands upon a few sick folk,
and healed them. And *he marvelled because of their
unbelief*" (Mark vi. 5, 6).

3. Neither *did* his miracles produce general conviction—nor the conclusion which would have followed
from conviction—in those who witnessed them, whether
friends, enemies, or indifferent spectators. Had they
appeared to the witnesses in that age in the same
form which they assume in the documents in which
they are handed down to us, conviction must have

been inevitable. Yet this was far from being the case. We read, indeed, frequently that the people "marvelled" and " glorified God "—and that "the fame of his wonderful works went throughout all the land "—but we also find several passages which point to a very opposite conclusion. " Then began he to upbraid the cities wherein most of his mighty works were done, because they repented not : Woe unto thee, Chorazin I woe unto thee, Bethsaida ! for if the mighty works, which were done in you, had been done in Tyre and Sidon, they would have repented long ago in sackcloth and ashes." (Matt. xi. 20, 21.) " But though he had done so many miracles before them (the people), yet they believed not on him." (John xii. 37.) Even his friends and disciples were not always convinced. The miracle of the loaves, even, seems to have produced little effect on their minds, for we are told (as a reason for their surprise at a subsequent marvel), " For they considered not the miracle of the loaves; for their hearts were hardened." (Mark vi. 52), an expression which a comparison with xvi. 14, shows to have signified incredulity. A still more significant statement is found in John vii. 5, " For neither did his brethren believe in him." A reference to John xi. 45, 46, shows that even so signal and unquestionable a miracle as is the raising of Lazarus, *in the form in which it has come down to us*, did not produce universal convic-tion. " Then many of the Jews w ch came to Mary, and had seen the things which Jesus did, believed on

him. *But some of them* went their way to the
Pharisees, and told them what things Jesus had done."

It is worthy of especial note, that to the last, in
defiance of the numerous, astonishing, and public
miracles recorded in the Gospels—of many of which,
as the raising of Lazarus, the cure of the blind man
(John ix.), the Pharisees and chief men among the
Jews are said to have been witnesses—the incredulity
of these Rulers and of the Sanhedrim remained un-
shaken.   It is evident, too, that it was genuine and
sincere disbelief—not merely a refusal to accept the
inference of the divine mission of Christ on the ground
of his miraculous power, but a disbelief in the miraculous power itself—or at least of its being miraculous
in our full modern acceptation of the term ; they were
exasperated, but no way *intimidated,* by the wonders
which he wrought before them.   Had they really supposed that he could cure the blind, heal the lame,
command spirits, still the waves, raise the dead (in a
different manner, and with a different degree or kind
of power from their own thaumaturgists)—still more,
had they seen any one of these awful evidences of
supernatural power—then, however hostile selfishness
and ambition or class prejudices might have made
them to his pretensions, they would have dreaded to
provoke his enmity, or to practise against his safety,
satisfied, as they must have been, that he could not
only foresee and baffle their machinations, but could
inflict a fearful retaliation.   But we see nothing of all
this ; we see just the reverse ;—they feared, not him,

but the people who were friendly to him ;—they more than once openly attacked him, and tempted him, even by taunts, to a display of his superhuman gifts ; —in a word, their whole conduct shows that his miracles, whatever they were, had not gone any way towards producing in *their* minds a conviction (*or even a fear*) of his supernatural power.

4. The minuter objections to the individual miraculous narratives in the Gospel, we need not dwell on. The discrepancies in the accounts where given by more than one Evangelist ;—the entirely distinct set of miracles recorded in the fourth, from those in the first three Gospels ; the remarkable circumstance that, of the three cases of the dead being restored to life, one is mentioned by John only, one by Luke only, and the third case, mentioned by three of the Evangelists, was no resurrection from the dead at all (for all accounts concur in representing Jesus to have said expressly, ·' The damsel is *not* dead, but sleepeth ;") —all these topics have been dwelt upon in detail by other critics, and need not be considered here.

The conclusion suggested by all these combined considerations seems to be this :—that the miracles spoken of in the New Testament had not the effect of real miracles upon the bystanders ;—that they were, probably, either remarkable occurrences elévated into supernatural ones by the general supernaturalistic tendencies of the age, or examples of wonderful healing powers, the original accounts of which have become strangely intermingled and overlaid with fiction in the process of transmission. The Gospels (we must bear constantly in mind) are not contemporaneous annals ; they merely narrate the occurrence of certain events, which, *at the time when the tradition was congealed into a record,* had assumed such and such a form and consistency in the public mind. They show us not the facts that occurred in the year A.D. 30, *but the form those facts had assumed in popular belief in the year* A.D. 70.

There is yet another objection to the plan of propounding miracles as the basis for a Revelation, which is all but insuperable. The assertion of a miracle having been performed, is not a *simple* statement ; it involves three elements—*a fact and two inferences.* It predicates, *first,* that such an occurrence took place ; *second,* that it was brought about by the act and will of the individual to whom it is attributed ; *third,* that it implied supernatural power in the agent—*i.e.,* that it could not have been produced by mere human means. Now, the fact may have been accurately observed, and yet one or both of the inferences may be unwarranted. Or, either inference may be rendered unsound by the slightest omission or deviation from accuracy in the observation or statement of the fact.[1] Nay, any new discovery in science—any advance in physiological knowledge—

---

[1] Bentham observes that the report of a man going up with a balloon would become a miracle, if a spectator told all the rest of the story truly, but omitted to tell of the balloon.

may show that the inference, which has always hitherto appeared quite irrefragable, was, in fact, wholly unwarranted and incorrect. In the process of time, and the triumphant career of scientific inquiry, any miracle may be—as so many thousand prodigies have been —reduced to a natural occurrence. No miracle can, therefore, be a safe foundation for so vast and weighty a superstructure as a Revelation. A miracle is an argument in some measure *ab ignorantia*— based upon scanty knowledge, and, therefore, defeasible by advancing knowledge. A miraculous revelation—a creed whose foundation is miracle—must always be at the mercy of Science, and must always dread it.

It should, then, be clearly understood that, when we decline to receive a miracle as evidence of a divine commission, we are not refusing simple testimony— *we are demurring to a proposition composed of one observation and two inferences*—a proposition, each of the three constituents of which contains the elements of possible inaccuracy ;—we are demurring, in fact, to a process of reasoning, *which assumes as its basis that the limits of human power and knowledge are indisputably known to us.*[1]

[" Roman Catholics fancy that Bible miracles and the

---

[1] " The miracle is of a most fluctuating character. The miracle worker of to-day is a matter-of-fact juggler to-morrow. Science each year adds new wonders to our store. The master of a locomotive steam engine would have been thought greater than Jupiter Tonans, or the Elohim thirty centuries ago."—Parker, p. 202.

miracles of their Church form a class by themselves :
Protestants fancy that Bible miracles, alone, form a
class by themselves.   This was eminently the posture
of mind of the late Archbishop Whately :—to hold
that all other miracles would turn out to be impostures,
or capable of a natural explanation, but that Bible
miracles would stand sifting by a London special jury
or by a committee of scientific men.   No acuteness
can save such notions, as our knowledge widens, from
being seen to be mere extravagances, and the Protestant notion is doomed to an earlier ruin than the
Catholic.   For the Catholic notion admits miracles in
the mass ; the Protestant notion invites to a criticism
by which it must finally itself perish.   When Stephen
was martyred, he looked up into heaven and saw the
glory of God, and Jesus standing on the right hand of
God. That, says the Protestant, is solid fact.   At the
martyrdom of St. Fructuosus, Babylas and Mygdone,
the Christian servants of the Roman governor, saw the
heavens open, and the saint and his deacon Eulogius
carried up on high with crowns on their heads.   That
is, says the Protestant, imposture or else illusion.   St.
Paul hears on his way to Damascus the voice of Jesus
say to him : ' Saul, Saul, why persecutest thou me ? '
That, again, is solid fact.   The companion of St.
Thomas Aquinas hears a voice from the crucifix say to
the praying saint : ' Thou hast written well of me,
Thomas ; what recompence dost thou desire ? '   That,
again, is imposture or else illusion.   Why ?   It is
impossible to find any criterion by which one of these

incidents may establish its claim to a solidity which we refuse to the others.

"One of two things must be made out in order to place either the Bible miracles alone, or the Bible miracles and the miracles of the Catholic Church with them, in a class by themselves. Either they must be shown to have arisen in a time eminently unfavourable to such a process as Shakespeare describes, to amplification and the production of legend; or they must be shown to be recorded in documents of an eminently historical mode of birth and publication. But surely it is manifest that the Bible miracles fulfil neither of these conditions. It was said that the waters of the Pamphylian Sea miraculously opened a passage for the army of Alexander the Great. Admiral Beaufort, however, tells us that, 'though there are no tides in this part of the Mediterranean, a considerable depression of the sea is caused by long-continued north winds, and Alexander, taking advantage of such a moment, may have dashed on without impediment;' and we accept the explanation as a matter of course. But the waters of the Red Sea are said to have miraculously opened a passage for the children of Israel; and we· insist on the literal truth of *this* story, and reject natural explanations as monstrous. Yet the time and circumstances of the flight from Egypt were a thousand times more favourable to the rise of some natural incident into a miracle, than the age of Alexander. They were a time and circumstances of less broad daylight."][1]

---

[1] Arnold's *Literature and Dogma*, p. 130.

CHAPTER XIV.

WE are now arrived at the most vitally important, and the most intensely interesting, portion of the Christian records—the resurrection of Jesus. This is the great fact to which the affections of Christians turn with the most cherished eagerness, the grand foundation on which their hopes depend, on which their faith is fixed. If, in consequence of our inquiries, the ordinary doctrine of Scriptural Inspiration be relinquished, we have reason to rejoice that Religion is relieved from a burden often too great for it to bear. If the complete verbal accuracy of the Gospel narratives is disproved, orthodoxy and not Christianity is a sufferer by the change, since it is only the more minute and embarrassing tenets of our creed that find their foundation swept away. If investigation shows the miracles of the Bible to be untenable, or at least unobligatory upon our belief, theologians are comforted by feeling that they have one weak and vulnerable outpost the less to defend. But if the resurrection of our Lord should prove, on closer scrutiny, to rest on no adequate evidence, and mental integrity should compel us to expunge it from our creed, the generality of Christians will feel that the whole basis of their faith and hope is gone, and their Christianity will vanish with the foundation on which, perhaps half unconsciously, they rested it. Whether this ought to be so is a point for future consideration. All that we have now to do is to remember that truth must be investigated without any side-glance to the consequences which that investigation may have upon our hopes. Our faith is sure to fail us in the hour of trial if we have based it on consciously or suspectedly fallacious grounds, and maintained it by wilfully closing our eyes to the flaws in its foundations.

The belief in the resurrection of our Lord, when based upon reflection at all, and not a mere mental habit, will be found to rest on two grounds :—*first*, the direct testimony of the Scripture narratives ; and *secondly*, the evidence derivable from the subsequent conduct of the Apostles.

I. The narratives of the resurrection contained in the four Gospels present many remarkable discrepancies. But discrepancies in the accounts of an event given by different narrators, whether themselves witnesses, or merely historians, by no means necessarily impugn the reality of the event narrated, but simply those *accessaries* of the event to which the discrepancies relate. Thus, when one evangelist tells us that the two malefactors, who were crucified along with Jesus, reviled him, and another evangelist relates that only one of

them riviled him, and was rebuked by the other for so
doing, though the contradiction is direct and positive,
no one feels that the least doubt is thereby thrown
upon the fact of two malefactors having been crucified
with Jesus, nor of some reviling having passed on the
occasion. Therefore the variations in the narratives
of the resurrection given by the four evangelists do
not, of themselves, impugn the fact of the resurrection.
Even were they (which they are not) the first-hand
accounts of eye-witnesses, instead of merely derived
from such, still it is characteristic of the honest testimony of eye-witnesses to be discrepant in collateral
minutiæ. But, on a closer examination of these accounts, several peculiarities present themselves for more
detailed consideration.

1. We have already seen reason for concluding that,
of the four Gospels, three at least were certainly not
the production of eye-witnesses, but were compilations
from oral or documentary narratives current among the
Christian community at the time of their composition,
and derived doubtless for the most part from very high
authority. With regard to the fourth Gospel the
opinions of the best critics are so much divided, that
all we can pronounce upon the subject with any certainty is, that if it were the production of the Apostle
John, it was written at a time when, either from
defect of memory, redundancy of imagination, or laxity
in his notions of an historian's duty, he allowed himself to take strange liberties with fact [1]. All, therefore,

---

[1] See chap. x.

that the Gospels now present to us is the narrative of the Resurrection, not as it actually occurred, but in the form it had assumed among the disciples thirty years or more after the death of Jesus.

Now, the discrepancies which we notice in the various accounts are not greater than might have been expected in historians recording an event, or rather traditions of an event, which occurred from thirty to sixty years before they wrote. These records, therefore, discrepant as they are, are, we think, quite sufficient to prove that *something of the kind* occurred, *i. e.*, that some occurrence took place which gave rise to the belief and the traditions ;—but no more. The agreement of the several accounts show that something of the kind occurred :—their discrepancies show that this occurrence was not exactly such as it is related to have been.

Something of the kind occurred which formed the groundwork for the belief and the narrative. What, then, was this something—this basis—this nucleus of fact ? The Gospel of Mark appears to contain this nucleus, and this alone.[1] It contains nothing but what all the other accounts contain, and nothing that is not simple, credible, and natural, but it contains enough to have formed a foundation for the whole subsequent superstructure. Mark informs us that

---

[1] We must bear in mind that the *genuine* Gospel of Mark ends with the 8th verse of chapter xvi. ; and that there is good reason to believe that Mark's Gospel was, if not the original one, at least the earliest.

when the women went early to the Sepulchre, they found it open, the body of Jesus gone, and some one in white garments who assured them that he was risen. *This all the four narratives agree in:—and they agree in nothing else.* The disappearance of the body, then, was certain;—the information that Jesus was risen came from the women alone, who believed it because *they were told it,* and who were also the first to affirm that they had seen their Lord. In the excited state of mind in which all the disciples must have been at this time, were not these three unquestioned circumstances—that the body was gone;—that a figure dressed in white told the women that their Lord was risen;—and that the same women saw *some one whom they believed to be him;*—amply sufficient to make a belief in his resurrection spread with the force and rapidity of a contagion?

2. It is clear that to prove such a miracle as the re-appearance in life of a man who had been publicly slain, the direct and concurrent testimony of eye-witnesses would be necessary:—that two or more should state that they saw him at such a time and place, and *knew* him;—and that this clear testimony should be recorded and handed down to us in an authentic document. This degree of evidence we *might* have had:— this we have not. We have epistles from Peter, James, John, and Jude—all of whom are said by the evangelists to have seen Jesus after he rose from the dead, in none of which epistles is the fact of the resurrection even stated, much less that Jesus was seen by the

wnter after his resurrection. This point deserves weighty consideration. We have ample evidence that the belief in Christ's resurrection [1] was very early and very general among the disciples, but we have not the direct testimony of any one of the twelve, nor of any eye-witness at all, that they saw him on earth after his death. Many writers say, "*he was seen;*"—no one says, "*I* saw him alive in the flesh."

There are three apparent exceptions to this, which, however, when examined, will prove rather confirmatory of our statement than otherwise. If the last chapter of the fourth Gospel were written by the Apostle John, it would contain the direct testimony of an eye-witness to the appearance of Jesus upon earth after his crucifixion. But its genuineness has long been a matter of question among learned men,[2] and few can read it critically and retain the belief that it is a real relic of the beloved Apostle, or even that it originally formed part of the Gospel to which it is appended. In the first place, the closing verse of the preceding chapter unmistakably indicates the termination of a history. Then, the general tone of the twenty-first chapter—its particularity as to the

---

[1] The belief in a general resurrection was, we know, prevalent among the Jews in general, and the disciples of Christ especially; and it appears from several passages that the opinion was that the resurrection would be immediate upon death (Luke xx. 38; xxiii. 43). In this case the belief that Christ was risen would follow immediately on the knowledge of his death.

[2] See Hug, 484.

II. K

distance of the bark from shore, and the exact number
of fishes taken—the fire ready made when the disciples
came to land—the contradiction between the fourth
verse and the seventh and twelfth, as to the recognition of Jesus—all partake strongly of the legendary
character, as does likewise the conversation between
Jesus and Peter. Again, the miraculous draught of
fishes which is here placed after the resurrection of
Christ, is by Luke related as happening at the very
commencement of his ministry. And finally, the last
two verses, it is clear, cannot be from the pen of John,
and we have no grounds for supposing them to be less
genuine than the rest of the chapter. On a review of
the whole question we entertain no doubt that the
whole chapter was an addition of later date, perhaps
by some elder of the Ephesian Church.

In the first Epistle of Peter (iii. 21, 22), the
resurrection and existence in heaven of Jesus are distinctly affirmed ; but when we remember that the
Jews at that time believed in a future life, and apparently in an immediate transference of the spirit
from this world to the next, and that this belief had
been especially enforced on the disciples of Jesus
(Matt. xvii. 1-4 ; xxii. 32. Luke xvi. 23-31 ; xxiii.
43), this will appear very different from an assertion
that Jesus had actually risen to an earthly life, and
that Peter had seen him. Indeed the peculiar expression that is made use of at ver. 18, in affirming
the doctrine (" being slain in flesh, but made alive

again in spirit,"[1]) indicates, in the true meaning of the original, not a fleshly, but a spiritual revivification.

There remains the statement of Paul (1 Cor. xv. 8), "And last of all, he was seen of me also." This assertion, taken with the context, negatives rather than affirms the reappearance of Christ upon the earth to the bodily eye of his disciples. The whole statement is a somewhat rambling one, and not altogether consistent with the Gospel narratives ; but the chief point to be attended to here is that Paul places the appearance of Jesus to the other disciples on the same footing as his appearance to himself. Now, we know that his appearance to Paul was *in a vision*—a vision visible to Paul alone of all the bystanders, and, therefore, *subjective* or mental merely. [Moreover, strictly speaking, there was no *vision*, at all ;—no one was *seen*; there was a bright light, and a voice was heard. In this all the accounts agree. In a subsequent verse, indeed (xxii. 18) Paul says that, when "in a trance in the Temple at Jerusalem," he "*saw*, him (the Lord) saying to him," &c. But this expression, again, seems to imply hearing, not sight.] The conclusion to be drawn from the language of Paul would, therefore, be that the appearance of Jesus to the other disciples was visionary likewise.[2] Our

---

[1] Θανατωθεὶς μὲν σαρκὶ ζωοποιηθεὶς δὲ πνεύματι. (Griesbach.) Our common translation alters the preposition, gratuitously and without warrant, and thus entirely loses the writer's antithesis.
[2] Bush's Anastasis, p. 164. ·

original statement, therefore, remains unqualified :—
We might have had, and should have expected to
have, the direct assertion of *four* Apostles, that they
had seen Jesus on earth and in the flesh after his death:
—we have not this assertion from any one of them.

3. The statements which have come down to us as
to when, where, by whom, and how often, Jesus was
seen after his death, present such serious and irreconcilable variations as to prove beyond question that
they are not the original statements of eye-witnesses,
but merely the form which the original statements had
assumed, after much transmission, thirty or forty years
after the event to which they relate.   Let us examine
them more particularly.   *It will be seen that they
agree in everything that is natural and probable, and
disagree in everything that is supernatural and difficult of credence.*   All the accounts agree that the
women, on their matutinal visit to the Sepulchre, found
the body gone, and saw some one in white raiment
who spoke to them.   *They agree in nothing else.*

(1.) They differ as to the number of the women.
John mentions only *one*, Mary Magdalene ; Matthew
two, Mary Magdalene and the other Mary ;—Mark
three, the two Marys and Salome ;—Luke *several*, the
two Marys, Joanna, and " certain others with them."

(2.) They differ as to the number of persons in
white raiment who appeared to the women.   Mark
speaks of one " young man ;"—Matthew of one
" angel ;"—Luke of two " men ;"—John of two

" angels."—According to John, also, the appearance of the two angels was not till Mary's second visit to the tomb, after Peter and John had been there.

(3.) They differ as to the words spoken by the apparitions. According to. Matthew and Mark they asserted the resurrection of Jesus, and his departure into Galilee, and sent a message to his disciples enjoining them to follow him thither. According to Luke they simply stated that he was risen, and referred to a former prediction of his to this effect.[1] According to John they only asked Mary, "Woman! why weepest thou ?"

(4.) They differ in another point. According to Matthew, Luke, and John, the women carried the information as to what they had seen at once to the disciples. According to Mark "they said nothing to any man."

(5.) They differ as to the parties to whom Jesus appeared.—According to Mark it was to no one. According to Matthew it was first to the two women, then to the eleven. According to John it was first to one woman then twice to the assembled Apostles.[2] According to Luke it was first to no woman, but to

---

[1] If, as we have reason to believe (chap. viii.), no such prediction was ever uttered, it follows that this reference to it most be purely fictitious.

[2] The text says simply " the disciples," but as they met in a room and with closed doors, and the absence of one of the Apostles on the first occasion is mentioned, it evidently means " the eleven."

Cleopas and his companion, then to Peter [1], and then to the assembled eleven.

(6.) They differ as to the locality. According to Mark it was nowhere. According to Matthew it was first at Jerusalem and then at Galilee, whither the disciples went in obedience to the angelic command. According to Luke it was in Jerusalem and its vicinity, and *there alone*, where the disciples remained in obedience to the reiterated command of Jesus himself.[2] According to the genuine part of John, also, the appearances were confined to Jerusalem.

The account of Paul differs slightly from all the others; it must have been second-hand; and is valuable only as showing the accounts which were current in the Christian Church at the time at which he wrote, and how much these varied from the evangelic documents, which were, in fact, a lection out of these current accounts. The epistle of Paul was written,

---

[1] This appearance to Peter is also mentioned by Paul (1 Cor. xv. 7), from whom probably Luke received it. We have nowhere else any trace of it.

[2] Luke xxiv. 49, 53; Acts i. 4. Luke and Matthew thus contradict each other past all possibility of reconciliation. Matthew tells us that Jesus commanded them to go into Galilee, and that they went thither;—Luke tells us that he positively commanded them " not to depart from Jerusalem," and that they remained there (xxiv. 53). But Luke contradicts himself quite as flatly on another point. In the Gospels he represents the ascension as taking place on the evening of the third day after the crucifixion: such is the clear meaning of the text (as may be seen from verses 21, 33, 36, 50):—in the Gospels he places the ascension forty days after the resurrection, and says that Jesus was seen by his disciples during the whole interval.

probably, about the year A.D. 57 ; the first three Gospels between the years A.D. 60 and 70. The appearance to James, which Paul mentions, was taken from the Gospel to the Hebrews, now lost.[1]

Now, we put it to any candid man whether the discrepancies in these accounts are not of a nature, and to an extent, entirely to disqualify them from being received as evidence of anything, except the currency and credit of such stories among Christians thirty years after the death of Christ?

4. A marked and most significant peculiarity in these accounts, which has not received the attention it deserves, is, that scarcely any of those who are said to have seen Jesus after his resurrection *recognized* him, though long and intimately acquainted with his person. According to Matthew (xxviii. 17), when Jesus appeared to the eleven in Galilee by his own appointment, some, even of them, " doubted ;" which could not have been the case had his identity been clearly recognizable. According to Luke, the two disciples, with whom he held a long conversation, and who passed many hours in his company, did not recognize him. " Their eyes were holden, that they should not know him."[2] And even after the disciples

---

[1] The passage, however, is preserved by Jerome. (See Hennell, p. 227.)

[2] Here another interesting point comes in for consideration. The conversation between Jesus and his two companions turned upon the Messianic prophecies, which the disciples held to have been disappointed by the death of Jesus, but which Jesus assured

had been informed, both of this reappearance and of
that to Peter (xxiv. 34-37), yet when Jesus appeared
to them, they were affrighted, and supposed that they
saw a spirit. According to John, even Mary Magdalene,
after Jesus had spoken to her, and she had turned to
look at him, still did not recognize him, but supposed
him to be the gardener.[1] In the spurious part of
John (xxi. 4-6) the same want of recognition is
observable. In the spurious part of Mark we see
traces of a belief that Jesus assumed various forms
after his resurrection, to account, doubtless, for the
non-recognition of some and the disbelief of others
(xvi. 11, 12, 13): "After that he appeared *in
another form* unto two of them." Now, if it really
were Jesus who appeared to these various parties,

them related to and were fulfilled in him. Now, if the conclusion
at which we arrived in a previous chapter (iv.) be correct, viz.,
that the Old Testament prophecies contain no real reference to a
suffering Messiah, or to Jesus at all, it follows, that at least half
the story of Cleopas must be fabulous, unless, indeed, we adopt
the supposition that Jesus held the same erroneous views respecting these prophecies as his disciples.

[1] Furness ("On the Four Gospels") dwells much on the fact
that it was "dark" when Mary visited the sepulchre (John xx. 1),
and that this was the reason why she did not recognize Jesus.
But, in the first place, it was not so dark but that she could see
that the sepulchre was open and the body gone. In the second
place, her sight of Jesus was on the occasion of her *second* visit to
the sepulchre, and the "darkness" of early dawn was during her
first visit, and in the interval she had gone to the city to find
Peter and John and had returned, by which time it must have
been broad day. In the third place, Mark tells us that the visit
of Mary was at *sunrise*—ἀνατείλαντος τοῦ ἡλίου—"the sun being
risen."

would this want of recognition have been possible ? If it were Jesus, he was so changed that his most intimate friends did not know him. How then can *we* know that it was himself ?

We will not attempt to construct, as several have endeavoured to do, out of these conflicting traditions, a narrative of the real original occurrence which gave rise to them, and of the process by which they attained the form and consistency at which they have arrived in the evangelical documents. Three different suppositions may be adopted, each of which has found favour in the eyes of some writers. We may either imagine that Jesus was not really and entirely dead when taken down from the cross, a supposition which Paulus and others show to be far from destitute of probability :[1] or we may imagine that the apparition of Jesus to his disciples belongs to that class of appearances of departed spirits for which so much staggering and bewildering evidence is on record ;[2] or, lastly, we may believe that the minds of the disciples, excited by the disappearance of the body, and the announcement by the women of his resurrection, mistook some passing individual for their crucified Lord, and that from such an origin multiplied rumours of his re-appearance arose and spread. We do not, ourselves, definitively adopt any of these hypotheses : we wish simply to call attention to the circumstance that we have no clear, consistent, credible account of

---

[1] Strauss, iii. 288.
[2] See Bush's Anastasis, 156.

the resurrection; that the only elements of the narrative which are retained and remain uniform in all its forms,—viz., the disappearance of the body, and the appearance of some one in white at the tomb, are simple and probable, and in no way necessitate, or clearly point to, the surmise of a bodily resurrection at all. Christ *may* have risen from the dead and appeared to his disciples; *but it is certain that if he did, the Gospels do not contain a correct account of such resurrection and re-appearance.*

II. The conduct of the Apostles subsequent to the death of Jesus,—the marked change in their character from timidity to boldness, and in their feelings from deep depression and dismay to satisfaction and triumph, —as depicted in the Acts, affords far stronger evidence in favour of the *bodily* resurrection of their Lord, than any of the narratives which have recorded the event. It seems to us certain that the Apostles *believed* in the resurrection of Jesus with absolute conviction. Nothing short of such a belief could have sustained them through what they had to endure, or given them enthusiasm for what they had to do; the question, therefore, which remains for our decision is, whether the Apostles could have believed it, had it not been fact; whether their reception of the doctrine of a general resurrection, or rather of a future life,[1] coupled

---

[1] The current belief in those days appears to have been not in an immediate liberation of the soul to a spiritual existence, but in an

with the disappearance of the body of Jesus from the sepulchre in which he had been laid, and the report of the women regarding the statement of the angelic vision, be sufficient to account for so vivid and actuating a faith, without the supposition of his actual appearance to themselves; whether, in fact, the Apostles, excited by the report that he was risen, could have believed that they had seen him if they had not really done so. This question will be differently answered by different minds; nor do we know that any arguments will weigh more on either side than the simple statement of the problem to be resolved.[1] Certainly, the bold faith of the Apostles, if sufficient, is the *only* sufficient evidence for the occurrence ; the narrative testimony would be inadequate to prove a far more credible event. All we can say is this, that a belief in the resurrection and bodily re-appearance of Jesus early prevailed and rapidly obtained currency in the Christian community ; that the Apostles shared the belief in the resurrection, and did not discourage

---

ultimate resurrection of all at the great day of account. John xi. 24 ; Luke xx. 33 ; Mark xii. 23. See *infra*, note, p. 255.

[1] It is certain that we, in these days, could not believe in the resurrection of an individual to an earthly life unless we had ascertained his death, and ourselves seen him afterwards alive. But we cannot justly apply this reasoning to the early followers of Christ; they were not men of critical, inquiring, or doubting minds, nor accustomed to sift or scrutinize testimony, but, on the contrary, inured to marvels, and trained to regard the supernatural as almost an ordinary part of the natural, given moreover to see visions, and unhesitatingly to accept them as divine communications.

that in the bodily reappearance ; that, however, none of them (the fourth Gospel not having been written by John) has left us his own testimony to having himself seen Jesus alive after his death ; and that some of the disciples doubted, and others long after disbelieved the fact.[1]

In order to mitigate our pain at finding that the fact of Christ's resurrection has been handed down to us on such inadequate testimony as to render it at best a doubtful inference, it is desirable to inquire whether, in reality, it has the doctrinal value which it has been the habit of theologians to attribute to it. We have been taught to regard it not only as the chief and crowning proof of the divinity of our Saviour's mission, but as the type, earnest, and assurance of our own translation to a life beyond the grave.   It is very questionable, however, whether either of these views of it is fully justified by reason.

There can be no doubt that the fact of an individual having been miraculously restored to life, is a signal proof of divine interposition in his behalf.   Such restoration may be viewed in three lights—either as a

---

[1] See 1 Cor. xv. 12.   The whole argument of Paul respecting the resurrection is remarkable—it is simply this, there must be a resurrection from the dead because Christ " is preached" to have risen ; and that if there were no resurrection, then Christ could not be risen.   It would seem as if he considered the truth of the resurrection of Christ to depend upon the correctness of the doctrine of the general resurrection (verse 13).

reward for a life of extraordinary virtue, or as an intimation that his mission upon earth had been prematurely cut short, and that his reanimation was necessary for its fulfilment, or as an announcement to the world that he was in a peculiar manner the object of divine regard and the subject of divine influence. The first point of view is evidently irrational, and the offspring of unregenerate and uncultivated thought. It is prompted either by the inconsiderate instincts of the natural man, or by disbelief in a future life. It implies either that there is no future world, or that this world is preferable to it, since no man, believing in another and a better state of existence, would regard it as an appropriate reward for distinguished excellence to be *reduced* to *this*. The second point of view is, if possible, still more unreasonable, since it assumes that God had permitted such an interference with and defeat of his plans, that he was obliged to interpose for their renewal. The third aspect in which such a fact is to be regarded alone remains, and is in effect the one in which it is commonly viewed throughout Christendom, viz., as a public announcement from the Most High, "This is my beloved Son, hear ye him." But this point of view is attended with many difficulties.

In the first place, if the Gospel narratives are to be taken as our standing-ground (and they are as valid for the one case as for the other), the restoration of the dead to life did not necessarily imply any such peculiar favour, or contain any such high announcement. The evangelists record *three* instances of such miraculous resuscitation, in none of which have we any reason for believing the subject of the miracle to be peculiarly an object of divine love or approbation, in all of which the miracle was simply one of mercy to mourning friends. The resuscitated parties were all obscure individuals, and only one of them appears to have been a follower of Christ. *Secondly*, this point of view was not the one taken by the Apostles. To them the value of Christ's resurrection consisted in its enabling them still to retain, or rather to resume, that belief in the Messiahship of Jesus which his death had shaken.[1] If restored to life, he might yet be, and probably was, that Great Deliverer whom, as Jews, they watched and waited and prayed for; if he were dead, then that cherished notion was struck dead with him. Now, if we are right in the conclusion at which we arrived in an earlier chapter,[2] viz., that Jesus had nothing in common with that liberating and triumphant conqueror predicted by the Jewish prophets and expected by the Jewish nation; it follows that the especial effect which the resurrection of Christ produced upon the minds of his disciples, was *to confirm them in an error*. This, to them, was its dogmatic value, the ground on which they hailed the announcement and cherished the belief. *Thirdly*, it will admit of question whether, in the eye of pure reason, the resurrection of Christ, considered as an attestation to

---

[1] This is especially manifest from the conversation on the journey to Emmaus.

[2] See chap. iv.

the celestial origin of his religion, be not superfluous —whether it be not human weakness, rather than human reason, which needs external miracle as sanction and buttress of a system which may well rely upon its own innate strength, whether the internal does not surpass and supersede the external testimony to its character, whether the divine truths which Christ taught should not be to us the all-sufficient attestation of his divine mission. We have seen in the preceding chapter that miraculous power in any individual is no guarantee for the correctness of his teaching. We have seen that if the doctrines which Jesus taught approve themselves to the enlightened understanding and the uncorrupted heart, they are equally binding on our allegiance whether he wrought miracles in the course of his career or not. And if the truth that God is a loving Father, and the precept, " Thou shalt love thy neighbour as thyself," derive no corroboration from the resurrection of Lazarus or the Youth of Nain, neither can they from that of Christ himself. Doubtless we should sit with more prostrate submission and a deeper reverence at the feet of a teacher who came to us from the grave, but it is probably only the infirmity of our faith and reason which would cause us to do so.[1] Rationally considered, Christ's resurrection cannot prove doctrines true that would else be false, nor certain that would else be doubtful. Therefore,

---

[1] Jesus seems to intimate as much when he says, " If they hear not Moses and the Prophets, neither will they be persuaded though one rose from the dead."

considered as a reward, it is contradictory and absurd; considered as the renewal of an interrupted mission, it involves an unworthy and monstrous conception of God's providence ; considered as an attestation to the Messiahship of Jesus, it is an attestation to an error ; considered as a sanction and corroboration of his doctrines, it is, or ought to be, superfluous.

Is the other view which we have been accustomed to take of Christ's resurrection,—viz., as the type, pledge, and foretelling of our own,—more consonant to sound reason ? We believe the reverse will prove nearer to the truth. That it was regarded in this view by the Apostles, is here no argument for us. For they looked for the coming of their Lord, and the end of the world, if not in their own lifetime, at least in that of the existing generation,—when they who were alive would be caught up into the clouds, and those who were dead would *come forth out of their graves*, and join together the glorious company of the redeemed. They looked for a *bodily* resurrection for themselves—which on their supposition of the date might appear possible,— a resurrection, therefore, of which that of Jesus *was* a prototype—a pattern—a cognate occurrence. But in *our* position the case is not only altered, but reversed. Christ's resurrection was believed, and is affirmed to have been, a reanimation of the body which he wore in life ; it could, therefore, be an earnest of the resurrection of those only whose bodies still remained to be reanimated : it was an exceptional case ; it refers not to us ; it conveys no hope to us ;—*we are not of those whose resurrection it could typify or assure ;* for our bodies, like those of the countless generations who have lived and passed away since Christ trod our earth, will have crumbled into dust, and passed into other combinations, and become in turn the bodies of myriads of other animated beings, before the great expected day of the resurrection of the just. To us a bodily resurrection is impossible. If, therefore, Christ's resurrection were *spiritual*—independent of his buried body—it might be a type and foreshadowing of our own;—if, on the other hand, as the evangelists relate, it was corporeal—if his body left the grave undecayed, and appeared on earth, and ascended into glory,—then its value as a pledge belonged to the men of that time alone,—we have neither part nor lot in its significance ;—it is rather an extinguisher than a confirmation of our hopes.

It will be seen that we make no scruple in negativing a doctrine held *verbally* by the Church, viz., "the resurrection of the body ;" since, whatever was intended by the authors of this phrase[1]—the meaning of which is by no means clear to us, and was probably no clearer to themselves,—thus much is certain, that

---

[1] " We can," says Pearson, "no otherwise expound this article teaching the resurrection of the body, than by asserting that the same bodies which have lived and died shall live again; that the same flesh which is corrupted shall be restored." Again, " That the same body, not any other, shall be raised to life which died, that the same flesh which was separated from the soul at the day of death shall be united to the soul at the last day," &c.—*Pearson on the Creed*, art. xi.

II. L

our "resurrection of the body" can bear no similarity to Christ's resurrection of the body;—for his body remained only a few hours in the grave, and, we are expressly told, "did not see corruption," and ours, we know, remains there for untold years, and moulders away into the original elements of its marvellous chemistry.

We conclude, then, as before :—that as we cannot hope to rise, as Christ is said to have done, with our own present uncorrupted body, his resurrection, if it were a reanimation of his earthly frame, can be no argument, proof, pledge, pattern, or foreshadowing of our own. If, on the contrary, his resurrection were spiritual, and his appearances to his disciples mental and apparitionary only, they would, *pro tanto*, countenance the idea of a future state. Our *interest*, therefore, as waiters and hopers for an immortality, would appear to lie in *dis*believing the letter of the Scripture narratives.

CHAPTER XV.

HAVING now arrived at this point of our inquiry, let us pause and cast a summary glance on the ground over which we have travelled, and the conclusions at which we have arrived. We have found that the popular doctrine of Scriptural Inspiration rests on no foundation whatever, but is a gratuitous as well as an untenable assumption. We have seen that neither the books of Moses nor the laws of Moses, as we have them, were (at least as a whole) the production of the great Leader and Lawgiver whose name they bear. We have seen ample reason for concluding that a belief in One only Supreme God was not the primary religion either of the Hebrew nation or the Hebrew priests ; but that their Theism—originally limited and impure —was gradually elevated and purified into perfect and exclusive monotheism, by the influence of their Poets and Sages, and the progressive advance of the people in intelligence and civilization. We have discovered that their Prophets were Poets and Statesmen, not Predictors—and that none of their writings contain a single prediction which was originally designed by them, or can be honestly interpreted by us, to foretell the appearance and career of Jesus of Nazareth. What have been commonly regarded as such, are happy and *applicable quotations :* but no more. We have seén further that none of the four histories of Christ which have come down to us are completely genuine and faithful ;—that while they are ample and adequate for showing us what Christ was, and what was the essence and spirit of his teaching, we yet do not possess sufficient certainty that they record, in any special instance, the precise words or actions of Christ, to warrant us in building upon those words or actions doctrines revolting to our uncorrupted instincts and our cultivated sense. We have found, moreover, that the Apostles—zealous and devout men as they were—were yet most imperfect and fallible expounders of the mind of their departed Lord. We have seen that miracles—even where the record of them is adequate and above suspicion, if any such case there be—are no sufficient guarantee of the truth of the doctrines preached by the worker of those wonders. And finally, we have been compelled to conclude that not only is the resurrection of our Lord, as narrated in the Gospels, encumbered with too many difficulties and contradictions to be received as unquestionable, but that it is far from having the dogmatic value usually attached to it, as a pledge and foreshowing of our own.

But however imperfect may be the records we possess of Christ's ministry, this imperfection does not affect the nature or authority of his mission. Another great question, therefore, here opens before us :—" Was Christ a divinely-commissioned Teacher of Truth ?" In other words, " Is Christianity to be regarded as a Religion revealed by God to man through Christ ? "

What is the meaning which, in ordinary theological parlance, we attach to the words " Divine Revelation ? " What do we intend to signify when we say that " God spoke" to this Prophet, or to that saint ?

We are all of us conscious of thoughts which *come to us*—which are not, properly speaking, *our own*—which we do not create, do not elaborate ;—flashes of light, glimpses of truth, or of what seems to us such, brighter and sublimer than commonly dwell in our minds, which we are not conscious of having *wrought out* by any process of inquiry or meditation. These are frequent and brilliant in proportion to the intellectual gifts and spiritual elevation of the individual : they may well be termed inspirations—revelations ; but it is not such as these that we mean when we speak of the Revelation by Christ.

Those who look upon God as a Moral Governor, as well as an original Creator,—a God at hand, not a God afar off in the distance of infinite space, and in the remoteness of past or future eternity,—who conceive of Him as taking a watchful and presiding interest in the affairs of the world, and as influencing the hearts and actions of men,—believe that through

the workings of the Spirit He has spoken to many,
has whispered His will to them, has breathed great
and true thoughts into their minds, has " wrought
mightily" within them, has in their secret communings
and the deep visions of the night, caused His Spirit
to move over the troubled waters of their souls, and
educed light and order from the mental chaos.   These
are the views of many religious minds ;—but these
are not what we mean when we speak of the Revelation made by God to Christ.

Those, again, who look upon God as the great
artificer of the world of life and matter, and upon
man, with his wonderful corporeal and mental frame,
as His direct work, conceive the same idea in a somewhat modified and more material form.   They believe
that He has made men with different intellectual
capacities ; and has endowed some with brains so
much larger and finer than those of ordinary men, as
to enable them to see and originate truths which are
hidden from the mass ; and that when it is His will
that Mankind should make some great step forward,
should achieve some pregnant discovery, He calls into
being some cerebral organization of more than ordinary magnitude and power, as that of David, Isaiah,
Plato, Shakspeare, Bacon, Newton, Luther, Pascal,
which gives birth to new ideas and grander conceptions of the truths vital to humanity.   But we mean
something essentially distinct from this when we
speak of Christ as the Teacher of a Religion revealed
to him by his Father.

When a Christian affirms Christianity to be a
"revealed religion," he intends simply and without
artifice to declare his belief that the doctrines and
precepts which Christ taught were not the production
of his own (human) mind, either in its ordinary operations, or in its flights of sublimest contemplation;
but were directly and supernaturally communicated to
him from on high.[1]   He means this, or he means
nothing definable and distinctive.   What grounds
have we, then, for adopting such an opinion?

It is evident that, if the conclusions to which our
previous investigations have led us be correct, our only
arguments for believing Christianity to be a divine
revelation in contradistinction to a human conception,
must be drawn from the *superhumanity* of its nature
and contents.   What human intellect could ascertain,
it would be superfluous for God to reveal.   The belief
of Christ himself, that his teaching " was not his, but
his Father's,"—even if we were certain that he used
these precise words, and intended them to convey
precisely the meaning we attach to them,—could not
suffice us, for the reasons assigned in the first chapter
of this work.   The belief in communications with
the Deity has in all ages been common to the most
exalted and poetical order of religious minds.   The
fact that Christ held a conviction which he shared

---

[1] Those who believe that Christ was God—if any such really
exist—must of course hold everything he taught was, *ipso facto*, a
divine revelation.   With such all argument and inquiry is necessarily superseded.

with the great and good of other times, can be no argument for ascribing to him divine communications distinct from those granted to the great and good of other times.   It remains, therefore, a simple question for our consideration, whether the doctrines and precepts taught by Jesus are so new, so profound, so perfect, so distinctive, so above and beyond parallel, that they could not have emanated naturally from a clear, simple, unsoiled, unwarped, powerful, meditative mind,—living four hundred years after Socrates and Plato—brought up among the pure Essenes, nourished on the wisdom of Solomon, the piety of David, the poetry of Isaiah—elevated by the knowledge, and illuminated by the love of the one true God.

Now on this subject we hope our confession of faith will be acceptable to all save the narrowly orthodox. It is difficult, without exhausting superlatives, even to unexpressive and wearisome satiety, to do justice to our intense love, reverence, and admiration, for the character and teaching of Jesus.   We regard him not as the perfection of the intellectual or philosophic mind, but as the perfection of the spiritual character,—as surpassing all men of all times in the closeness and depth of his communion with the Father.   In reading his sayings, we feel that we are holding converse with the wisest, purest, noblest Being that ever clothed thought in the poor language of humanity.   In studying his life we feel that we are following the footsteps of the highest ideal yet presented to us upon earth.   " Blessed be

God, that so much manliness has been lived out, and stands there yet, a lasting monument to mark how high the tides of divine life have risen in the world of man !"

But these convictions — strong, deep-seated, and well-grounded as they are—do not bring us to the conclusion that either the rare moral or mental superiorities of Jesus were supernatural endowments, in the common acceptation of the word. The Old Testament *contained* his teaching ; it was reserved for him to elicit, publish, and enforce it. A thoughtful perusal of Job, the Psalms, Ecclesiastes, and Isaiah will show beyond question the germs of those views which in the purer and sublimer genius of Christ rose to so high an elevation.[1] The doctrine of a future world, though not enforced, perhaps probably not found, in the Old Testament, was we know currently believed among the Jews before the time of Jesus, and must have been familiar to him from his infancy. We have no hesitation in concluding that a pure and powerful mind, filled with warm affections and devo-

---

[1] A quotation of texts is scarcely the right mode of proving this. See Hennell for an exposition of how much of Christianity was already extant in Jewish teaching ; also Mackay's Progress of the Intellect, ii. 376. [Em. Deutch's paper on the Talmud, *Quart. Review*, No. 246, and Renan, *Vie de Jesus*, ch. v.] But it must not be forgotten that though many of the Christian precepts were *extant* before the time of Jesus, yet it is to him that *we* owe them; to the energy, the beauty, the power of his teaching, and still more to the sublime life he led, which was a daily and hourly exposition and enforcement of his teaching.

tional feelings, and studying the Hebrew Scriptures
discriminatively, appropriating and assimilating what
was good and noble, and rejecting what was mean and
low, could and might naturally arrive at the conclusion which Jesus reached, as to the duties of men, the
attributes of God, and the relation of man to God.
Christianity is distinguished from Judaism rather by
what it excluded than by what it added.   It is an
eclecticism and an expansion of the best elements of
its predecessor.   It selects the grand, the beautiful,
the tender, the true, and ignores or suppresses the
exclusive, the narrow, the corrupt, the coarse, and the
vindictive.   It is Moses, David, Solomon, Isaiah,
purified, sublimated and developed.   If this be so,
then the supposition that Christianity was supernaturally communicated, falls to the ground as needless,
and therefore inadmissible.   What man could discover
naturally, God would not communicate supernaturally.

  But we may go further.   Not only is there no
necessity for supposing that Christ's views as to God
and duty were supernaturally revealed to him, but
there is almost a necessity for adopting an opposite
conclusion.   If they were the elaboration of his own
mind, we may well imagine that they may contain
some admixture of error and imperfection.   If they
were revealed to him by God, this could not be the
case.   If, therefore, we find that Jesus was in error
in any point either of his practical or his speculative
teaching, our conclusion, hitherto a probability,

becomes a certainty. It is evident that we could treat of this point with far more satisfaction if we were in a position to pronounce with perfect precision what Christ did, and what he did not, teach. But as we have seen that many words are put into his mouth which he never uttered, we cannot ascertain this as undoubtedly as is desirable. There must still remain some degree of doubt as to whether the errors and imperfections which we detect, originated with or were shared by Christ, or whether they were wholly attributable to his followers and historians.

There are, however, some matters on which the general concurrence of the evangelical histories, and their undesigned and incidental intimations, lead us to conclude that Jesus did share the mistakes which prevailed among his disciples, though, in going even so far as this, we speak with great diffidence. He appears to have held erroneous views respecting demoniacal possession, the interpretation of Scripture,[1] his own Messiahship, his second coming, and the approaching end of the world. At least, if he held the views ascribed to him (and the preponderance of evidence is

---

[1] See on this subject chap. viii. Perhaps the most singular instance of this misinterpretation of Scripture is in the sophistical argument ascribed to Christ, concerning the supposed address of David to the Messiah. " The Lord said unto my Lord," &c. (Matth. xxii. 41, and parallel passage.) It appears clear that this Psalm was not composed by David, but was addressed *to* David by Nathan, or some Court Prophet, on the occasion of some of his signal victories. —See " Hebrew Monarchy," p. 92. David did not call the Messiah " Lord ; " it was the Poet that called David " Lord."

in favour of the assumption that he did), we know that on these topics he was mistaken. Now if he was so in error, his teaching could not have been an infallible revelation from the God of truth, in the sense in which Christendom employs that phrase.

But we now come upon another question, which, if answered in the negative, at once closes the inquiry to which this chapter is devoted. " Is the revelation of an undiscoverable truth possible ? " That is, " Can any doctrine be taught by God to man—be supernaturally infused, that is, into his mind, which he might not by the employment of his own faculties have discerned or elicited ? " In other words, " Can the human mind *receive* an idea which it could not *originate ?* " We think it plain that it cannot; though the subject is one which may be better illuminated by reflection than by discussion. At least it is difficult to conceive the nature and formation of that intellect which can comprehend and grasp a truth when presented to it, and perceive that it is a truth, and which yet could not, in the course of time and under favourable conditions, work out that truth by the ordinary operation of its own powers. It appears to us that, by the very nature of the statement, the faculties necessary for the one mental process must be competent to the other.[1] If an idea (and a truth is

---

[1] It may be objected that external *facts* may be revealed which could not be discovered. We may be assured by revelation that the inhabitants of Saturn have wings or have no heads, but then we do not recognise the truth of the assurance. We may be assured

only an idea, or a combination of ideas, which approves itself to us), can find entrance into the mind and take up its abode there, does not this very fact show *a fitness for the residence of that idea ?*—a fitness, therefore, which would have insured admittance to the idea if suggested in any of those mental processes which we call thought, or by any of those combinations of occurrences which we call accident—a fitness, there-fore, which, as the course of time and the occurrence of a thousand such possible suggesting accidents must almost necessarily have ensured the *presentation* of the idea, would also have ensured its *reception ?* If, on the other hand, the idea, from its strangeness, its immensity, its want of harmony with the nature and existing furniture of the mind, could never have pre-sented itself naturally, would not the same strangeness, the same vastness, the same incompatibility of essence incapacitate the mind from receiving it if presented supernaturally ?

" Revealed religion," says one of our acutest writers, " is an *assumption* of some truths, and an *anticipa-tion* or *confirmation* of others. . . . . It is obvious that a truth which is announced from heaven in one age, may be discovered by man in another. A truth is a real and actual relation of things subsisting somewhere,—either in the ideas within us, or the

---

by revelation of ·the existence of a future world; but could we receive the assurance unless our minds were already so prepared for it, or so constituted, that it would naturally have occurred to them ?

objects without us,—and capable therefore of making itself clear to us by evidence either demonstrative or moral. We may not yet have advanced to the point of view from which it opens upon us; but a progressive knowledge must bring us to it ; and we shall then see that which hitherto was sustained by authority, resting on its natural support ; we shall behold it, indeed, in the same light in which it has all along appeared to the superior Intelligence who tendered it to our belief. Thus revelation is an anticipation only of Science ; a forecast of future intellectual and moral achievements ; a provisional authority for governing the human mind, till the regularly-constituted powers can be organised." In this case it is evident that the question whether a truth were discovered or revealed, depends upon a previous inquiry ; viz., whether the truth were too far before the age to have been discovered by that age ? and if so, whether the Teacher of it were not far enough before his age to make the truth which was hidden from his contemporaries visible to him ? It thus becomes a mere question of time and degree ; and what is justly called a revelation now, would be justly called a discovery a century hence. It is obvious that this is too narrow and shifting a ground to form a safe foundation for a theory of revelation.

Further, we are at a loss to imagine how a man can *distinguish* between an idea revealed to him and an idea conceived by him. In what manner and by what sure token, can it be made clear to him that

a thought came to him from without, not arose within ?
He may perceive that it is resplendently bright, unquestionably new ; he may be quite unconscious of
any process of ratiocination or meditation by which it
can have been originated ; but this is no more than
may be said of half the ideas of profound and, con-
templative genius. Shall we say that it was breathed
into him " in a dream, in a vision of the night, when
deep sleep falleth upon man ; " and that, therefore, he
assumes that it is not his, but God's ? Yet what is
this but to declare that God chooses for his communications with the mind of man the period of its most
unquestionable imperfection, when the phantasy is
ascendant and the judgment is torpid and in abeyance ?
Shall we say that the thought was spoken to him
aloud, in the ordinary language of humanity, and that,
therefore, he knows it to have been a divine communication, not a human conception ? But what singular
logic is this ! Is the voice of God, then, only, or then
most, recognisable when it borrows the language of
man ? Is that unprecise and feeble instrument of
thought and utterance, invented by man's faulty
faculties, God's best and surest mode of communication
with the spirit he has created ? Nay, is not imperfect
language an *impossible* medium for the conveyance of
absolute and infinite truth ? And do we really mean
that we feel *certain* it is God's voice which we hear
from the clouds, and *doubtful* that it is His which
spoke to us silently, and in the deep and sacred

musings of the Soul? We cannot intend to maintain this monstrous thesis.

Our reflections, then, bring us to this conclusion :—
that the only certain proof we can have of a revelation
must lie in the truths it teaches being such as are
inaccessible to, and therefore incomprehensible by, the
mind of man ; that if they are such as he can conceive and grasp and accept, they are such as he might
have discovered, and he has no means of knowing
that he has not discovered them ; if they are such as
he could not have discovered, they are such as he
cannot receive, such as he could not recognise or
ascertain to be truth.

Since, then, we can find no adequate reason for
believing Jesus to be the Son of God, nor his doctrines
to be a direct and special revelation to him from the
Most High—using these phrases in their ordinary
signification—in what light *do* we regard Christ and
Christianity ?

We do not believe that Christianity contains anything which a genius like Christ's, brought up and
nourished as his had been, might not have disen-
tangled for itself. We hold that God has so arranged
matters in this beautiful and well-ordered, but mys-
teriously-governed universe, that one great mind after
another will arise from time to time, as such are
needed, to discover and flash forth before the eyes of
men the truths that are wanted, and the amount of
truth that can be borne. We conceive that this is

effected by endowing them, or (for we pretend to no scholastic nicety of expression) by having arranged that Nature and the course of events shall send them into the world endowed with that superior mental and moral organisation, in which grand truths, sublime gleams of spiritual light, will spontaneously and inevitably arise. Such a one we believe was Jesus of Nazareth, the most exalted religious genius whom God ever sent upon the earth ; in himself an embodied revelation; humanity in its divinest phase, "God manifest in the flesh," according to Eastern hyperbole; an exemplar vouchsafed, in an early age of the World, of what man may and should become, in the course of ages, in his progress towards the realisation of his destiny ; an individual gifted with a grand clear intellect, a noble soul, a fine organisation, marvellous moral intuitions, and a perfectly balanced moral being; and who, by virtue of these endowments, saw further than all other men—

> " Beyond the verge of that blue sky
> Where God's sublimest secrets lie ; "

an earnest, not only of what humanity may be, but of what it will be, when the most perfected races shall bear the same relation to the finest minds of existing times, as these now bear to the Bushmen or the Esquimaux. He was, as Parker beautifully expresses it, "the possibility of the race made real." He was a sublime poet, prophet, moralist, and hero ; and had the usual fate of such—misrepresented by his enemies,

II.   M

—misconstrued by his friends ; unhappy in this, that his nearest intimates and followers were not of a calibre to understand him ; happy in this, that his words contained such undying seeds of truth as could survive even the media through which they passed. Like the wheat found in the Egyptian Catacombs, they retain the power of germinating undiminished, whenever their appropriate soil is found. They have been preserved essentially almost pure, notwithstanding the Judaic narrowness of Peter, the orthodox passions of John, and metaphysical subtleties of Paul. Everything seems to us to confirm the conclusion that we have in the Christianity of Scripture, not a code of law, still less a system of dogma, but a mass of beautiful, simple, sublime, profound, *not perfect*, truths, obscured by having come down to us through the intervention of minds far inferior to that of its Author— narrowed by their uncultivation—marred by their misapprehensions—and tarnished by their foreign admixtures. It is a collection of grand truths, transmitted to us by men who only half comprehended their grandeur, and imperfectly grasped their truth.[1]

---

[1] " The character of the record is such that I see not how any stress can be laid on particular actions attributed to Jesus. That he lived a divine life, suffered a violent death, taught and lived a most beautiful religion—this seems the great fact about which a mass of truth and error has been collected. That he should gather disciples, be opposed by the Priests and Pharisees, have controversies with them—this lay in the nature of things. His loftiest sayings seem to me the most likely to be genuine. The great stress laid on the person of Jesus by his followers, shows what the person

The question whether Christ had a *special* mission —were specially inspired by the Spirit of God—will be decided by each man according to the views he may entertain of Providence, and to the meaning which he attaches to words which, in the lips of too many, have no definite meaning at all. We are not careful to answer in this matter. We believe that God has arranged this glorious but perplexing world with a purpose, and on a plan. We hold that every man of superior capacity (if not *every* man sent upon the earth) has a duty to perform—a mission to fulfil—a baptism to be baptized with—" and how is he straitened till it be accomplished !" We feel a deep inward conviction that every great and good man possesses some portion of God's truth, to proclaim to the world, and to

---

must have been; they put the person before the thing, the fact above the idea. But it is not about common men that such mythical stories are told."—Theodore Parker, Discourse, p. 188.

[" Les évangélistes eux-mêmes, qui nous ont légué l'image de Jésus, sont si fort au-dessous de celui dont ils parlent que sans cesse ils le défigurent, faute d'atteindre à sa hauteur. Leurs écrits sont pleins d'erreurs et de contre-sens. On entrevoit à chacque ligne un original d'une beautè divine trahi par des rédacteurs qui ne le comprennent pas, et qui substituent leurs propres ideés à celles qu'ils ne saisissent qu'à demi."—Rénan, *Vie de Jesus*, p. 466.

" The more we conceive of Jesus as almost as much over the heads of his disciples and reporters as he is over the heads of so-called Christians now, the more we sec his disciples to have been, as they were, men raised by a truer moral susceptiveness above their countrymen, but in intellectual conceptions and habits much on a level with them,—all the more do we make room, so to speak, for Jesus to be inconceivably great and wonderful; as wonderful as his reporters imagined him to be, though in a different manner." —*Literature and Dogma*, p. 153.]

fructify in his own bosom. In a true and simple, but not the orthodox, sense, we believe all the pure, wise, and mighty in soul, to be inspired, and to be inspired for the instruction, advancement, and eleva-tion of mankind. "Inspiration, like God's omnipre-sence, is not limited to the few writers claimed by the Jews, Christians, or Mahometans, but is co-extensive with the race. . . . . The degree of inspiration must depend upon two things : first, on the natural ability, the particular intellectual, moral, and religious endow-ment or genius wherewith each man is furnished by God ; and next, on the use each man makes of this endowment. In one word, it depends on the man's *Quantity of Being* and his *Quantity of Obedience.* Now, as men differ widely in their natural endowments, and much more widely in their use and development thereof, there must of course be various degrees of inspiration, from the lowest sinner up to the loftiest saint. All men are not by birth capable of the same degree of inspiration, and by culture and acquired character they are still less capable of it. A man of noble intellect, of deep, rich, benevolent affections, is by his endowments capable of more than one less gifted. He that perfectly keeps the Soul's law, thus fulfilling the conditions of inspiration, has more than he who keeps it imperfectly ; the former must receive all his soul can contain at that stage of its growth. . . . . Inspiration, then, is the consequence of a faithful use of our faculties. Each man is its subject—God its source—truth its only test, ... Men may call it miraculous, but nothing is more natural. It is co-extensive with the faithful use of man's natural powers. . . . . Now, this inspiration is limited to no sect, age, or nation. It is wide as the world, and common as God. It is not given to a few men, in the infancy of mankind, to monopolize inspiration, and bar God out of the Soul. You and I are not born in the dotage and decay of the world. The stars are beautiful as in their prime ; ' the most ancient Heavens are fresh and strong.' God is still everywhere in nature. Wherever a heart beats with love—where Faith and Reason utter their oracles—there also is God, as formerly in the hearts of seers and prophets. Neither Gerizim, nor Jerusalem, nor the soil that Jesus blessed, is so holy as the good man's heart; nothing so full of God. This inspiration is not given to the learned alone, not only to the great and wise, but to every faithful child of God. Certain as the open eye drinks in the light, do the pure in heart see God ; and he that lives truly feels Him as a presence not to be put by." [1]

This, however, to minds nourished on the positive and sententious creeds of orthodox Christendom, is not enough. Truths that are written by the finger of God upon the heart of man, are not definite enough for them. Views of religion and duty wrought out by the meditations of the studious, confirmed by the allegiance of the good and wise, stamped as sterling

---

[1] Theodore Parker, p. 161, et seq.

by the response they find in every uncorrupted mind
—are not *sure* enough for them. " They cannot trust
God unless they have his bond *in black and white,
given under oath, and attested by witnesses.*" They
cling to dogmatic certainties, and vainly imagine such
certainty to be attainable. It is this feeling which
lies at the root of the distaste so generally evinced by
orthodox Christians for natural religion and for free
and daring theological research ; and. the mental defect in which it has its origin is not difficult to discover.
It belongs to understandings at once dependent, indolent, and timid, in which the practical predominates
over the spiritual, to which external testimony is more
intelligible than internal evidence—which prefer the
ease derived from reposing on authority to the labour
inseparable from patient and original reflection. Such
men are unwilling to rest the hopes which animate
them, and the principles which guide them, either on
the deductions of fallible reason, or the convictions of
corruptible instincts. This feeling is natural, and is
shared by even the profoundest thinkers at some period
or other of their progress towards that serenity of faith
which is the last and highest attainment of the devout
searcher after truth. But the mistake is, to conceive
it *possible* to attain certainty by some change in the
process of elaborating knowledge ;—to imagine that any
surer foundation *can* be discovered for religious belief
than the deductions of the intellect and the convictions
of the heart. If reason proves the existence and attributes of God—if those spiritual instincts, which we

believe to be the voice of God in the soul, infuse into
the mind a sense of our relation to Him, and a hope
of future existence—if reason and conscience alike
irresistibly point to virtue as the highest good and
the destined end and aim of man,—we doubt, we hesitate, we tremble at the possibility of a mistake ; we
cry out that this is not certainty, and that on anything
short of certainty our souls cannot rest in peace. But
if we are told, on the authority of certain ancient
documents, and venerable but still modified and metamorphosed traditions, that some centuries ago a saint
and sage came into the world, and assured his hearers
that they had one God and Father who commanded
virtue as a law, and promised futurity as a reward ;
and that this sage, to prove that he was divinely
authorized to preach such doctrines, wrought miracles,
which fallible disciples witnessed, and which fallible
narrators have transmitted—then we bow our heads
in satisfied acquiescence, and feel that we have attained
the unmistakable, unquestionable, infallible certainty
we sought ! What is this but the very spirit of
Hindoo Mythology, which is not contented till it has
found a resting-place for the Universe, yet is content
to rest it on an elephant, and on a tortoise ?

The same fallible human reason is the foundation of
our whole superstructure in the one case equally as in
the other. The whole difference is, that in the one
case we apply that reason to the evidence for the
doctrine itself; in the other case we apply it to the
credentials of the individual who is said to have

taught that doctrine. But is it possible we can so blind ourselves as to believe that reason can ever give us half the assurance that Matthew is correct when he tells us that Christ preached the Sermon on the Mount and fed 5000 men with five loaves and two fishes—as it gives us that a mighty and benevolent Maker formed the Universe and its inhabitants, and made man "the living to praise him?" What should we think of the soundness of that man's understanding, who should say, "I have studied the wonders of the Heavens, the framework of the Earth, the mysterious beauties and adaptations of animal existence, the moral and material constitution of the human creature, who is so fearfully and wonderfully made; and I have risen from the contemplation unsatisfied and uncertain *whether* God is, and *what* He is. But I have carefully examined the four Gospels, weighed their discrepancies, collated their reports, and the result is a perfect certainty that Christ was the miraculous Son of God, commissioned to make known His existence, to reveal His will, to traverse or suspend His laws. It is *doubtful* whether a wise and good Being be the Author of the starry heavens above me, and the moral world within me; but it is *unquestionable* that Jesus walked upon the water, and raised the Widow's Son at Nain. I may be mistaken in the one deduction—I cannot be mistaken in the other." Strange conformation of mind! which can find no adequate foundation for its hopes, its worship, its principles of action, in the far-stretching universe, in the glorious firmament, in the deep, full soul, bursting with unutterable thoughts, in the vast and rich store-house of the material and · moral world—yet can rest all, with a trusting simplicity approaching the sublime, on what a book relates of the sayings and doings of a man who lived eighteen centuries ago !

If the change which resulted from our inquiries were indeed a descent from certainty to probability, it would involve a loss beyond all power of compensation. But it is not so. It is merely an exchange of conclusions founded on one chain of reasoning for conclusions founded on another. The plain truth, if we dared but look it in the face, is this,—that absolute certainty on these subjects is not attainable, and was not intended. We have already seen that no miraculous revelation could make doctrines credible which are revolting to our reason ; nor can any revelation give to doctrines greater certainty than that which attaches to its own origin and history. Now, we cannot conceive the proofs of any miraculous revelation to be so perfect, flawless, and cogent, as are the proofs of the great doctrines of our faith, independent of miracle or revelation. Both set of proofs must, philosophically speaking, be *imperfect;* but the proof that any particular individual was supernaturally inspired by God, must always be *more* imperfect than the proof that Man and the Universe are the production of His fiat ; that goodness is His profoundest essence ; that doing good is the noblest worship we can pay Him. To seek that more cogent and compelling certainty of

these truths which orthodoxy yearns after, is to strive
· for a shadow—to fancy that we have attained it, is to
be satisfied with having affixed Man's indorsement to
" the true sayings of God."[1]

[In truth, however, it is not for the sake of these
grand foundation-stones of all religion which are so
much more certain than the authority or inspiration of
any ancient documents or traditions possibly can be,
that positive, unquestioning, dogmatic, absolute conviction of the genuineness and infallibility of the letter
of the Bible is so urgently insisted upon by the
orthodox.   This conviction, this proposition, is
essential to their entire system of doctrine, for the
simple reason (which can never be too plainly realised
or kept in mind, and which was discussed in chapter
xi.) that this doctrinal system · is founded not on the
New Testament narratives *as a whole*, nor even on the
Scriptures as a whole, but on special texts, often
isolated, often unharmonizing, often absolutely incon-

---

[1] " Having removed the offence we took in fancying God speaking with a human voice, and saying, ' This is my beloved Son :
hear ye him,'—we certainly do not incline to call that a loss.   But
we do not lose anything else ; for considering the godliness and
purity of the life of Jesus, and then thinking of God and his holiness on the one side, and of our destination on the other, we know,
without a positive declaration, that God must have been pleased
with a life like that of Jesus, and that we cannot do better than
adhere to him.   We do not lose, therefore, with those voices from
heaven, more than is lost by a beautiful picture from which a ticket
is taken away that was fastened to it, containing the superfluous
assurance of its being a beautiful picture."—Strauss's Letter to
Professor Orelli, p. 20.

gruous. Only if the whole Bible is unassailable in its absolute and omnipresent accuracy and authority, can the more difficult and startling doctrines of the popular creed hold their ground.]

In grasping after this certainty, which can be but a shadow, ordinary Christianity has lost the substance ——it has sacrificed in practical more than it has gained in dogmatic value. In making Christ the miraculous Son of God, it has destroyed Jesus as a human exemplar. If he were in a peculiar manner " the only begotten of the Father," a partaker in his essential nature, then he is immeasurably removed from us ; we may revere, we cannot imitate him. We listen to his precepts with submission, perhaps even greater than before. We dwell upon the excellence of his character, no longer for imitation, but for worship. We read with the deepest love and admiration of his genius, his gentleness, his mercy, his unwearying activity in doing good, his patience with the stupid, his compassion for the afflicted, his courage in facing torture, his meekness in enduring wrong ; and then we turn away and say, " Ah ! he was a God ; such virtue is not for humanity, nor for us." It is useless by honeyed words to disguise the truth. If Christ were a man, he is our *dattern;* " the possibility of our race made real." If he were God—a partaker of God's nature, as the orthodox maintain—then they are guilty of a cruel mockery in speaking of him as a type and model of human excellence. How can one endowed with the perfections of a God be an example to beings encumbered with the weaknesses of humanity? Adieu, then, to Jesus as anything but a Propounder of doctrines, an Utterer of precepts! The *vital* portion of Christianity is swept away. His *Character*—that from which so many in all ages have drawn their moral life and strength—that which so irresistibly enlists our deepest sympathies, and rouses our highest aspirations—it becomes an irreverence to speak of. The character, the conduct, the virtues of a God!— these are felt to be indecent expressions. Verily, orthodoxy has slain the life of Christianity. In the presumptuous endeavour to exalt Jesus, it has shut him up in the Holy of Holies, and hid him from the gaze of humanity. It has displaced him from an object of imitation into an object of worship. It has made his life barren, that his essence might be called divine.

" But *we* have no fear that we should lose Christ by being obliged to give up a considerable part of what was hitherto called Christian creed! He will remain to all of us the more surely, the less anxiously we cling to doctrines and opinions that might tempt our reason to forsake him. But if Christ remains to us, and if he remains to us as the highest we know and are capable of imagining within the sphere of religion, as the person without whose presence in the mind no perfect piety is possible ; we may fairly say that in Him do we still possess the sum and substance of the Christian faith." [1]

---

[1] Strauss's Soliloquies, p. 67.

"But," it will be objected, "what, on this system, becomes of the religion of the poor and ignorant, the uneducated, and the busy? If Christianity is not a divine revelation, and therefore entirely and infallibly true,—if the Gospels are not perfectly faithful and accurate expositors of Christ's teaching and of God's will,—what a fearful loss to those who have neither the leisure, the learning, nor the logical habits of thought requisite to construct out of the relics that remain to them and the nature that lies before them a faith for themselves!"

To this objection we reply that the more religion can be shown to consist in the realization of great moral and spiritual truths, rather than in the reception of distinct dogmas, the more the position of these classes is altered for the better. In no respect is it altered for the worse. Their *creeds*, *i.e.*, their collection of dogmas, those who do not or cannot think for themselves must always take on the authority of others. They do so now: they have always done so. They have hitherto believed certain doctrines because wise and good men assure them that these doctrines were revealed by Christ, and that Christ was a Teacher sent from God. They will in future believe them because wise and good men assure them of their truth, and their own hearts confirm the assurance. The only difference lies in this,—that, in the one case, the authority on which they lean vouches for the truth; in the other, for the Teacher who proclaimed it.

Moreover, the Bible still remains; though no longer

as an inspired and infallible record. Though not the word of God, it contains the words of the wisest, the most excellent, the most devout men, who have ever held communion with Him. The poor, the ignorant, the busy, need not, do not, will not, read it critically. To each of them, it will still, through all time, present the Gospels and the Psalms,—the glorious purity of Jesus, the sublime piety of David and of Job. Those who read it for its spirit, not for its dogmas—as the poor, the ignorant, the busy, *if unperverted*, will do— will still find in it all that is necessary for their guidance in life, their support in death, their consolation in sorrow, their rule of duty, and their trust in God.

A more genuine and important objection to the consequences of our views is felt by indolent minds on their own account. They shrink from the toil of working out truth for themselves, out of the materials which Providence has placed before them. They long for the precious metal, but loathe the rude ore out of which it has to be extricated by the laborious alchemy of thought. A ready-made creed is the Paradise of their lazy dreams. A string of authoritative dogmatic propositions comprises the whole mental wealth which they desire. The volume of nature, the volume of history, the volume of life, appal and terrify them. Such men are the materials out of whom good Catholics —of all sects—are made. They form the uninquiring and submissive flocks which rejoice the hearts of all Priesthoods. Let such cling to the faith of their forefathers—if they can. But men whose minds are cast in a nobler mould and are instinct with a diviner life, who love truth more than rest, and the peace of Heaven rather than the peace of Eden, to whom "a loftier being brings severer cares,"—

> " Who know Man does not live by joy alone
> But by the presence of the power of God,"—

such must cast behind them the hope of any repose or tranquillity save that which is the last reward of long agonies of thought ;[1] they must relinquish all prospect of any Heaven save that of which tribulation is the avenue and portal ; they must gird up their loins and trim their lamp for a work which cannot be put by, and which must not be negligently done. " He," says Zschokke, " who does not like living in the *furnished lodgings of tradition*, must build his own house, his own system of thought and faith, for himself."[2]

---

[1] " O Thou ! to whom the wearisome disease
Of Past and Present is an alien thing,
Thou pure Existence ! whose severe decrees
Forbid a living man his soul to bring
Into a timeless Eden of sweet ease,
Clear-eyed, clear-hearted—lay thy loving wing
In death upon me—if that way alone
Thy great Creation-thought thou wilt to me make known."
R. M. MILNES.

[2] Zschokke's Autobiography, p. 29.   The whole section is most deeply interesting.

CHAPTER XVI.

CHRISTIANITY, then, not being a revelation, but a conception—the Gospels not being either inspired or accurate, but fallible and imperfect human records—the practical conclusion from such premises must be obvious to all. Every doctrine and every proposition which the Scriptures contain, whether or not we believe it to have come to us unmutilated and unmarred from the mouth of Christ, is open, and must be subjected, to the scrutiny of reason. Some tenets we shall at once accept as the most perfect truth that can be received by the human intellect and heart;—others we shall reject as contradicting our instincts and offending our understandings ;—others, again, of a more mixed nature, we must analyze, that so we may extricate the seed of truth from the husk of error, and elicit "the divine idea that lies at the bottom of appearance."[1]

I. I value the Religion of Jesus, not as being ab-

---

[1] Fichte.

solute and perfect truth, but as containing more truth, purer truth, higher truth, stronger truth, than has ever yet been given to man. Much of his teaching I unhesitatingly receive as, to the best of my judgment, unimprovable and unsurpassable—fitted, if obeyed, to make earth all that a finite and material scene can be, and man only a little lower than the angels. *The worthlessness of ceremonial observances, and the necessity of essential righteousness*—" Not every one that saith unto me, Lord! Lord! but he that doeth the will of my Father which is in Heaven ;" " By their fruits ye shall know them ;" " I will have mercy, and not sacrifice ;" " Be not a slothful hearer only, but a doer of the word ;" " Woe unto ye, Scribes and Pharisees, for ye pay tithes of mint and anise and cummin, and neglect the weightier matters of the Law, justice, mercy, and temperance :"—*The enforcement of purity of heart as the security for purity of life, and of the government of the thoughts, as the originators and forerunners of action*—"He that looketh on a woman, to lust after her, hath committed adultery with her already in his heart ;" " Out of the heart proceed murders, adulteries, thefts, false witness, blasphemies: these are the things which defile a man;"— *Universal good-will towards men*—" Thou shalt love thy neighbour as thyself ;" " Whatsoever ye would that men should do unto you, that do ye also unto them, for this is the Law and the Prophets:"—*Forgiveness of injuries*—" Love your enemies ; do good to them that hate you ; pray for them which despitefully

II.   N

use you and persecute you; " "Forgive us our
trespasses, as we forgive those that trespass against us;"
"I say not unto thee, until seven times, but until
seventy times seven;" "If ye love them only that love
you, what reward have ye? do not even publicans the
same ?"—*The necessity of self-sacrifice in the cause of
duty*—"Blessed are they which are persecuted for
righteousness' sake;" "If any man will be my disciple, let him deny himself, and take up his cross daily,
and follow me;" "If thy right hand offend thee, cut
it off and cast it from thee;" "No man, having put
his hand to the plough and looking back, is fit for the
kingdom of God;"—*Humility*—"Blessed are the
meek, for they shall inherit the earth;" "He that
humbleth himself shall be exalted;" "He that is
greatest among you, let him be your servant :"—*Genuine sincerity; being, not seeming*—"Take heed
that ye do not your alms before men, to be seen of
them;" "When thou prayest, enter into thy closet
and shut thy door;" "When thou fastest, anoint thine
head, and wash thy face, that thou appear not unto
men to fast;"—all these sublime precepts need no
miracle, no voice from the clouds, to recommend them
to our allegiance, or to assure us of their divinity;
they command obedience by virtue of their inherent
rectitude and beauty, and vindicate their author as
himself the one towering perpetual miracle of history.

II. Next in perfection come the views which
Christianity unfolds to us of God in his relation to man,
which were probably as near the truth as the minds of

men could in that age receive. God is represented as Our *Father* in Heaven—to be whose especial children is the best reward of the peace-makers—to see whose face is the highest hope of the pure in heart—who is ever at hand to strengthen His true worshippers—to whom is due our heartiest love, our humblest submission—whose most acceptable worship is righteous conduct and a holy heart—in whose constant presence our life is passed—to whose merciful disposal we are resigned by death. It is remarkable that, throughout the Gospels, with the exception, I believe, of a single passage,[1] nothing is said as to the *nature* of the Deity :—his *relation* to us is alone insisted on:—all that is needed for our consolation, our strength, our guidance, is assured to us:—the purely speculative is passed over and ignored.

Thus, in the two great points essential to our practical life—viz., our feelings towards God, and our conduct towards man—the Gospels, relieved of their unauthentic portions, and read in an understanding spirit, not with a slavish and unintelligent adherence to the naked letter, contain little about which men can differ—little from which they can dissent. He is our Father, we are all brethren. This much lies open to the most ignorant and busy, as fully as to the most leisurely and learned. This needs no Priest to teach it—no authority to indorse it. The rest is Speculation—intensely interesting, indeed, but of no practical necessity.

---

[1] God is a spirit.

III. There are, however, other tenets taught in Scripture and professed by Christians, in which reflective minds of all ages have found it difficult to acquiesce. Thus :—however far we may stretch the plea for a liberal interpretation of Oriental speech, it is impossible to disguise from ourselves that the New Testament teaches, in the most unreserved manner, and in the strongest language, the doctrine of *the efficacy of Prayer* in modifying the divine purposes, and in obtaining the boons asked for at the throne of grace. It is true that one passage (John xi. 42) would seem to indicate that prayer was a form which Jesus adopted for the sake of others ; it is also remarkable that the model of prayer, which he taught to his disciples, contains only one simple and modest request for personal and temporal good ;[1] yet not only are we told that he prayed earnestly and for specific mercies (though with a most submissive will), on occasions of peculiar suffering and trial, but few of his exhortations to his disciples occur more frequently than that to constant prayer, and no promises are more distinct or reiterated than that their prayers shall be heard and answered. "Watch and pray ;" "This kind goeth not out but by prayer and fasting ;" "What things soever ye desire, when ye pray, believe that ye shall receive them, and ye shall

---

[1] "It is a curious fact that the Lord's prayer may be reconstructed," says Wetstein, "almost verbatim out of the Talmud, which also contains a prophetic intimation that all prayer will one day cease, except the prayer of Thanksgiving." (Mackay's Progress of the Intellect ii. 379.)

have them;" "Verily, verily, I say unto you, what-soever ye shall ask of the Father in my name, he will give it you;" "Ask, and it shall be given you;" "Thinkest thou that I cannot now pray to my Father, and he shall presently give me more than twelve legions of angels?" The parable of the unjust Judge was delivered to enforce the same conclusion, and the writings of the apostles are at least equally explicit on this point. "Be constant in prayer;" "Pray without ceasing;" "Let him ask in faith, nothing wavering;" "The fervent effectual prayer of a righteous man availeth much."

No one can read such passages, and the numberless others of a similar character with which both Testaments abound, and doubt that the opinion held both by Christ and his disciples was that "Jehovah is a God that heareth and answereth prayer;"—that favours are to be obtained from Him by earnest and reiterated entreaty; that whatever good thing His sincere worshippers petition for, with *instance* and with faith, shall be granted to them, if consonant to his purposes, and shall be granted *in consequence* of their petition; that, in fact and truth, apart from all metaphysical subtleties and subterfuges the designs of God can be modified and swayed, like those of an earthly father, by the entreaties of His children. This doctrine is set forth throughout the Jewish Scriptures in its coarsest and nakedest form and it reappears in the Christian Scriptures in a form only slightly modified and refined.

Now, this doctrine has in all ages been a stumbling-block to the thoughtful.   It is obviously irreconcilable with all that reason and revelation teach us of the divine nature ; and the inconsistency has been felt by the ablest of the Scripture writers themselves.[1] Various and desperate have been the expedients and suppositions resorted to, in order to reconcile the conception of an immutable, all-wise, all-foreseeing God, with that of a father who is turned from his course by the prayers of his creatures.   But all such efforts are, and are felt to be, hopeless failures.. They involve the assertion and negation of the same proposition in one breath.   The problem remains still insoluble ; and we must either be content to leave it so, or we must abandon one or other of the hostile premises.

The religious man, who believes that all events, mental as well as physical, are pre-ordered and arranged according to the decrees of infinite wisdom, and the philosopher, who knows that, by the wise and eternal laws of the universe, cause and effect are indissolubly chained together, and that one follows the other in inevitable succession,—equally feel that this ordination—this chain—cannot be changeable at the cry of man.   To suppose that it can is to place the whole harmonious system of nature at the mercy of the weak reason and the selfish wishes of humanity.   If the purposes of God were not wise, they would not be

---

[1] "God is not a man that he should lie, nor the son of man, that he should repent."

formed :—if wise, they cannot be changed, for then they would become unwise. To suppose that an all-wise Being would alter his designs and modes of proceeding at the entreaty of an unknowing creature, is to believe that compassion would change his wisdom into foolishness. It has been urged that prayer may render a favour wise, which would else be unwise ; but this is to imagine that events are not foreseen and pre-ordered, but are arranged and decided *pro re natâ:* it is also to ignore utterly the unquestionable fact, that no event in life or in nature is isolated, and that none can be changed without entailing endless and universal alterations.[1] If the universe is governed by fixed laws, or (which is the same proposition in different language) if all events are pre-ordained by the fore-seeing wisdom of an infinite God, then the prayers of thousands of years and generations of martyrs and saints cannot change or modify one iota of our destiny. The proposition is unassailable by the

---

[1] "Immediate proof of that system of interminable connection which binds together the whole human family, may be obtained by every one who will examine the several ingredients of his physical, intellectual, and social condition ; for he will not find one of these circumstances of his lot that is not directly an effect or consequence of the conduct, or character or constitution of his progenitors, and of all with whom he has had to do ; if *they* had been other than what they were, he *also* must have been other than he is. And then our predecessors must in like manner trace the qualities of their being to theirs ; thus the linking ascends to the common parents of all ; and thus must it descend—still spreading as it goes—from the present to the last generation of the children of Adam."—Nat. Hist. of Enthusiasm, p. 149.

subtlest logic.[1] The weak, fond affections of humanity struggle in vain against the unwelcome conclusion.

It *is* a conclusion from which the feelings of almost all of us shrink and revolt. The strongest sentiment of our nature, perhaps, is that of our helplessness in the hands of fate, and against this helplessness we seek for a resource in the belief of our dependence on a Higher Power, which can control and will interfere with fate. And though our reason tells us that it is inconceivable that the entreaties of creatures as erring and as blind as we are, can influence the all-wise purposes of God, yet we feel an internal voice, more potent and persuasive than reason, which assures us that to pray to Him in trouble is an irrepressible instinct of our nature—an instinct which precedes

---

[1] The author of the Natural History of Enthusiasm has a singular theory on this point. He is not very clear, because clearness would make his inconsistency and the strangeness of his position too manifest; but as far as we can decipher his notion, it is this: He divides all events into two classes—the certain and fortuitous. He conceives, as we do, that the great mass of events occur according to established laws, and in the regular process of causation : and these he regards as settled and immutable : but in addition to these he considers that there are many others which are mere *fortuities*, at the command of God's will and of man's prayers; and that these fortuities are the special province and *means* of the divine government " (chap. vi.). Yet this writer allows that all events and all men's lots are inextricably woven together (pp. 132, 149); how then can one thing be more fortuitous or alterable than another? Moreover, fortuity, as he elsewhere intimates, is merely an expression denoting our ignorance of causation : that which seems a chance to us is among the most settled and certain of God's ordainments.

teaching—which survives experience—which defies philosophy.

> " For sorrow oft the cry of faith
> In bitter need will borrow."

It would be an unspeakable consolation to our human infirmity, could we, in this case, believe our reason to be erroneous, and our instinct true ; but we greatly fear that the latter is the result, partly of that anthropomorphism which pervades all our religious conceptions, which our limited faculties suggest, and which education and habit have rooted so fixedly in our mental constitution, and partly of that fond weakness which *recoils from the idea of irreversible and inescapable decree.* The conception of subjection to a law without exception, without remission, without appeal, crushing, absolute, and universal, is truly an appalling one ; and, most mercifully, can rarely be perceived in all its overwhelming force, except by minds which, through stern and lofty intellectual training, have in some degree become qualified to bear it.

Communion with God, we must ever bear in mind, is something very different from *prayer for specific blessings,* and often confers the submissive strength of soul for which we pray; and we believe it will be found that the higher our souls rise in their spiritual progress, the more does entreaty merge into thanksgiving, the more does *petition* become absorbed in communion with the " Father of the spirits of all

flesh." That the piety of Christ was fast tending to
this end is, we think, indicated by his instructions to
his disciples (Matt. vi. 8, 9) ; " When ye pray, use not
vain repetitions, for your father knoweth what things ye
have need of before ye ask him. After this manner,
therefore, pray ye," &c. ; and by that last sublime
sentence in Gethsemane, uttered when the agonizing
struggle of the spirit with the flesh had terminated
in the complete and final victory of the first, " Father,
if this cup may not pass from me except I drink it,
thy will be done."

Prayer may be regarded as the form which devotion
naturally takes in ordinary minds, and even in the
most enlightened minds in their less spiritual moods.
The highest intellectual efforts, the loftiest religious
contemplations, dispose to devotion, but check the
impulses of prayer. The devout philosopher, trained
to the investigation of universal system,—the serene
astronomer, fresh from the study of the changeless
laws which govern innumerable worlds,—shrinks from
the monstrous irrationality of asking the great
Architect and Governor of all to work a miracle in his
behalf—to interfere, for the sake of *his* convenience,
or *his* plans, with the sublime order conceived by the
Ancient of Days in the far Eternity of the Past ; for
what is a special providence but an interference with
established laws ? And what is such interference but
a miracle ? There is much truth and beauty in the
following remarks of Isaac Taylor, but much also
of the inconsistency, irreverence, and insolence of
orthodoxy.

" The very idea of addressing *petitions* to Him who worketh all things according to the counsel of his own eternal and unalterable will, and the enjoined practice of clothing sentiments of piety in articulate forms of language, though these sentiments, before they are invested in words, are perfectly known to the searcher of hearts, imply that, in the terms and mode of intercourse with God and man, no attempt is made to lift the latter above his sphere of limited notions and imperfect knowledge. *The terms of devotional communion rest even on a much lower ground than that which man, by efforts of reason and imagination, might attain to.*[1] Prayer, by its very conditions, supposes not only a condescension of the divine nature to meet the human, *but a humbling of the human nature to a lower range than it might easily reach. The region of abstract conceptions, of lofty reasonings, of magnificent images, has an atmosphere too subtle to support the health of true piety ;* and in order that the warmth and vigour of life may be maintained in the heart, the common level of the natural affections is chosen as the scene of intercourse between heaven and earth. . . . . The utmost distances of the material universe are finite ; but the disparity of nature which separates man from his Maker is infinite ; nor can the interval be filled up or brought under any process of

---

[1] Is it not a clear deduction from this, that prayer is a form of devotion conceded only to our imperfect spiritual capacities, and to be outgrown as those capacities are raised and strengthened ?

measurement. . . . Were it indeed permitted to man to
gaze upward from step to step, and from range to range
of the vast edifice of rational existences, and could his
eye attain its summit, and then perceive, at an infinite
height beyond that highest platform of created beings,
the lowest beams of the Eternal Throne—what liberty
of heart would afterwards be left to him in drawing
near to the Father of Spirits ? How, after such a
revelation of the upper world, could the affectionate
cheerfulness of earthly worship again take place ? Or
how, while contemplating the measured vastness of the
interval between heaven and earth, could the dwellers
thereon come familiarly as before to the Hearer of
Prayer ; bringing with them the small requests of their
petty interests of the present life. . . . These
spectacles of greatness, if laid open to perception,
would present such an interminable perspective of
glory, and so set out the immeasurable distance
between ourselves and the Supreme Being with a long
gradation of·splendours, and we should henceforth feel
as if thrust down to an extreme remoteness from the
divine notice ; and it would be hard or impossible to
retain, with any comfortable conviction, the belief in
the nearness of Him who is revealed as ' a very present
help in every time of trouble.' . . . Every ambitious
attempt to break through the humbling conditions on
which man may hold communion with God, must then
fail of success ; since the Supreme has fixed the
scene of worship and converse, not in the skies, but
on the earth. The Scripture models of devotion, far

from encouraging vague and inarticulate contemplations, consist of such utterances of desire, hope and
love, as seem to suppose the existence of correlative
feelings, and of every *human* sympathy in Him to
whom they are addressed.[1] *And though reason and
scripture assure us that He neither needs to be informed of our wants, nor waits to be moved by our
supplications, yet will he be approached with the
eloquence of importunate desire, and He demands,
not only a sincere feeling of indigence and dependence
but an undissembled zeal and diligence in seeking the
desired boons by persevering request.* He is *to be
supplicated with arguments as one who needs to be
swayed and moved, to be wrought upon and
influenced;* nor is any alternative offered to those who
would present themselves at the throne of heavenly
grace, or any exception made in favour of superior
spirits, *whose more elevated notions of the divine perfections may render this accommodated style distasteful.*
As the Hearer of Prayer stoops to listen, so also must
the suppliant stoop from the heights of philosophical or
meditative abstractions, and either come in genuine
simplicity of petition, as a son to a father, *or be utterly
excluded from the friendship of his Maker."* [2]

The expressions in this last paragraph—those par-

---

[1] That is, they are based on erroneous premises, supported by a
natural feeling, the very feeling which, pushed a little further, has
originated prayers to Christ in the English Church, and to Saints
and to the Virgin Mary in the Roman Communion.

[2] Nat. Hist. of Enthusiasm, pp. 27-32.

ticularly which we have italicised—appear to us, we
confess, monstrous, and little, if at all, short of blas-
phemy, *i.e.*, speaking evil of God. What! He, who
"both by reason and Scripture" has taught us that
He is *not* moved by our supplications, requires us—
"on pain of being utterly excluded from his favour"
—to act as if He were! He, who has given us the
understanding to conceive His entire exemption from
all human weaknesses, requires us to proceed as if. we
"thought that He was altogether such a one as ourselves!" He, who has made us to know that all
things are ordered by Him from the beginning—"that
with Him is no variableness, neither shadow of turning"
—requires us to supplicate, "argue," importune, *as if
we believed* that supplication, argument, and impor-
tunity could sway and turn Him from His purposes,—
commands us, in a word, to enact in His august presence a comedy, which He knows, and we know, to be
a mockery and a pretence! He, who has given us, as
His divinest gift, to elevate, to perfect, and to purify,
an intellect bearing some faint analogy to His own,—
punishes with "exclusion from His friendship," those
nobler conceptions of His nature which are the finest
achievements of this intellect, unless we consent to
abnegate and disavow them, *or pretend that we do so!*
—for this appears to be the signification of the last
sentence we have quoted. Such are the bewildering
positions into which Orthodoxy drives its more intellectual disciples!

The following remarks are thrown out rather as

suggestions for thought than as digested reflections, but they may contain a clue to some truth.

The inadmissibility of the idea of the *bona fide* efficacy of prayer, would appear to be enforced rather by our conviction that all things in life are arranged by *law*, than by a belief in the foreknowledge (which in a supreme Being is equivalent to foreordainment) of the Deity. This latter doctrine, however metaphysically true and probable, we *cannot* hold, so as to follow it out fairly to its consequences. It negatives the free-will of man at least as peremptorily as the efficacy of prayer :—yet in the free-will of man we do believe, and must believe, however strict logic may struggle against it. Why, then, should we not also hold the efficacy of prayer ?—a doctrine, *so far,* certainly not more illogical ? Because if, as we cannot doubt, the immutable relation of cause and effect governs everything, in all time, through all space—then prayer—*except in those cases where it operates as a natural cause*—cannot affect the sequence of events. If bodily pain and disease be the legitimate and traceable consequence of imprudence and excess—if pleurisy or consumption follow, by natural law, exposure to inclement weather in weak frames—if neuralgia be the legal progeny of organic decay or shattered nerves—if storms follow laws as certain as the law of gravitation —how can prayer bring about the cessation of pain, or the lulling of the storm, for the relief of the suffering, or the rescue of the imperilled, man ? Is not the prayer for such cessation clearly a prayer for a miracle ?

Prayer may be itself *a natural* cause;—it may, by its mental intensity, suspend bodily pain :—it may, by the moral elevation it excites, confer strength to dare and to endure. Prayer, to a fellow-creature of superior power and science, may induce such to apply a lenitive or a cure, which, however, is simply a natural cause, placed by our ignorance beyond our reach. If, therefore, there be around us, as many think, superior spiritual beings, our prayers, if heard by them, may induce them to aid us by means unknown to our inferior powers. But such aid would then be the natural result of natural though obscure causes. " If, however," it may be asked, "superior beings may be moved by prayer to aid us by their knowledge of natural agencies unknown to us, why not God ? " The answer is : that for Prayer to be a *bonâ fide* effective agent in obtaining any boon, it must operate on an impressible and *mutable* will :—therefore, if there be superior intermediate beings, sharing human sympathies and imperfections, but possessing more than human powers and knowledge—prayer may secure their aid ; but not that of a supreme God. Still, the question remains much one of *fact :—are* our prayers —*are* the most earnest prayers of the wisest, the best, the most suffering—generally answered ? Does toothache or sciatica last a shorter time with those who *pray*, than with those who only *bear ?*

On the whole, however, we are content that man should rest in the Christian practice, though not in the Christian theory, of Prayer—just as we are obliged to rest satisfied with a conception of Deity, which, though utterly erroneous in the sight of God, and consciously imperfect even in our own, is yet the nearest approach to truth our minds can frame, and practically adequate to our necessities. The common doctrine we cannot but regard as one of those fictions which imperfect and unchastened man is fain to gather round him, to equalize his strength with the requirements of his lot, but which a stronger nature might dispense with ; —one of those fictions which may be considered as the imperfect expression—the approximative formula—of mighty and eternal verities.

IV. Remotely connected with the doctrine of an interposing and influencible Providence, is the fallacy, or rather the imperfection, which lies at the root of the ordinary Christian view of *Resignation* as a duty and a virtue. Submission, cheerful acquiescence in the dispensations of Providence, is enjoined upon us, not because these dispensations are just and wise—not because they are the ordinances of His will who cannot err,—but because they are ordained for our benefit, and because He has promised that "all things shall work together for good to them that love Him." We are assured that every trial and affliction is designed solely for our good, for our discipline, and will issue in a blessing, though we see not how ; and that *therefore* we must bow to it with unmurmuring resignation. These grounds, it is obvious, are purely self-regarding; and resignation, thus represented and thus motived, is no virtue, but a simple calculation of self-interest.

II.   O

This narrow view results from that incorrigible egotism of the human heart which makes each man prone to regard himself as the special object of divine consideration, and the centre round which the universe revolves. Yet it is unquestionably the view most prominently and frequently presented in the New Testament,[1] and by all modern divines.[2] It may be, that the prospect of "an exceeding, even an eternal weight of glory," may be needed to support our frail purposes under the crushing afflictions of our mortal lot; it may be, that, by the perfect arrangements of omnipotence, the sufferings of all may be made to work out the ultimate and supreme good of each; but this is not, cannot be, *the reason why* we should submit with resignation to whatever God ordains. His will must be wise, righteous, and we believe beneficent, whether it allot to *us* happiness or misery: it *is* His will; we need inquire no further. Job, who had no vision of a

---

[1] See especially Matt. v. 11, 12; xvi. 25–27. Romans viii. 18, 28. 2 Cor. iv 17. Gal. vi. 9. There is one sublime exception, from the mouth of Christ. "The cup that my Father has given me, shall I not drink it?"

[2] The sublimest and purest genius among modern divines goes so far as to maintain that, apart from the hope of future recompense, "a deviation from rectitude would become the part of wisdom, and should the path of virtue be obstructed by disgrace, torment, or death, to persevere would be madness and folly." (Modern Infidelity, p. 20, by Robert Hall.) It is sad to reflect how mercenary a thing duty has become in the hands of theologians. Were their belief in a future retribution once shaken, they would become, on their own showing, the lowest of sensualists, the worst of sinners.

future compensatory world, had in this attained a sublimer point of religion than St. Paul :—"Though He slay me, yet will I trust in Him." "What! shall we receive good at the hands of God, and shall we not receive evil ?" (Job xiii. 15 ; ii. 10).

To the orthodox Christian, who fully believes all he professes, cheerful resignation to the divine will is comparatively a natural, an easy, a simple thing. To the religious philosopher, it is the highest exercise of intellect and virtue. The man who has *realized* the faith that his own lot, in all its minutest particulars, is not only directly regulated by God,—but is so regulated by God as unerringly to work for his highest good,—with an express view to his highest good,—with such a man, resignation, patience, nay, cheerful acquiescence in all suffering and sorrow, appears to be in fact only the simple and practical expression of his belief. If, believing all this, he still murmurs and rebels at the trials and contrarieties of his lot, he is guilty of the childishness of the infant which quarrels with the medicine that is to lead it back to health and ease. But the religious Philosopher,—who, sincerely holding that a Supreme God created and governs this world, holds also that He governs it by laws which, though wise, just, and beneficent, are yet steady, unwavering, inexorable ;—who believes that his agonies and sorrows are not specially ordained for *his* chastening, *his* strengthening, *his* elaboration and development. —but are incidental and necessary results of the operation of laws the best that could be devised for the happiness and purification of the species,—or perhaps not even that, but the best adapted to work out the ⌐ st, awful, glorious, eternal designs of the Great Spirit of the universe ;—who believes that the ordained operations of Nature, which have brought misery to him, have, from the very unswerving tranquillity of their career, showered blessing and sunshine upon every other path,—that the unrelenting chariot of Time, which has crushed or maimed him in its allotted course, is pressing onward to the accomplishment of those serene and mighty purposes, to have contributed to which—even as a victim—is an honour and a re-compense :—he who takes this view of Time, and Nature, and God, and yet bears his lot without mur-mur or distrust, because it is portion of a system, the best possible, *because ordained by God,*—has achieved a point of virtue, the highest, amid passive excellence, which humanity can reach ;—and his reward and sup-port must be found in the reflection that he is an unreluctant and self-sacrificing co-operator with the Creator of the universe, and in the noble conscious-ness of being worthy, and capable, of so sublime a conception, yet so sad a destiny.[1]

---

[1] " ' Pain is in itself an evil. It cannot be that God, who, as we know, is perfectly good, can choose us to suffer pain, unless either we are ourselves to receive from it an antidote to what is evil in ourselves, or else as such pain is a necessary part in the scheme of the universe, which as a *whole* is good. In either case I can take it thankfully. . . . . I should not be taken away without it was ordered so. . . . . Whatever creed we hold, if we believe that God is, and that he cares for his creatures, one cannot doubt that. And

In a comparison of the two resignations, there is no measure of their respective grandeurs. The orthodox sufferer fights the battle only on condition of surviving to reap the fruits of victory :—the other fights on, knowing that he must fall early in the battle, but content that his body should form a stepping-stone for the future conquests of humanity.[1]

Somewhat similar remarks may be made with reference to the virtues of action as to those of endurance. It is a matter suggestive of much reflection, that, throughout the New Testament, the loftiest and purest motive to action—love of duty *as* duty, obedience to the will of God *because* it is His will—is rarely appealed to ; one or two expressions of Christ, and the 14th chapter of John, forming the only exceptions. The almost invariable language—pitched to

---

it would not have been ordered so without it was better either for ourselves, or for some other persons, or some things. To feel sorrow is a kind of murmuring against God's will, which is worse than unbelief.'

" ' But think of the grief of those you leave.'

" ' They should not allow themselves to feel it. It is a symptom of an unformed mind.' "—*Shadows of the Clouds,* pp. 146, 148.

This is a somewhat harshly-expressed philosophy, but full of truth.

[1]   " Is selfishness—
For time, a sin—spun out to eternity
Celestial prudence ?   Shame ! oh, thrust me forth,
Forth, Lord, from self, until I toil and die
No more for Heaven or bliss, but duty, Lord—
Duty to Thee—although my meed should be
The Hell which I deserve."

                         Saint's Tragedy.

the level of ordinary humanity—is, " Do your duty at
all hazards, for your Father which seeth in secret shall
reward you openly." " Verily, I say unto you, ye shall
in no wise lose your reward." [1]

Yet this is scarcely the right view of things. The
hope of success, not the hope of reward, should be our
stimulating and sustaining might. Our object, not
ourselves, should be our inspiring thought. The
labours of philanthropy are comparatively easy, when
the effect of them, and their recoil upon ourselves, is
immediate and apparent. But this it can rarely be,
unless where the field of our exertions is narrow, and
ourselves the only or the chief labourers. In the
more frequent cases where we have to join our efforts
to those of thousands of others to contribute to the
carrying forward of a great cause, merely to till the
ground or sow the seed for a very distant harvest, or
to prepare the way for the future advent of some
great amendment ; the amount which each man has

---

[1] " When thou art bidden, take the lowest room, that when he
that bade thee cometh, he may say, ' Friend, go up higher ;' *so
shalt thou have honour in the presence of them that sit at meat with
thee.*" " Every one that humbleth himself *shall be exalted.*"
" Seek ye first the Kingdom of Heaven, ... and *all these things
shall be added unto you.*" " Lord, we have left all and followed
thee, *what shall we have therefore ?* Verily I say unto you, that
ye which have followed me, in the regeneration, when the Son
of Man shall sit on the throne of his glory, ye also shall sit upon
twelve thrones, judging the twelve tribes of Israel." " No man
that hath left father or mother for my sake but *shall receive a
hundred fold more in this present life,* and *in the world to come life
everlasting.*"

contributed to the achievement of ultimate success, the portion of the prize which justice should assign to each as his especial production, can never be accurately ascertained. Perhaps few of those who have laboured, in the patience of secrecy and silence, to bring about some political or social change which they felt convinced would ultimately prove of vast service to humanity, may live to see the change effected, or the anticipated good flow from it. Fewer still of them will be able to pronounce what appreciable weight their several efforts contributed to the achievement of the change desired. And discouraging doubts will therefore often creep in upon minds in which egotism is not wholly swallowed up by earnestness, as to whether, in truth, their exertions had any influence whatever — whether in sad and sober fact they have not been the mere fly upon the wheel. With many men these doubts are fatal to active effort. To counteract them we must labour to elevate and purify our *motives*, as well as sedulously cherish the conviction—assuredly a true one—that in this world there is no such thing as effort thrown away—that " in all labour there is profit "— that all sincere exertion in a righteous and unselfish cause is necessarily followed, in spite of all appearance to the contrary, by an appropriate and proportionate success—that no bread cast upon the waters can be wholly lost—that no good seed planted in the ground can fail to fructify in due time and measure ; and that, however we may in moments of despondency be apt to doubt, not only whether our cause will triumph, but whether we shall have contributed to its triumph,—there is One who has not only seen every exertion we have made, but who can assign the exact degree in which each soldier has assisted to gain the great victory over social evil.[1] The Augæan stables of the world — the accumulated uncleanness and misery of centuries—require a mighty river to cleanse them thoroughly away : every drop we contribute aids to swell that river and augment its force, in a degree appreciable by God, though not by man ;— and he whose zeal is deep and earnest, will not be over anxious that his individual drop should be distinguishable amid the mighty mass of cleansing and fertilizing waters, far less that, for the sake of distinction, it should flow in ineffective singleness away. He will not be careful that his name should be inscribed upon the mite which he casts into the treasury of God. It should suffice each of us to know that, *if* we have laboured, with purity of purpose, in any good cause, we *must* have contributed to its success ; that the degree in which we have contributed is a matter of infinitely small concern ; and

---

[1] " Yet are there some to whom a strength is given,
    A Will, a self-constraining Energy,
    A Faith which feeds upon no earthly hope,
    Which never thinks of victory, but content
    In its own consummation, *combating*
    Because it ought to combat, ...
    Rejoicing fights, and still rejoicing falls."
            The Combat of Life.—R. M. Milnes.

still more, that the consciousness of having so contributed, however obscurely and unnoticed, should be our sufficient, if our sole, reward. Let us cherish this faith; it is a duty. He who sows and reaps is a good labourer, and worthy of his hire. But he who sows what shall be reaped by others who know not and reck not of the sower, is a labourer of a nobler order, and worthy of a loftier guerdon.

V. The common Christian conception of the pardon of sin upon repentance and conversion seems to us to embody a very transparent and pernicious fallacy. "Who can forgive sins but God only?" asked the Pharisees. There is great confusion and contradiction in our ideas on this subject. God is the only being who can *not* forgive sins. "Forgiveness of sins" means one of two things :—it either means saving a man from the consequences of his sins, that is, interposing between cause and effect, in which case it is *working a miracle* (which God no doubt can do, but which we have no right to expect that He will do, or ask that He shall do) ; or it means *an engagement to forbear retaliation*, a suppression of the natural anger felt against the offender by the offended party, *a foregoing of vengeance* on the part of the injured—in which meaning it is obviously quite inapplicable to a Being exempt and aloof from human passions. When we entreat a fellow-creature to forgive the offences we have committed against him, we mean to entreat that he will not, by any act of his, punish us for them, that he will not revenge nor repay them, that he will retain no rancour in his breast against us on account of them ; and such a prayer addressed to a being of like passions to ourselves is rational and intelligible, because we know that it is natural for him to feel anger at our injuries, and that, unless moved to the contrary, he will probably retaliate. But when we pray to our Heavenly Father to " forgive us our trespasses, as we forgive those who trespass against us," we overlook the want of parallelism of the two cases, and show that our notions on the subject are altogether misty and confused ; for God cannot be *injured* by our sins, and He is inaccessible to the passions of anger and revenge. Yet the plain expression of the Book of Common Prayer—" Neither take Thou vengeance of our sins "—embodies the real signification attached to the prayer for forgiveness, by all who attach any definite signification to their prayers. Now, this expression is an *Old Testament* or a *Pagan* expression, and can only be consistently and intelligibly used by those who entertain the same low ideas of God as the ancient Greeks and Hebrews entertained —that is, who think of Him as an irritable, jealous, and avenging Potentate.

If, from this inconsistency, we take refuge in the other meaning of the Prayer for forgiveness, and assume that it is a prayer to God that he will exempt us from the natural and appointed consequences of our misdeeds, it is important that we should clearly define to our minds what it is that we are asking for. In our view of the matter, punishment for sins by the divine law is a wholly different thing and process from punishment for violations of human laws. It is not an infliction for crime, imposed by an external authority and artificially executed by external force, but a natural and inevitable result of the offence—a child generated by a parent—a sequence following an antecedent—a consequence arising out of a cause.

" The Lord is just: He made the chain .
Which binds together guilt and pain."

The punishment of sin *consists* in the consequences of sin. These form a penalty most adequately heavy. A sin without its punishment is as impossible, as complete a contradiction in terms, as a cause without an effect.

To pray that God will forgive our sins, therefore, appears, in all logical accuracy, to involve either a most unworthy conception of His character, or an entreaty of incredible audacity—viz., that He will work daily miracles in our behalf. It is either beseeching Him to renounce feelings and intentions which it is impossible that a Nature like His should entertain : or it is asking Him to violate the eternal and harmonious order of the universe, for the comfort of one out of the infinite myriads of its inhabitants.

It may, perhaps, be objected, that Punishment of sins may be viewed, not as a vengeance taken for injury or insult committed, nor yet as the simple and necessary sequence of a cause—but as *chastisement*, inflicted to work repentance and amendment. But, even when considered in this light, prayer for forgiveness remains still a marvellous inconsistency. It then becomes the entreaty of the sick man to his Physician not to heal him. " Forgive us our sins," then means, " Let us continue in our iniquity." It is clear, however, that the first meaning we have mentioned, as attached to the prayer for forgiveness of sins, is both the original and the prevailing one ; and that it arises from an entire misconception of the character of the Deity, and of the feelings with which He may be supposed to regard sin—a misconception inherited from our Pagan and Jewish predecessors ; it is a prayer to deprecate the just resentment of a Potentate whom we have offended—a petition which would be more suitably addressed to an earthly foe or master than to a Heavenly Father. The misconception is natural to a rude state of civilisation and of theology. It is the same notion from which arose sacrifices (*i.e.*, offerings to appease wrath), and which caused their universality in early ages and among barbarous nations. It is a relic of anthropomorphism;—a belief that God, like man, is *enraged* by neglect or disobedience, and can be *pacified* by submission and entreaty ; a belief consistent and intelligible among the Greeks, inconsistent and irrational among Christians, appropriate as applied to Jupiter, unmeaning or blasphemous as applied to Jehovah.

We have, in fact, come to regard sin, not as an injury done to our own nature, an offence against our own souls, a disfiguring of the image of the Beautiful and Good, but as a personal affront offered to a power- .

ful and avenging Being, which, unless *apologised* for, will be chastised as such. We have come to regard it as an injury to *another* party, for which atonement and reparation can be made and satisfaction can be given ; not as a deed which cannot be undone, eternal in its consequences ; an act which, once committed, is numbered with the irrevocable Past. In a word, Sin *contains* its own retributive penalty as surely, and as naturally, as the acorn contains the oak. Its consequence is its punishment, it needs no other, and can have no heavier; and its consequence is involved in its commission, and cannot be separated from it. *Punishment* (let us fix this in our minds) *is not the execution of a sentence, but the occurrence of an effect.* It is ordained to follow guilt by God, not as a Judge, but as the Creator and Legislator of the Universe. This conviction, once settled in our understandings, will wonderfully clear up our views on the subject of pardon and redemption. Redemption becomes then, of necessity, not a saving but a regenerating process. We can be saved from the punishment of sin only by being saved from its commission. Neither *can* there be any such thing as vicarious atonement or punishment (which, again, is a relic of heathen conceptions of an angered Deity, to be propitiated by offerings and sacrifices). Punishment, being not the penalty, but the result of sin, being not an arbitrary and artificial annexation, but an ordinary and logical consequence, cannot be borne by other than the sinner.

It is curious that the votaries of the doctrine of the

Atonement admit the correctness of much of the above reasoning, saying (see "Guesses at Truth," by J. and A. Hare), that Christ had to suffer for the sins of men, because God *could not* forgive sin ; He must punish it in some way. Thus holding the strangely inconsistent doctrine that God is so just that He could not let sin go unpunished, yet so unjust that He could punish it in the person of the innocent. It is for orthodox dialectics to explain how Divine Justice can be *impugned* by pardoning the guilty, and yet *vindicated* by punishing the innocent !

If the foregoing reflections are sound, the awful, yet wholesome, conviction presses upon our minds, that *there can be no forgiveness of sins;* that is, no interference with, or remittance of, or protection from their natural effects; that God will not interpose between the cause and its consequence ;[1]—that "whatsoever a man soweth, that shall he also reap." An awful consideration this; yet all reflection, all experience, confirm its truth. The sin which has debased our soul may be repented of, may be turned from, but the injury is done : the debasement may be redeemed by after efforts, the stain may be obliterated by bitterer struggles and severer sufferings, by faith in God's love

---

[1] Refer to Matt. ix. 2-6. "Whether is it easier to say, Thy sins be forgiven thee! or to say, Arise, take up thy bed and walk?" Jesus seems here clearly to intimate that the view taken above (of forgiveness of sins, namely, involving an interference with the natural order of sequence, and being therefore a *miracle*) is correct. He places the two side by side, as equally difficult.

and communion with His Spirit ; but the efforts and the endurance which might have raised the soul to the loftiest heights, are now exhausted in merely regaining what it has lost. "There must always be a wide difference (as one of our divines has said) between him who only ceases to do evil, and him who has always done well ; between the man who began to serve his God as soon as he knew that he had a God to serve, and the man who only turns to Heaven after he has exhausted all the indulgences of Earth."

Again, in the case of sin of which you have induced another to partake. You may repent—*you* may, after agonising struggles, regain the path of virtue— *your* spirit may re-achieve its purity through much anguish, and after many stripes ; but the weaker fellow-creature whom you led astray, whom you made a sharer in your guilt, but whom you cannot make a sharer in your repentance and amendment, whose downward course (the first step of which you taught) you cannot check, but are compelled to witness, what " forgiveness" of sins can avail you˙ there ? *There* is your perpetual, your inevitable punishment, which no repentance can alleviate, and no mercy can remit.

This doctrine, that sins can be forgiven, and the consequences of them averted, has in all ages been a fertile source of mischief. Perhaps few of our intellectual errors have fructified in a vaster harvest of evil, or operated more powerfully to impede the moral progress of our race. While it has been a source of unspeakable comfort to the penitent, a healing balm to the wounded spirit, while it has saved many from hopelessness, and enabled those to recover themselves who would otherwise have flung away the remnant of their virtue in despair ; yet, on the other hand, it has encouraged millions, *feeling what a safety was in store for them in ultimate resort,* to persevere in their career of folly or crime, to ignore or despise those natural laws which God has laid down to be the guides and beacons of our conduct, to continue to do " that which was pleasant in their own eyes," convinced that nothing was irrevocable, that however dearly they might have to pay for re-integration, repentance could at any time redeem their punishment, and *undo the past.* The doctrine has been noxious in exact ratio to the baldness and nakedness with which it has been propounded. In the Catholic Church of the middle ages we see it perhaps in its grossest form, when pardon was sold, bargained for, rated at a fixed price ; when one hoary sinner, on the bed of sickness, refused to repent, because he was not *certain* that death was close at hand, and he did not wish for the trouble of going through the process twice, and was loth, by a premature amendment, to lose a chance of any of the indulgences of sin. Men would have been far more scrupulous watchers over conduct, far more careful of their deeds, had they believed that those deeds would inevitably bear their natural consequences, exempt from after intervention, than when they held that penitence and pardon could at any time unlink the chain of sequences ; just as now they are little scrupulous of indulging in hurtful excess, when medical aid is at hand to remedy the mischief they have voluntarily encountered. But were they on a desert island, apart from the remotest hope of a doctor or a drug, how far more closely would they consider the consequences of each indulgence, how earnestly would they study the laws of Nature, how comparatively unswerving would be their endeavours to steer their course by those laws, obedience to which brings health, peace, and safety in its train !

Let any one look back upon his past career—look inward on his daily life—and then say what effect would be produced upon him, were the conviction once fixedly imbedded in his soul, that everything done is done irrevocably—that even the Omnipotence of God cannot *uncommit* a deed—cannot make that undone which has been done ; that every act *must* bear its allotted fruit according to the everlasting laws —must remain for ever ineffaceably inscribed on the tablets of universal Nature. And then let him consider what would have been the result upon the moral condition of our race, had all men ever held this conviction.

Perhaps you have led a youth of dissipation and excess which has undermined and enfeebled your constitution, and you have transmitted this injured and enfeebled constitution to your children. They suffer, in consequence, through life ; suffering, perhaps even sin, is *entailed* upon them ; your repentance, were it in sackcloth and ashes, cannot help you or them. Your punishment is tremendous, but it is legitimate,

II.   P

and inevitable. · You have broken Nature's laws, or you have ignored them ; and no one violates or neglects them with impunity. What a lesson for timely reflection and obedience is here !

Again,—You have broken the seventh commandment. You grieve, you repent, you resolutely determine against any such weakness in future. It is well. But "you know that God is merciful, you feel that he will forgive you." You are comforted. But no— there is no forgiveness of sins : the injured party may forgive you, your accomplice or victim may forgive you, according to the meaning of human language ; *but the deed is done*, and all the powers of Nature, were they to conspire in your behalf, could not make it undone : the consequences to the body, the consequences to the soul, though no man may perceive them, *are there*, are written in the annals of the Past, and must reverberate through all time.[1]

But all this, let it be understood, in no degree militates against the value or the necessity of repentance. Repentance, contrition of soul, bears, like every other act, its own fruit, the fruit of purifying the heart, of amending the future, not, as man has hitherto conceived, of effacing the Past. The commission of sin is an irrevocable act, but it does not incapacitate the soul for virtue. Its consequences cannot be expunged, but its course need not be

---

[1] [I have left this whole argument just as it was written five-and-twenty years ago ; because, though I recognise its painful harshness, I am unable to detect any flaw in the substance of its logic.]

unworthy portion of existence, have done most injury to our virtue, by demanding feelings which are unnatural, and which, therefore, if *attained*, must be morbid, if merely *professed*, must be insincere—or to the cause of social progress, by teaching us to look rather to a future life for the compensation of social evils, than to this life for their cure.   It is only those who feel a deep interest in and affection for this world, who will work resolutely for its amelioration ; —those whose affections are transferred to Heaven acquiesce easily in the miseries of earth ; give them up as hopeless, as befitting, as ordained ; and console themselves with the idea of the amends which are one day to be theirs.[1]   If we had looked upon this earth as our only scene, it is doubtful if we should so long have tolerated its more monstrous anomalies and more curable evils.   But it is easier to look to a future paradise than to strive to make one upon earth ; and the depreciating and hollow language of preachers has played into the hands both of the insincerity and the indolence of man.

I question whether the whole system of professing Christians is not based in a mistake, whether it be

---

[1] " I sorrowfully admit, that when I count up among my personal acquaintances all whom I think to be the most decidedly given to spiritual contemplation, and to make religion rule in their hearts, at least three out of four appear to have been apathetic towards all improvement of this world's systems, and a majority have been virtual *conservatives of evil*, and hostile to political and social reform as diverting men's energies from Eternity."—Note by a Friend.

pursued. Sin, though it is ineffaceable, calls for no despair, but for efforts more energetic than before. Repentance is still as valid as ever ; but it is valid to secure the future, not to obliterate the past.

The moral to be drawn from these reflections is this :—God has placed the lot of man—not, perhaps, altogether of the Individual, but certainly of the Race —in his own hands, by surrounding him with *fixed laws*, on knowledge of which, and on conformity to which, his well-being depends. The study of these, and the principle of obedience to them, form, therefore, the great aim of education, both of men and nations. They must be taught—

1. The *physical laws*, on which God has made *health* to depend.

2. The *moral laws*, on which He has made *happiness* to depend.[1]

3. The *intellectual laws*, on which He has made *knowledge* to depend.

4. The *social* and *political laws*, on which He has made *national prosperity* and advancement to depend.

5. The *economic laws*, on which he has made *wealth* to depend.

---

[1] "There is nothing which more clearly marks the Divine Government than the difficulty of distinguishing between the natural and the supernatural; between the *penalty* attached to the breach of the written law, and the *consequence*, which we call natural, though it is in fact the penalty attached to the breach of the unwritten law. . . . In the divine law, the penalty always grows out of the offence."— State of Man before the Promulgation of Christianity, p. 108.

A true comprehension of all these, *and of their
unexceptional and unalterable nature*, would ultimately rescue mankind from all their vice and nearly
all their suffering—save casualties and sorrows.

VI. The ascetic and depreciating view of life,
inculcated by ordinary Christianity, appear to us
erroneous, both in its form and in its foundation.
How much of it belongs to Christ, how much to the
Apostles, and how much was the accretion of a
subsequent age, is not easy to determine. It appears
in the Epistles as well as in the Gospels ; and in the
hands of preachers of the present day it has reached a
point at which it is unquestionably unsound, noxious,
and insincere. In Christ this asceticism assumes a
mild and moderate form ; being simply the doctrine of
the Essenes, modified by his own exquisite judgment
and general sympathies, and dignified by the conviction that to men, who had so arduous and perilous a
work before them as that to which he and his disciples
were pledged, the interests, the affections, the enjoyments of this life must needs be of very secondary
moment. With him it is confined almost entirely to
urging his hearers not to sacrifice their duties (and by
consequence their rewards) to earthly and passing
pleasures, and to teaching them to seek consolation
under present privations in the prospect of future
blessedness. " Lay not up for yourselves treasures
upon earth, where moth and rust do corrupt, and
where thieves break through and steal." " What
shall it profit a man if he should gain the whole world

and lose his own soul? or what shall a man give in exchange for his soul?" Luke xiv. 26, 33, appears at first sight to go further than this; but even these verses are only a hyperbolical expression of a universal truth, viz., that a man cannot cast himself with effect into any great or dangerous achievement, unless he is prepared to subdue and set at nought all interfering interests and feelings.

That the Apostles, called to fight against principalities and powers, obliged to hold life and all its affections cheap, because the course of action in which they were engaged perilled these at every step, finding the great obstacle to their success in the tenacity with which their hearers clung to those old associations, occupations, and enjoyments, which embracing the new faith would oblige them to forswear,—impressed, moreover, with the solemn and tremendous conviction that the world was falling to pieces, and that their own days and their own vision would witness the final catastrophe of nature;—that the Apostles should regard with unloving eyes that world of which their hold was so precarious and their tenure so short, and should look with amazement and indignation upon men who would cling to a doomed and perishing habitation, instead of gladly sacrificing everything to obtain a footing in the new Kingdom was natural, and, granting the premises, rational and wise.

But for Divines in this day, when the profession of Christianity is attended with no peril, when its practice even demands no sacrifice, save that pre-

ference of duty to enjoyment which is the first law of
cultivated humanity, to repeat the language, profess
the feelings, inculcate the notions of men who lived in
daily dread of such awful martyrdom, and under the
excitement of such a mighty misconception ; to cry
down this world, with its profound beauty, its thrilling
interests, its glorious works, its noble and holy affections ; to exhort their hearers, Sunday after Sunday,
to detach their hearts from the earthly life as inane,
fleeting, and unworthy, and fix it upon Heaven, as the
only sphere deserving the love of the loving or the
meditation of the wise,—appears to us, we confess,
frightful insincerity, the enactment of a wicked and
gigantic lie. The exhortation is delivered and listened
to as a thing of course ; and an hour afterwards the
preacher, who has thus usurped and profaned the
language of an Apostle who wrote with the faggot and
the cross full in view, is sitting comfortably with his
hearer over his claret ; they are fondling their children,
discussing public affairs or private plans in life with
passionate interest, and yet can look at each other
without a smile or a blush for the sad and meaningless
farce they have been acting !

Yet the closing of our connection with this earthly
scene is as certain and probably as near to us as it
was to the apostles. Death is as close to us as the
end of the world was to them. It is not, therefore,
their misconception on this point which makes their
view of life unsound and insincere when adopted by
us. We believe it to be erroneous in itself, and to

proceed upon false conceptions of our relation to time and to futurity. The doctrine, as ordinarily set forth, that this world is merely one of probation and preparation, we entirely disbelieve. The idea of regarding it as merely a portal to another is simply an attempt to solve the enigma of life ; a theory to explain the sufferings of man, and to facilitate the endurance of them ; to supply the support and consolation which man's weakness cannot dispense with, but which he has not yet learned to draw from deeper and serener fountains. We, on the contrary, think that everything tends to prove that this life is, not perhaps, not probably, our only sphere, but still an *integral* one, and *the* one with which we are meant to be concerned. The present is our scene of action —the future is for speculation, and for trust. We firmly believe that man was sent upon the earth to live in it, to enjoy it, to study it, to love it, to embellish it—to make the most of it, in short. It is his country, on which he should lavish his affections and his efforts. *Spartam nactus es—hanc exorna.* It should be to him a house, not a tent—a home, not only a school. If, when this house and this home are taken from him, Providence in its wisdom and its bounty provides him with another, let him be deeply grateful for the gift—let him transfer to that future, *when it has become his present*, his exertions, his researches, and his love. But let him rest assured that he is sent into this world, not to be constantly hankering after, dreaming of, preparing for, another which may, or may not, be in store for him—but to do his duty and fulfil his destiny on earth—to do all that lies in his power to improve it, to render it a scene of elevated happiness to himself, to those around him, to those who are to come after him. So will he avoid those tormenting contests with Nature —those struggles to suppress affections which God has implanted, sanctioned, and endowed with irresistible supremacy—those agonies of remorse when he finds that God is too strong for him—which now embitter the lives of so many earnest and sincere souls : so will he best prepare for that future which we hope for—if it come ;—so will he best have occupied the present, if the present be his all. To demand that we shall love Heaven more than Earth —that the Unseen shall hold a higher place in our affections than the Seen and the Familiar—is to ask that which cannot be obtained without subduing Nature, and inducing a morbid condition of the Soul. The very law of our being is love of life and all its interests and adornments.

This love of the world in which our lot is cast, this engrossment with the interests and affections of Earth, has in it nothing necessarily low or sensual. It is wholly apart from love of wealth, of fame, of ease, of splendour, of power, of what is commonly called worldliness. It is the love of Earth as the garden on which the Creator has lavished such miracles of beauty, as the habitation of humanity, the arena of its conflicts, the scene of its illimitable progress, the dwelling-place of the wise, the good, the active, the loving, and the dear.

" It is not the purpose and end of this discourse, to raise such seraphical notions of the vanity and pleasures of this world, as if they were not worthy to be considered, or could have no relish with virtuous and pious men. They take very unprofitable pains who endeavour to persuade men that they are obliged wholly to despise this world and all that is in it, even whilst they themselves live here : God hath not taken all that pains in forming, and framing, and furnishing, and adorning the world, that they who were made by Him to live in it should despise it ; it will be enough if they do not love it so immoderately as to prefer it before Him who made it : nor shall we endeavour to extend the notions of the Stoic Philosophers, and stretch them further by the help of Christian precepts, to the extinguishing all those affections and passions which are and will always be inseparable from human nature. As long as the world lasts, and honour, and virtue, and industry have reputation in the world, there will be ambition and emulation and appetite in the best and most accomplished men in it ; if there should not be, more barbarity and vice and wickedness would cover every nation of the world, than it yet suffers under." [1]

It is difficult to decide whether exhortations to ascetic undervaluing of this life, as an insignificant and

---

[1] Lord Clarendon's Essay on Happiness.

not an error to strive after *spirituality*—after a frame of mind, that is, which is attainable only by incessant conflict with the instincts of our unsophisticated nature, by macerating the body into weakness and disorder ; by disparaging what we see to be beautiful, know to be wonderful, feel to be unspeakably dear and fascinating ; by (in a word) putting down the nature which God has given us, to struggle after one which He has not bestowed. Man is sent into the world, not a spiritual, but a composite being, a being made up of body and mind—the body having, as is fit and needful in a material world, its full, rightful, and allotted share. Life should be guided by a full re-cognition of this fact; not denying it as we do in bold words, and admitting it in weaknesses and inevitable failings. *Man's spirituality will come in the next stage of his being*, when he is endowed with the σωμα πνευματικον. Each in its order : " first, that which is natural ; afterwards, that which is spiritual." The body will be dropped at death :—till then God meant it to be commanded, but never to be neglected, despised, or ignored, under pain of heavy consequences.

The two classes of believers in future progress— those who believe in the future perfection of the individual, and those who believe in the future per-fection of the race—are moved to different modes of action. Perhaps they ought not to be ; but from the defects of our reason, and from personal feelings, they generally are. It is a question, however, whether the world, *i.e.*, the human race, will not be more benefited by the labours of those who look upon Heaven as a state to be attained on earth by future generations, than by those who regard it as the state to be attained by themselves after death, in another world. The latter will look only, or mainly, to the improvement of their own character and capacities ;—the former will devote their exertions to the amelioration of their kind and their habitation. The latter are too easily induced to give up earth as hopeless and incorrigible ;—the former, looking upon it as the scene of blessed existence to others hereafter, toil for its amendment and embellishment. There is a vast fund of hidden selfishness, or what, at least, has often the practical effect of such, in the idea of Heaven as ordinarily conceived ; and much of the tolerated misery of earth may be traced to it.[1]

Do we then mean that our future prospects have no claim on our attention here ? Far from it. The fate of the Soul after it leaves those conditions under which alone we have any cognizance of its existence, the possibility of continued and eternal being, and the character of the scenes in which that being will be developed, must always form topics of the profoundest interest, and the most ennobling and refining contem-

---

[1] See some very interesting reflections on this subject (with which, however, I do not at all agree), by Sir James Mackintosh (Life, 120-122). See also some curious speculations by a Communistic Frenchman, Pierre Leroux, in his work De l'Humanité.

plation. These great matters will of necessity, from their attractions, and ought, from their purifying tendencies, to occupy much of the leisure of all thinking and aspiring minds. Those whose affections are ambitious, whose conceptions are lofty, whose imagination is vivid, eloquent, and daring—those to whom this life has been a scene of incessant failure—those

" Whom Life hath wearied in its race of hours,"

who, harassed and toil-worn, sink under the burden of their three-score years—those who, having seen friend, parent, child, wife, successively removed from the homes they beautified and hallowed, find the balance of attraction gradually inclining in favour of another life, — all such will cling to these lofty speculations with a tenacity of interest which needs no injunction, and will listen to no prohibition. All we wish to suggest is that they should be regarded rather as the consoling privilege of the aspiring, the way-worn, the weary, the bereaved, than as the inculcated duty of youth in its vigour, or beauty in its prime.

Yet, having said thus much by way of combating an erroneous view of life which appears to lead to a perilous and demoralizing insincerity, I would not be thought incapable of appreciating the light which the contemplation of the future may let in upon the present, nor the effect which that contemplation is fitted to produce on the development of the higher portions of our nature. One of the most difficult, and at the

same time the gravest, of the practical problems of
life, is the right adjustment of the respective claims of
heaven and earth upon the time and thought of man :
—how much should be given to performing the duties
and entering into the interests of the world, and how
much to preparation for a better ;—how much to
action, and how much to meditation ;—how much to
the cultivation and purification of our own character,
and how much to the public service of our fellow-men.
Nor is this nice problem adequately solved by saying
that Heaven is most worthily served, and most surely
won, by a scrupulous discharge of the duties of our
earthly station ; and that constant labour for the good
of others will afford the best development for the
purer portions of our own character.   There is much
truth in this ; but there is not complete truth.   The
man whose whole life is spent in discharging with
diligence and fidelity the toils of his allotted position
in society, or whose every hour is devoted to the details
of philanthropic exertions, is in a rare degree " a good
and faithful servant ; " yet it is impossible not to perceive that he may pass through life with many depths
of his being altogether unsounded, with the richest
secrets of the soul undiscovered and unguessed, with
many of the loftiest portions of his character still latent
and unimproved; and that when he passes through the
portals of the grave, and reaches the new Existence,
he will enter it a wholly unprepared and astonished
stranger.   Much quiet meditation, much solitary intro-
spection, which the man involved in the vortex of

active and public life has rarely leisure to bestow, seem requisite to gain a clear conception of the true objects and meaning of existence—of the relation which our individual entities hold with the Universe around us and the Great Spirit which pervades it. Without this deep and solitary communing with our inner Nature, the most energetic and untiring Philanthropist or Duty-doer among us appears little more than an instrument in the hands of the Creator—a useful and noble one, certainly, yet still an instrument—for the production of certain results, but scarcely to have attained to the dignity of a distinct and individual Intelligence — an agent who comprehends himself and the nature of the work in which he is engaged, as well as the mere routine of its performance.

Again, notwithstanding all that has been said as to the admirable effect of *action* on the character, it is certain that there are many points of personal morality from which a life of busy and even meritorious activity almost unavoidably diverts our attention. The temper, the appetites, the passions, require a ceaseless and guarded watchfulness, to which incessant exertion is, to say the least, certainly not favourable.

On the other hand, too frequent a reflection, too deep an insight—too vivid a realization of the great mysteries of Being, would be apt so to shrivel up into microscopic insignificance all the cares, toils,.and interests of this life, as entirely to paralyze our zeal and energy concerning them. If we were literally to " live as seeing Him who is invisible," the common works of earth could no longer be performed, save as a duty, and in a dream. It is well for us that we " walk by faith, and not by sight." If we could *realize* both the nearness and the fulness of Eternity, we should be unfitted for the requirements of this earthly state.

CHAPTER XVII.

WE are accustomed to say that Christ brought life and immortality to light by his Gospel ; by which we mean,—not that he first taught the doctrine of a future life, scarcely even that he threw any new light on the nature of that life ; for the doctrine was held, long before he lived, by many uncivilized tribes ; it was the received opinion of most, if not all, among the Oriental nations ; and it was an established tenet of the most popular and powerful sect among the Jews ; —but that he gave to the doctrine, for the first time, an authoritative sanction : he announced it as a direct revelation from the Deity; and, as it were, exemplified and embodied it in his own resurrection. But, as we have already come to the conclusion that Christianity was not a Revelation in the ordinary sense of the word, Christ's inculcation of the doctrine becomes simply the added attestation of the most pious and holy man who ever lived, to a faith which has been cherished by the pious and the holy of all times and of all lands.

In this view of Christianity, a future life becomes

II.   Q

to us no longer a matter of positive knowledge—a revealed fact—but simply a matter of faith, of hope, of earnest desire ; a sublime possibility, round which meditation and inquiry will collect all the probabilities they can. Christianity adds nothing certain to our convictions or to our knowledge on the subject, however rich it may be in suggestions of the truth. Let us, therefore, by a short statement of its views of futurity, see how far they are such as can be accepted by a cultivated and inquiring age.

It may seem to many a strange observation, but we greatly question whether the views of Christ regarding the future world (so far as we can gather them from the imperfect and uncertain records of his sayings, which alone we have to go by) were not *less* in advance of those current in his age and country, than his views upon any other topic. The popular opinion—that he made that a matter of certainty which before was only a matter of speculation—has blinded our perceptions on this point. When we put aside this common misconception, and come to examine what the notions inculcated by the Gospel concerning the *nature* of this futurity really were, we shall be surprised and pained to find how little they added, and how little they rose superior, to those current among the Pharisees and the Essenes at the date of its promulgation ; and perhaps even how far they fell short of those attained by some pious Pagans of an earlier date.

The scriptural idea of Heaven, so far as we can collect it from the Gospels, seems to have been :—

1. That it was a scene hallowed and embellished by the more immediate, or at least more perceptible, presence of God, who is constantly spoken of as " *Our Father who is in Heaven.*" It is the local dwelling-place of the Creator, lying exterior to and above the Earth, and into which Christ visibly *ascended.* Indeed, notwithstanding the distinct and repeated assertions of the perpetual superintendence of God, He is depicted much more as a local and limited, and much less as a pervading and spiritual Being, in the New Testament than in many of the Psalms and in Job. The delineations of the former are far more simple, affectionate, and human—far more tinged with anthropomorphism, in the *tone* at least ; those of the latter more vague, more sublime, more spiritual. In this point, the Gospel idea of one of the attributes of Heaven, though eminently beautiful, natural, and attractive, will scarcely bear scrutiny. That in a future state we shall be more conscious of God's presence, is not only probable, but is a necessary consequence of the extension and purification of our faculties :—that He dwells there more than here is an obviously untenable conception. The notion may be said to be subjectively true, but objectively false.

2. That Heaven would be a scene of retribution for the deeds and characters of earth has been the view of its essential nature taken by nearly all nations which have believed in its existence : to this idea the Gospel has added nothing new. That it would also be a state of *compensation*, to rectify the inequalities and atone

for the sufferings of our sublunary life, has long been
the consolatory notion of the disappointed and the
sorrow-stricken. This idea Christianity especially en-
courages; nay, unless we are to allow an unusually
free deduction for the hyperbolical language which the
New Testament habitually employs, it would appear
to carry it to an extent scarcely reconcilable with sober
reason or pure justice; almost countenancing the notion
—so seducing to the less worthy feelings of the dis-
contented and the wretched—not only that *their*
troubles will be compensated by a proportionate excess
of future joy, but that earthly prosperity will, *per se*,
and apart from any notion of 'moral retribution, constitute a title to proportionate suffering hereafter—
that, in truth, Heaven will be the especial and exclusive patrimony of the poor and the afflicted.
" Blessed are they that mourn, for they shall be comforted." " Blessed be ye poor, for yours is the Kingdom of God. Blessed are ye that hunger now, for ye
shall be filled. Blessed are ye that weep now, for ye
shall laugh. But woe unto ye that are rich, for ye
have received your consolation. Woe unto ye that
are full, for ye shall hunger. Woe unto ye that laugh
now, for ye shall weep." The parable of Dives and
Lazarus inculcates the same notion. " Son, remember
that thou in thy lifetime receivedst thy good things,
and likewise Lazarus evil things; but now he is comforted, and thou art tormented." It is very difficult
to discover on what worthy conception of Divine Providence the ideas inculcated in these last quotations

can be justified, or how they can be reconciled with the doctrine of a just moral retribution ; and it is equally difficult to shut our eyes to the encouragement they may give and have given to the envious and malignant feelings of grovelling and uncultured minds.[1]

3. The eternal duration of the future existence has, we believe, with all nations formed a constituent element of the doctrine ; though it is so far from being a necessary one, that it is not easy to discover whence its universal adoption is to be traced. To this idea Scripture has added another, which presents a stumbling-block to our moral and our metaphysical philosophy alike—viz., the *unchanging* character of both its pains and pleasures. We attempt in vain to trace in the Gospel the least evidence that the future state is to be regarded as one of *progress*—that its sufferings are to be probationary and purifying, and therefore terminable ; or its joys elevating and improving, and therefore ever advancing. If any doctrine be distinctly taught by Scripture on this point, it clearly is, that the lot of each individual is fixed for ever at the judgment day. In this it stands below some both Pagan and Oriental conceptions. The Gospel view of the eternity of the future life, which fully approves itself

---

[1] See Eugene Aram, chap. viii., for an illustration. A Calvinist peasant considered that the choicest bliss of Heaven would be " to look down into the other place, and see the folk grill." Tertullian has a passage, part of which Gibbon quotes (c. xv.), expressing the same idea in language quite as horrible. We believe there is a similar passage in Baxter's Saints' Rest.

to our reason, is one which it shares with all theories:
its conception of the eternity of future punishments,
in which probably it stands almost alone, is one, the
revolting character of which has been so strongly felt,
that the utmost ingenuity both of criticism and logic,
has been strained for centuries—the first, to prove that
the doctrine is not taught, the second, to prove that it
ought to be received.   Neither have quite succeeded.
It is difficult to maintain that the doctrine is not
taught in Scripture, if the clear language of special
texts is to be taken as our guide; and it was probably
held by the Apostles and the first Christians; and all
the attempts yet made to reconcile the doctrine with
divine justice and mercy are calculated to make us
blush alike for the human heart that can strive to
justify such a creed, and for the human intellect which
can delude itself into a belief that it has succeeded in
such justification.

That would be a great book, and he would be a
great man, that should detect and eliminate the latent
and disfigured truth that lies at the root of every falsehood ever yet believed among men.   In Scripture we
meet with several doctrines which may be considered
as the *approximate formula*, the imperfect, partial,
and inaccurate expression, of certain mighty and
eternal verities.   Thus, the spirituality of Christ's
character and the superhuman excellence of his life,
lie at the bottom of the dogma of the Incarnation;
which was simply "a mistake of the morally for the
physically divine," an idea carnalized into a fact.   In

the same manner, the doctrine of the eternity of future
punishments, false as it must be in its ordinary signification, contains a glimpse of one of the most awful
and indisputable truths ever presented to the human
understanding—viz., the eternal and ineffaceable consequences of our every action, the fact that every word
and every deed produces effects which must, by the
very nature of things, reverberate through all time, so
that the whole of futurity would be different had that
word never been spoken, or that deed enacted.[1]

---

[1] "The pulsations of the air, once set in motion by the human
voice, cease not to exist with the sounds to which they gave rise.
Strong and audible as they may be in the immediate neighbour-
hood of the speaker, and at the immediate moment of utterance,
their quickly-attenuated force soon becomes inaudible to human
ears. But the waves of air thus raised perambulate the earth's
and ocean's surface, and in less than twenty hours every atom of
its atmosphere takes up the altered movement due to that infinitesimal portion of primitive motion which has been conveyed to it
through countless channels, and which must continue to influence
its path throughout its future existence.

"But these aerial pulses, unseen by the keenest eye, unheard by
the acutest ear, unperceived by human senses, are yet demonstrated
to exist by human reason ; and in some few and limited instances,
by calling to our aid the most refined and comprehensive instrument of human thought (mathematical analysis), their courses are
traced, and their intensities measured. . . . . Thus considered,
what a strange chaos is this wide atmosphere we breathe! Every
atom impressed with good and with ill, retains at once the motions
which philosophers and sages have imparted to it, mixed and combined in ten thousand ways with all that is worthless and base.
The air itself is one vast library, on whose pages is for ever written
all that man has ever said or even whispered. There, in their
mutable, but unerring characters, mixed with the earliest as well
as the latest sighs of mortality, stand for ever recorded vows un-

There is therefore a sense in which the eternity of
future punishment may be irrefragably and terribly
true—if that very enhancement of our faculties in a
future life which enables us to perceive and trace the
ineffaceable consequences of our idle words and our
evil deeds, should render our remorse and grief as

---

redeemed, promises unfulfilled, perpetuating, in the united move-
ments of each particle, the testimony of man's changeful will.

" But if the air we breathe is the never-failing historian of the
sentiments we have uttered, earth, air, and ocean, are in like manner the eternal witnesses of the acts we have done. . . . . No
motion impressed by natural causes or by human agency is ever
obliterated. The track of every canoe which has yet disturbed the
surface of the ocean, remains for ever registered in the future moments of all succeeding particles which may occupy its place.

" Whilst the atmosphere we breathe is the ever-living witness
of the sentiments we have uttered, the waters and the more solid
materials of the globe, bear equally enduring testimony of the acts
we have committed. If the Almighty stamped on the brow of the
earliest murderer the visible and indelible mark of his guilt, he
has also established laws by which every succeeding criminal is not
less irrevocably chained to the testimony of his crime ; for every
atom of his mortal frame, through whatever changes its severest
particles may migrate, will still retain, adhering to it through
every combination, some movement derived from that very mus-
cular effort by which the crime itself was perpetrated."—Babbage,
Ninth Bridgewater Treatise, c. ix.

" If we imagine the soul in an after stage of existence, connected
with an organ of hearing so sensitive as to vibrate with motions
of the air, even of infinitesimal force, and if it be still within the
precincts of its ancient abode, all the accumulated words pronounced from the creation of mankind will fall at once on that
ear ; . . . . and the punished offender may hear still vibrating on
his ear the very words uttered perhaps thousands of centuries
before, which at once caused and registered his own condemnation."—*Ibid.* c. xii.

eternal as those consequences themselves. No more fearful punishment to a superior Intelligence can be conceived than to see still in action—with the consciousness that it must continue in action for ever—a cause of wrong put in motion by itself ages before. Let us trust either that our capacities will be too limited for this awful retribution, or that the resources of omnipotence may be adequate to cancel or to veil the Past.

4. It is remarkable that while in the New Testament the delights of Heaven are always depicted as consisting in the exercise and development of the spiritual affections, the pains of Hell are as constantly delineated as *physical*. The joys of the one state are those of the intellect and the Soul; the sufferings of the other those of the body only. In the Gospel pictures, Heaven is "to sit at the right hand of the Father;" Hell is "to burn in unquenchable fire." Unless there be some deep meaning hidden under this apparent inconsistency; unless it be intended to intimate to us that the blessed will be made purely spiritual, and that the damned will be wholly absorbed in their corporeality—an idea which it is difficult to admit; it seems strange that the description of Heaven as consisting in communion with God and with the Just made perfect, should not have suggested the correlative idea that Hell must consist in "living with the Devil and his angels;" in fact, what more horrible conception of it could be formed ?

5. But perhaps the most imperfect and inadmissible

point in the Scriptural conception of the Future
World is that which represents it as divided into two
distinct states, separated by an impassible barrier,
decidedly on one or other side of which the eternal ·
destiny of every one is cast. Such an arrangement, it
is obvious, is incompatible with any but the rudest
idea of righteous retribution, and could only be the
resource of imperfect justice and imperfect power.
For as in this world there is every possible gradation
of virtue and of vice, which run into each other by
the most imperceptible degrees, and are often only
distinguishable by the minutest shade—so in the next
world there must be every possible gradation of reward
and punishment. A trenchant line of demarcation,
which from its nature must be arbitrary, and which
every one who overpasses by a hair's-breadth must
overpass by a great gulph, could only be the invention
of a judge of finite and imperfect capacity, for the
more convenient dispatch of judgment. That, of
two individuals whose degree of virtue is so similar
that the question of precedence can neither be decided
by the keenest human insight, nor expressed by the
finest minutiæ of human language, one should be
rewarded with eternal joy, and the other condemned
to everlasting torment, is assuredly among the rudest
of religious conceptions. Yet, to all appearance, such
is the notion of future retribution held by the New
Testament writers.

The doctrine of a future life has been firmly held in

all ages and by every order of minds. The reasonings ordinarily adduced in proof of this doctrine have
always appeared to me deplorably weak and inconclusive ; so much so as clearly to indicate that they
do not form the grounds on which it has been believed,
but are merely subsequent attempts to justify that
belief. *The creed being there,* human reason, in the
endeavour to account for it, has surrounded it with
props and crutches of every conceivable degree of
weakness ; and these post-dated supports have been
mistaken for the foundation. But they are not so ;
and we must at once distinguish between the conviction and the arguments by which the mind (*erroneously
supposing it to be based on argument, and to need
argument for its justification*) has sought to build it
up. Logic never originated it, logic can never
establish it. All that can properly be called reasoning, *i.e.*, inference deduced from observation, appears
to point the other way. It is remarkable, too, that
while the doctrine is announced with the utmost
clearness and positiveness in the New Testament, all
the attempts there made to bring arguments in its
favour, to prove it logically, or even to establish a
reasonable probability for it, are futile in the extreme.[1]

------

[1] The reasoning ascribed to Jesus (Luke xx. 37)—" Now, that
the dead are raised, even Moses showed at the bush, when he
called the Lord the God of Abraham, and the God of Isaac, and
the God of Jacob ; for he is not a God of the dead, but of the
living "—it is scarcely possible to regard as anything but a verbal
ingenuity. Paul's logic (Romans viii. 16, 17 ; and 1 Thess. iv.

Nature throws no light upon the subject; the phenomena we observe could never have suggested the idea
of a renewed existence beyond the grave ; physiological
science, as far as it speaks at all, distinctly negatives
it. Appearances all testify to the reality and permanence of death ; a fearful onus of proof lies upon
those who contend that these appearances are deceptive.
When we interrogate the vast universe of organization,
we see, not simply life and death, but gradually growing life, and gradually approaching death. After
death, all that we have ever *known* of a man is gone;[1]
all we have ever *seen* of him is dissolved into its com-
ponent elements ; it does not *disappear,* so as to

---

14) is, to say the least of it, feeble and far-fetched. While the
well known passage in 1 Cor. xv. 12-16, is one of the most
marvellous specimens extant of reasoning in a circle. On this see
Newman on the Soul, p. 185 ; Bush's Anastasis, p. 170.

In one point of the view of a future existence there would
appear to be a remarkable coincidence between the notions of the
Pagan philosophers and those of the more enlightened among the
Jews and some of the early Christians. The Ancients seem to
have imagined that only *the Great* would live again ; that the mass
of souls, the οἱ πολλοί, were not worth resuscitating. Thus Tacitus
(Vit. Agr.), " Si quis *piorum* manibus locus, si, ut sapientibus
placet, non cum corpore extinguuntur *magnæ animæ,*" &c. Cicero
de Senect,—" O prœclaram diem, cum ad illud *divinum animorum*
concilium cœtumque proficiscar, &c. See the above passages in
the Epistles. Also Anastasis, 169, 252 ; in Luke xx. 35 ; remarkable impression, " They which shall be accounted worthy," &c.

[1] [A modification of this phrase would seem to be necessary,
"There is one indication of immortality which must not be left
out of consideration, though, of course, its value will be very
differently estimated by different minds. I refer to that
spontaneous, irresistible, and perhaps nearly universal feeling we

leave us at liberty to imagine that it may have gone to exist elsewhere, but is actually used up as materials for other purposes. So completely is this the case that, as Sir James Mackintosh observes, "the doctrine of a resurrection could scarcely have arisen among a people who buried their dead." Moreover, the growth, decay, and dissolution we observe, are, to all appearance, those of the mind as well as the body. We see the mind, the affections, the Soul (if you will), gradually arising, *forming* (for no other expression adequately describes the phenomenon), as the body waxes, sympathizing in all the permanent changes and temporary variations of the body, diseased with its

---

experience on watching, just after death, the body of one we have intimately known; the conviction, I mean, (a sense, a consciousness, an impression *which you have to fight against if you wish to shake it off*,) that the form lying there is somehow *not* the EGO you have loved. It does not produce the effect of that person's personality. You miss the Ego, though you have the frame. The visible Presence only makes more vivid the sense of actual absence. Every feature, every substance, every *phenomenon* is there—and is unchanged. You have seen the eyes as firmly closed, the limbs as motionless, the breath almost as imperceptible, the face as fixed and expressionless, before, in sleep or in trance—without the same peculiar sensation. The impression made is indefinable, and is not the result of any conscious process of thought, that that body, quite unchanged to the eye, IS not, and never was, your friend— the *Being* you were conversant with—that his or her individuality was not the garment before you *plus* a galvanic current; that, in fact, the EGO you knew once, and seek still, *was not that—is not there.* And if not *there*, it must be *elsewhere* or *nowhere*, and ' nowhere,' I believe modern science will not suffer us to predicate of either force or substance that once has been."—*Enigmas of Life, Preface vii.*]

diseases, enfeebled by its weakness, disordered by
dyspepsia or suppressed gout, utterly metamorphosed
past recognition by cerebral affection, hopelessly
deranged by a spicula of bone penetrating the brain,
actually suppressed by a vascular effusion or a cranial
depression, wearied as the body ages, and gradually
sinking into imbecility as the body dies away in helplessness.   The sudden destruction of the corporeal
frame by an accident, at a moment when the MIND
was in its fullest vigour, might possibly suggest the
idea of a transference to other scenes of so manifest an
Entity, so undeniable a Power—the slow and
synchronous extinction of the bodily and mental
faculties never could.   Look, again, at an infant
three years old—two years old—one year old : we
say it has a Soul.   But take a new-born babe, an
hour or a minute old : has *it* a soul, an immortal part
or inmate ?   If so, when does it come to it ? at the
time of its separation from the Mother's life ? or a
moment before, or a moment after ?   Does the awful
decision whether it is to be a mere perishable animal
or a spiritual being depend upon whether it dies an
instant before or an instant after it first sees the light ?
Can the question of its immortality—of its being an
embryo angel, or a senseless clod—hang upon such an
accident as a maternal movement, or a clumsy
accoucheur ?   Inquiries these, our answers to which
can only display either hopeless acquiescence in a
gloomy conclusion, or equally hopeless struggles to
escape from it.

" Admitting all this," urges one reasoner, "the phenomena of life and death, nay, even the doctrine of materialism in all its nakedness, need present no insuperable difficulty ; for the same power which bestowed life is surely competent to restore it under another form and in another scene." Unquestionably ; but if we are material merely—if our inferences from observation are correct—a renewed existence must be a new creation ; where then is our identity ? We are not *continued*, but *succeeded*.[1]

" But," says another speculator, " how can you tell that there is not some unascertained portion of the human frame, infinitesimal, indeed, and evanescent to our senses, which does not perish with the rest of the corporeal fabric, but forms the germ which is expanded into the new existence ? "[2] It may be that there is such ; but no shadow of a probability can be adduced for such an assumption. It is at best only a mode

---

[1] Life of Sir James Mackintosh, ii. 120, 121.

[2] The ancient Jews held the existence of such a nucleus. " They contended that there was an immortal bone in the human body (called by them *ossiculum Luz*) which is the germ of the resurrection-body. This bone, they held, one might burn, boil, bake, pound, bruise, or attempt to bruise, by putting it on the anvil and submitting it to the strokes of the sledge-hammer ; but all in vain. No effect would be produced upon it. It was indestructible—incorruptible—immortal."—Bush's Anastasis, p. 177. The author of the " Physical Theory " seems to imagine that the body contains some imperishable nucleus, or particle, or element, in which soul or life resides; something as imponderable as light, as imperceptible as electricity, which does not perish with the coarser elements of our frame, but assumes a higher life, and collects about it, or evolves, a nobler and subtler organization.

of *conceiving the possibility* of that which, on other grounds, or without grounds, we have decided to believe. It offers no escape from the overwhelming weight of inference drawn from natural appearances.

The philosophical value of the arguments ordinarily adduced to demonstrate the reality, or at least the high probability, of an existence after death, will be variously estimated by different minds. That they possess, accurately speaking, no logical cogency, will be admitted by all candid and competent reasoners ; to us, we confess, they appear lamentably feeble and inadequate.

By some we are told that the soul is immaterial, and that by reason of its immateriality it *cannot* die. How can human beings, professing to have cultivated their understandings, be content to repeat, and rest in, such wretched inanities as these ?—at best but the convulsive flounderings of an intellect out of its depth, deluding itself into the belief that it has grasped an idea, when it has only got hold of a word. That the immaterial must of necessity be immortal seems to us an unmeaning assertion on a matter of which we know absolutely nothing. Of the nature of the Soul, science has taught us, indeed, little—far too little to allow us to decide and dogmatize; but honesty must admit that the little it has taught us all points to an opposite conclusion. Alas ! for the Spirit's immortal trust, if it rested on such scholastic trivialities as these !

Again. Much stress is laid on the inference to be drawn from the general belief of mankind. But this consideration will lose nearly all its force when we reflect how easily, in the fond, tender, self-deceptive weakness of humanity, a belief can grow out of a wish. Regarded from this point of view, the universal belief in a future state is only the natural result of universal love of life. Man, for his preservation, is endowed with an instinctive love of life, an instinctive horror of destruction—an instinct which is strengthened every hour by the manifold joys and interests of existence. The prolongation of this existence becomes a natural desire, which soon ripens into a passion; in earlier times the possibility of a deathless existence *upon earth* was, we know, the dream, the hope, the pursuit of many; but as accumulated experience speedily dissipated this form of the longings of nature, and compelled men to transfer their aspirations to the other side of the grave, the notion of an invisible futurity arose. The first natural desire was for an earthly immortality; out of the reluctantly acknowledged impossibility of realizing this may have sprung the glorious conception of a heavenly existence. If this view of the genesis of the Universal Creed be correct, the argument drawn from it falls to the ground; since the fact of our desire for any blessing, even when that desire has grown into a conviction, can offer no proof that it will be bestowed.

It is true that now, thousands who have no wish for a prolonged existence upon earth, yet long for and believe in a future life elsewhere. But this is the result partly of a conviction that the weariness and decay of both physical and moral powers would make

II.   R

continued life here a penalty and not a blessing, and partly of a desire for those higher capacities and nobler pursuits which they anticipate hereafter. The origin of the aspiration still remains the same: it is the desire for a happy existence *after their conceptions of happiness;* and they transfer the scene of it to heaven, because they do not see how these conceptions could be realised on earth, *i.e.,* under the ordinary conditions of humanity.

It will be urged that the belief is strongest in the most spiritual and religious minds, that is, in those which dwell most constantly on unseen and superhuman realities. This is true: and we cannot venture to say that to such minds, raised and purified by heavenly contemplations, may not be given a deeper insight into divine truths than can be attained by those occupied with the things of earth and time. Still the fact will admit of another and more simple explanation; since it is a well-known law of our intellectual constitution that topics and scenes on which the mind habitually and intently dwells, acquire, *ipso facto,* an increasing degree of reality and permanence in our mental vision, out of all proportion to their certainty or actuality. There is no fancy, however baseless— no picture, however shadowy and unreal—to which constant and exclusive contemplation will not impart a consistence, substance, and tenacity, sufficient to render it unassailable by reason, by experience, and almost by the information of the senses. And it cannot be doubted that, however inadequate were the original grounds for the belief in a future state, yet when once it was assumed as an article of faith, daily meditation would soon inevitably confer upon it a firmness and solidity with which the most demonstrable truths of exact science would compete in vain.

Much, and as it appears to us undeserved, stress is laid on the argument derived from the unequal, and apparently unjust, apportionment of human lots. A future life, it is said, is needed to redress the inequalities of this. But it is evident that this argument proceeds upon two assumptions, one of which is clearly untenable, and the other at least questionable. It assumes that the Presiding Deity is *bound* to allot an equal portion of good to all his creatures; that to permit the condition of one human being to be happier than that of another, is to perpetrate an injustice, —a position for which it is difficult to imagine any rational defence, and which must probably be assigned to the unconscious operation of one of the least worthy passions of our nature—envy. What possible law can that be which shall make it *the duty* of Him who confers his unpurchased gifts " with a mysterious and uncontrollable sovereignty " to mete out to every being an equal proportion of his boons ? The very statement of the proposition confutes it. All that the creature can demand from the justice and the love of his Creator, is that he shall not be created for wretchedness—that on the average of his career, happiness shall predominate over misery—that existence shall, on the whole, have been a blessing—or, what perhaps is the same thing, that it shall be fairly attributable to the voluntary fault—the option—of the individual, if it be not so. Now, without going so far as to assert that there are not, and never have been, exceptions to the general fact that life presents to all a preponderating average of enjoyment, we may well question whether there are such; we are sure they must be incalculably few; and it is to these exceptional cases only that the argument can have any application.

But are human lots as unequal in the amount of happiness they confer as at first sight would appear? It is generally acknowledged that they are not. Without wishing to maintain even an apparent paradox; without arguing that the aggregate balance of enjoyment may not at the end of life be widely different with the cultivated and the brutish—the intellectual and the sensual—the obtuse and the sensitive—the man who has never known a day's sickness, and the man who has never known a day's health—the savage who lives beset with perils and privations, and the noble who lives embosomed in peace and luxury—the wretched pauper, and the wealthy millionaire—the man on whom fortune always smiles, and the man on whom she always frowns—the man whose children are a glory and a blessing, and him to whom they are a plague and a reproach—the man who is hated, and the man who is loved—the man whose life is a ceaseless struggle, and the man whose life is an unbroken sleep ;—it is not to be denied that every fresh insight we obtain into the secrets of each man's lot, equalizes them more and more ; discovers undreamed-of compensations for good and for evil ; discloses a vigorous spirit of enjoyment among the most obviously unfortunate, and a dark cloud of care brooding over the prosperous, which go far to rectify our first hasty judgment of the inequality of their condition. The inner life of every man is hidden from his fellows by a thick veil : whenever accident draws this partially aside, are we not invariably amazed at the unexpected incongruities it lays bare ? Are we not on such occasions made aware that we are habitually forming the most egregiously mistaken estimates of the essential condition of those around us ? For myself I can truly say that whenever circumstance has made me intimately acquainted with the deeper secrets of my fellow-men, I have been utterly confounded at the unlooked-for nature of the revelations. Among the lowest I have found " seeds of almost impossible good ; " among the most virtuous in appearance (and in some respects in reality), guilt or frailty that scarcely any evidence could make credible ; among the most wretched in outward condition, either strange insensibility to suffering, or an inextinguishable spirit of delight ; among the most favoured of the children of fortune, some inchoate, or acted, tragedy hanging like a black thunder-cloud over their path.

Compensation is the great law everywhere inscribed on the procedures of Nature. It prevails likewise

over human destinies even in this life, not perhaps—
not probably—altogether to the extent of equalization,
but to an extent that certainly approaches nearer and
nearer to this point, the wider our knowledge and the
deeper our meditation.[1]   Still, I do not wish to push
this argument too far : I merely wish to show how invalid a foundation it must be for such a superstructure
as we build upon it.

"But the ideal of moral retribution (we are told)
necessitates a future state.   God is a righteous Judge,
who will recompense virtue and punish sin.   In this
life virtue, we know, often goes without its reward,
and vice without its punishment :—there must therefore be a future life in which these respectively await
them."   Such is the syllogism on which reason most
relies for the establishment of the Great Tenet.   I do
not dispute the conclusion :—I question the soundness
of the premisses.

---

[1] The class whose destiny is by far the most perplexing to the
thinker, is that whose element, whose atmosphere, whose almost
necessary condition, we may say, is that of vice ; *classes danger-
euses* of large towns, who are born and bred in squalor and iniquity,
and never have a chance afforded them to rise out of it.   Their intellect and moral sense are seldom sufficiently developed to afford
them the compensation these bring to others.   The apparently
hopeless, objectless, noxious existence of these beings, and their
fearful power of mischief and of multiplication, have always been,
and still remain to me, " God's most disturbing mystery."   Still
we do not know that, on the whole, even they are miserable.   If,
however, they are, *it would rather drive us to the startling conclusion
that those have most claim on a future life who are least fit for it—*
that the least intellectual, the least moral, the least spiritual of the
species, are the surest denizens of Heaven !

It is evident that the whole cogency of the above syllogism depends upon the correctness of the assumption that virtue and vice are not equitably recompensed in this life. It assumes, *first*, that we can read the heart and the circumstances, and see where virtue and vice—merit and demerit—really lie ;—and, *secondly*, that we can look into the lot, and discern where there is, or is not, retribution ;—that guilt and innocence are what we deem such, and that Nemesis executes no sentences but such as meet our eye. Alas ! for the argument that rests on two postulates so disputable as these.

What do we know—what can we predicate—of the sinfulness of any fellow-creature ? Can we say, " this man is more guilty than that ? " or even, " this man is very wicked ? " We may, indeed, be able to say, " this man has lied, has pilfered, has forged; and that man has apparently gone through life with clean hands." But can we say that the first has not struggled long, though unsuccessfully, against temptations under which the second would have succumbed without an effort ? We can say which has the cleanest hands before man ;—can we say which has the cleanest soul before God ? We may be able to say, " this man has committed adultery, and that man has never been guilty of unchastity ; "—but can we tell that the innocence of the one may not have been due to the coldness of his heart—to the absence of a motive— to the presence of a fear ? And that the fall of the other may not have been preceded by the most vehement self-contest—caused by the most over-mastering phrenzy—and atoned for by the most hallowing repentance ?　We know that one man is generous and open-handed, and another close, niggardly and stern ; but we do not know that the generosity of the one as well as the niggardliness of the other, may not be a mere yielding to native temperament.　In the eye of Heaven, a long life of beneficence in the one may have cost less exertion, and may indicate less virtue, than a few rare hidden acts of kindness wrung by duty out of the reluctant and unsympathizing nature of the other.　There may be more real merit—more self-sacrificing effort—more of the noblest struggles of moral grandeur in a life of failure, sin, and shame, than in a career, to our eyes, of stainless integrity. " God seeth not as man seeth."　Let this be a consoling thought to the sinner who, black as he may be before the world, has yet contrived to keep some little light burning in his own soul ;—a humbling and a warning thought to many who now walk proudly in the sunshine of immaculate fame.

But *do* we know even the outside life of men ?　Are we competent to pronounce even on their *deeds ?*　Do we know half the acts of wickedness or of virtue even of our most immediate fellows ?　Can we say with any certainty, even of our nearest friend, " this man has, or has not, committed such a sin—broken such a commandment ? "　Let each man ask his own heart.　Of how many of our best and of our worst acts and qualities are our most intimate associates utterly unconscious? How many virtues does the world give us credit for that we do not possess? How small a portion of our evil deeds and thoughts ever come to light? Even of our few redeeming goodnesses, how large a portion is known to God only! Truly, we walk in a vain show![1]

When we see one whom we know only as a good man overtaken by a strange calamity, we call it a perplexing dispensation. But in the secret recesses of that man's heart, perhaps, how well does he feel to have deserved it, nay, often, how precisely can he trace back the open suffering to the secret sin! Sorrow and darkness come upon us; and the World pities us and says, "Poor man! he has little deserved such a fate." But *we* know that if the world knew us as we know ourselves, it would deem such fate far too light a chastisement for our iniquities. If it be so with

---

[1] " Or what if Heaven for once its searching light
     Sent to some partial eye, disclosing all
   The rude, bad thoughts, that in our bosom's night
     Wander at large, nor heed Love's gentle thrall;

" Who would not shun the dreary uncouth place?
     As if, fond leaning where her infant slept,
   A mother's arm a serpent should embrace;
     So might we friendless live, and die unwept.

" Then keep the softening veil in mercy drawn,
     Thou who canst love us, though Thou read us true."
                                    Keble's Christian Year.

ourselves, may it not be so with others ?   Men accustomed to self-study, and honest with themselves, often
think their prosperity unmerited ; rarely indeed do
they think their calamities heavier than their demerits;
—though they may be often at a loss—though it may
often be impossible—to trace the connection between
them.

We are wholly in the dark, then, as to what retribution is *deserved :*—we are equally in the dark as to
what retribution is *awarded.*   We could not tell, if it
were left to us, where to reward and where to punish:
—neither can we tell where reward and punishment
now actually fall, nor in what proportion.   The retribution may be in a man's heart or in his lot.   In the
one case we see it not at all—in the other we see it
very imperfectly.   But it is probable that could we
see even half the retribution that takes place in life,
the argument we are considering would never have
arisen.   In the weary satiety of the idle—in the
healthy energy of honest labour ;—in the irritable
temper of the selfish—in the serene peace of the
benevolent ;—in the startling tortures of the Soul
where the passions have the mastery—in the calm
Elysium which succeeds their subjugation ;—may be
traced materials of retribution sufficient to satisfy the
severest justice.   Deeds and states of mind are their
own avengers.   The consequence of an act is its reward or punishment.   Our actions in the long run
carry their own retribution along with them.   If it

were not ᷈o, the arrangements of nature would be at fault.[1]

" What did the preacher mean by assuming that judgment is not executed in this world ; by saying that the wicked are successful, and the good are miserable, in the present life ? Was it that houses and lands, offices, wine, horses, dress, luxury, are had by unprincipled men, whilst the saints are poor and despised ; and that a compensation is to be made to these last hereafter, by giving them the like gratifications another day—bank stock and doubloons, venison and champagne ? This must be the compensation intended, for what else ? Is it that they are to have leave to pray and praise ? to love and serve men ? why, they can do these now. The legitimate inference the disciple would draw, was, ' We are to have *such* a good time as the sinners have now ;'—or, to push it to its extreme import, ' You sin now ; we shall sin by-and-by ; we would sin now if we could ; —not being successful, we expect our revenge to-morrow.'

" The fallacy lay in the immense concession that

---

[1] " Men call the circumstance the retribution. The casual retribution is in the thing, and is seen by the Soul. The retribution in the circumstance is seen by the understanding ; it is inseparable from the thing, but is often spread over a long time, and so does not become distinct for many years. The specific stripes may follow late after the offence, but they follow because they accompany it. Crime and punishment grow out of one stem. Punishment is a fruit that, unsuspected, ripens within the flower of the pleasure that concealed it."—*Emerson*, Essay iii.

the bad are successful, that justice is not done now. The blindness of the preacher consisted in deferring to the base estimate of the market of what constitutes a manly success, instead of confronting and convicting the world from the truth ; announcing the presence of the Soul ; the omnipotence of the will, and so establishing the standard of good and ill, of success and falsehood, and summoning the dead to its present tribunal." [1]

Our false view of the whole subject arises from the hold still possessed over our minds by the old Jewish notion, that the good things of this life are the fitting and the promised recompense of virtue,—that virtue and prosperity, vice and poverty, are linked together by the decrees of divine justice. This unacknowledged fallacy lies at the root of much of our disappointment, and much of our surprise and perplexity at the dispensations of Providence. There is much sound wisdom on this subject in Mrs Barbauld's Essay on " Inconsistency in our Expectations ;" still more perhaps in Pope's " Essay on Man." [2]

Much reliance is placed upon the assertion that

---

[1] Emerson's Essay on Compensation.

[2] " But is it not some reproach on the economy of Providence that such a one, who is a mean, dirty fellow, should have amassed wealth enough to buy half a nation? Not in the least. He made himself a mean, dirty fellow for that very end. He has paid his health, his conscience, his liberty for it ; and will you envy him his bargain ? "—*Barbauld*, i. 187.

" But sometimes Virtue starves, while Vice is fed :
What then ? *Is the reward of Virtue bread!*

Man possesses faculties which can find no fitting aliment, and can attain no adequate development, on earth ; and which, therefore, are supposed to indicate the necessity of a future scene for their perfection. Many of our powers, we are told, do not ripen till the close of life ; and reach their acme just as the approach of death renders them, if this life be all, of no further use to us. It is contradictory to all the analogies of nature, it is said, to imagine that Providence has bestowed any capacities or desires for which an appropriate scope and object have not been appointed. I confess I do not appreciate the force of this argument; it appears to me as if its setters-forth had satisfied themselves too easily with mere words. It is not true that our powers—our active powers at least—whether physical or intellectual, reach their highest development as life draws to a close. On the contrary, they commonly attain their height in middle life, and gradually weaken and decay as age creeps over the frame. Wisdom, indeed, may be said in well-constituted minds to increase to the end of life ; but wisdom is but the accumulated inference from our experience and our reflection, and will naturally

---

That, Vice may merit ; 'tis the price of toil ;
The knave deserves it when he tills the soil.
The good man may be weak, be indolent ;
Nor is his claim to plenty, but content.
What nothing earthly gives, or can destroy,
The Soul's calm sunshine, and the heartfelt joy,
Is Virtue's prize."

Pope, Essay iv.

augment with the perpetual increase of its materials. But memory, imagination, the power of acquisition, the power of intellectual creation, unquestionably do not continue to ripen and strengthen after maturity is passed. Nor is it easy to discover what those faculties are, for which this earth may not afford a fitting field and ample occupation. Love, Hope, Fancy, are probably the noblest endowments of man's moral Being. Cannot Love—even in its richest profusion and its tenderest refinements—find adequate exercise amid the varied relations of our mortal existence, in soothing sorrow, in conferring good, in brightening all the dark passages of life, and turning earth into an anticipated Paradise ? Will any one who has once loved a fellow-creature with all the passionate energy of an earnest soul, or who has once melted into rapture with genuine gratitude to the God who has bestowed such happiness, dare to say that Love finds no ample development, and reaps no teeming harvest *here* ? And Hope ;—is not hope the spring of all exertion—the origin of all progress—the conferrer of all strength—along the toilsome and dusty pathways of the world ? And can it find no worthy object in the dream of what Humanity, through the efforts which it stimulates and rewards, may yet become ? And is Imagination entitled to complain of the narrow field in which it is permitted to expatiate, because Time and Space are the allotted limits of its range, so long as it has the mighty possibilities of human destiny

before it, and Suns and Systems, and Firmaments—
countless, infinite, inscrutable—above it ?

" But (it is said) the character, at least, continues
growing till the end of life, and many of our best
virtues are the fruit only of the discipline of Life,
especially humility, forbearance, resignation, and con-
tentment. Shall then existence terminate just when
the human being is most fitted to appreciate it, to
understand it, to fulfil its aims ? Is its success to be
the signal for its extinction ? Is supreme excellence
to be achieved only to be eclipsed for ever ? Is our
goal to be our grave ? " I feel the weight of these
considerations, and have nothing to urge against
them.

But in truth all these arguments we have been
considering are to be taken, not so much as proofs of
the doctrine of a future life, as proofs of man's resolu-
tion to hold that doctrine. They are inadequate to
demonstrate its soundness ; but amply sufficient to
show that *the belief being in man's mind,* he knows
not how nor whence, he is determined to maintain
it, curious to account for it, anxious to justify it.
Erroneously conceiving that it must be a product of
reason, he diligently looks about to discover the
logical processes which have generated it ; and clings
to the shallowest crudities rather than surrender (as
he conceives) the title-deeds of his faith.

The truth we believe to be, that a future existence
is, and must be, a matter of *information* or *intuition*
not of *inference.* The intellect may imagine it, but

could never have *discovered* it, and can never prove
it—the Soul must have revealed it ; must, and does,
perpetually reveal it. It is a matter which comes
properly within the cognizance of the Soul [1]—of that
spiritual sense, to which on such topics we must look
for information, as we look to our bodily senses for
information touching the things of earth—things that
lie within their province. We never dream of doubting what *they* tell us of the external world, though a
Berkeley should show us that their teaching is at
variance with, or indefensible by logic. We therefore
at once cut the Gordian knot by conceding to the
Soul the privilege of instructing us as to the things of
itself ;—we apply to the spiritual sense for information on spiritual things. We believe that there is no
other solution of the question. To the man who dis-
believes the Soul's existence, this will of course appear

---

[1] " That a purely *historical* is as unsatisfactory as a metaphysical basis for a spiritual doctrine is obvious ; indeed Paul gives
us clearly to understand that the future hopes of the soul were to
be discerned by the soul itself, for itself ; and did not depend upon
man's wisdom, as a question of history does and must. . . . Paul
may have had more of direct insight into this deepest of subjects
than the passages quoted denote : God forbid that I should pre-
sumptuously limit the insight enjoyed by his most favoured servants. Yet his light does us little or no good, while it is a light
outside of us ; so long we are depending on the soundness of
Paul's faculties. If he in any way confused the conclusions of his
logic (which is often extremely inconsequent and mistaken) with
the perceptions of his divinely-illuminated soul, our belief might
prove baseless. Faith by proxy is really no faith at all, and certainly is not what Paul would have ever recommended."—*Newman
on the Soul*, pp. 187-9.

an unwarrantable and illogical admission. To him the Soul has not spoken. My sources of information are unavailable to him. *My* soul can tell *him* nothing. Providence has denied to him a *sense* which has been granted to me ; and all the knowledge which comes to me through the avenues of that sense must seem foolishness to him.

The only occasions on which a shade of doubt has passed over my conviction of a future existence, have been when I have rashly endeavoured to make out a case, to give a reason for the faith that is in me, to assign ostensible and logical grounds for my belief. At such times, and still more when I have heard others attempting to prove the existence of a future world by arguments which could satisfy no one by whom arguments were needed, I confess that a chill dismay has often struck into my heart, and a fluctuating darkness has lowered down upon my creed, to be dissipated only when I had again left inference and induction far behind, and once more suffered the Soul to take counsel with itself.

This appears to me the only foundation on which the belief in a future life can legitimately rest, to those who do not accept a miraculous external revelation. *Et tibi magna satis.* It is a belief anterior to reasoning, independent of reasoning, unproveable by reasoning ; and yet *as no logic can demonstrate its unsoundness,* or can bring more than negative evidence to oppose to it—I can hold it with a simplicity, a tenacity, an undoubting faith, which is never

II.   S

granted to the conclusions of the understanding. *" Ld, où finit le raisonnement, commence la veritable certitude."* It is a kind provision in man's moral nature that he is not made dependent on the tardy, imperfect, fallible, and halting processes of logic, for any convictions necessary either to happiness or action.[1] These are all instinctive, primary, intuitive. Reason examines them, combines them, confirms them, questions them ; but there they remain, heedless alike

---

[1] " There are instances of common convictions—firm ones too —which you cannot put to proof in a logical form. There is our reliance on *permanency of the laws of Nature.* One of the ablest reasoners, and with no bias towards Christianity, or any particular form of religion in his mind, has found himself unable to account for this reliance but by terming it a human instinct, something analogous to the instincts of animals. That the Sun rose to-day is no logical proof that he will rise to-morrow. That the grain grew last year does not argue, by a syllogistic deduction, that it will grow next year. Yet where is there a confidence stronger than this ?—where a belief more firm ? Our conviction of *the reality of external nature* is another instance of the same description. That, too, baffles the logician. You cannot show that there is matter, or existence at all, beyond yourself ; and yet you believe it, rely upon it, act upon it. It may all be only impression on our consciousness. The Berkeleian can dispose of the whole material universe in this way with the greatest ease. There may be no stars shining in Heaven, no trees growing in the forest—all may be but sensation, thought, in us : still, who does not rest upon, who does not act upon, the reality of something which is out of us, with an assurance as strong as that of our belief in our own existence ? Those who require direct agencies of demonstration in such matters as these—who contend that belief and the logical form of proof have an inseparable union — must find their way out of this dilemma as well as they can."—*Fox*, On the Religious Ideas, p. 20.

of her patronage or her hostility ;—" asking no leave to shine of our terrestrial star."

It is an immense advantage gained, when we have discovered and decided that it is not from the logical faculty that our knowledge on spiritual topics is to be gained. We can then afford to be honest—to give reason and analysis fair play—to shrink from no conclusion, however unwelcome to our speculations, which they may force upon us ; for after they have done all they can to correct, to negative, to ascertain, we feel that their function is critical merely—*that our light comes to us from elsewhere.*

There are three points especially of religious belief, regarding which intuition (or instinct) and logic are at variance—the efficacy of prayer, man's free-will, and a future existence. If believed, they must be believed, the last without the countenance, the two former in spite of the hostility, of logic. Hence the belief in them is most resolute, and undoubting the nearer men and nations approach to the *instinctive condition.*[1] Savages never doubt them; sufferers

---

[1] This is the idea that lies at the root of Wordsworth's sublimest poem—The Ode on the Intimations of Immortality.

" Heaven lies about us in our infancy !
Shades of the prison-house begin to close
    Upon the growing boy,
But he beholds the light, and whence it flows,
    He sees it in his joy ;
The youth who daily further from the East
Must travel, still is Nature's Priest,
And by the vision splendid
Is on his way attended ;

never doubt them; men in the excitement of vehement action never doubt them. It is the quiet, even tenour of comfortable and refined existence—it is the fireside, the library, the arm-chair that doubt, that question, that speak of darkness, that ask for proofs.

We have already intimated that we think it questionable whether the doctrine of a future life has been of that practical service to mankind, either in kind or degree which is commonly assumed. Of its inestimable value, as a consolation to the sorrowing, as a hope to the aspiring, as a rest to the weary and heavy-laden, it is not easy to speak in language strong enough for the occasion. But we incline to doubt whether it exercises much influence on the actual morals of mankind at large—whether, except in isolated instances, the expectation of future retribution operates strongly to deter from crime or to stimulate to virtue.[1] And, as we said in the last section, it is

At length the Man perceives it die away
And fade into the light of common day."
* * * * *
"Mighty Prophet! Seer blest!
On whom those truths do rest,
Which we are toiling all our lives to find,
In darkness lost, the darkness of the grave;
Thou, over whom thine immortality
Broods like the day, a Master o'er a Slave,
A Presence which is not to be put by;
Thou little child!"

[1] "Such remarks, I fear, may be felt as exceedingly painful by those who are accustomed to regard a fixed logical dogma on this

more than doubtful whether the happiness and social progress of mankind has not rather been retarded than promoted by the doctrine.

But as to the deep paramount interest of the doctrine to every believer, there can be no difference of opinion. Speculation as to the nature of that strange and new existence, and as to the influence which our proceedings *here* may exert upon . our position *there*, cannot fail to engross much of the thoughts of the serious mind. On this latter point the philosophical Theist and the mere Biblical Christian differ less than either is willing to assume. Both believe that actually, and by *some* operation, the condition of the Soul on earth must determine at least the outset of its future destiny. The Christian conceives that, by a formal decree of the Most High, the virtuous Soul will be assigned to happiness, and the vicious Soul to misery. The Theist conceives that this precise allotment will result from the, very nature of the Soul itself. The Christian believes that, as each Soul appears before its Maker, it will receive

---

subject to be of first-rate importance, and even of necessity; but a little reflection as to the high tone of spiritual elevation maintained by the Hebrew bards ought to suffice to show that that 'necessity' is extremely exaggerated. But this is not all. Need we ask what sort of influence the current views exert over the irreligious? Are they less profane for the dreadful doctrine of an eternal Hell? . . . . That a firm belief of immortality, *arising out of insight* ᴜust have very energetic force, I regard as an axiom; but as an ᴄ⊥ᴋₗₙₐₗ dogma, I cannot but think that its efficacy is prodigiously over-rated."—*Newman on the Soul.*

from His lips the dread sentence which will fix it for
ever on one side or other of that great gulph which
separates the space where He *is* from the space where
He is *not.* The Theist believes that the quickened
perceptions, the intensified faculties, the unclouded
vision, which we imagine as proper to the disembodied
spirit, will constitute its sure Heaven or its inevitable
Hell.   The one creed is, that the pure, the loving, the
aspiring Soul, *must* be happy ; and that the grovelling,
the tarnished, the malignant Soul, *cannot* be so.   The
other creed is, that God will pronounce to them this
irreversible fiat at the last great day.

We cannot agree with those who say that Earth can
give us no conception, no foretaste, of the felicities of
Heaven. How then can we affect honestly to desire it?
If we could not conceive of it, how could we long for
it ?   And how can we conceive of it, but from the
basis of experienced feelings ?   " What can we reason
but from what we know ?"   Why should we regard
this life as so wretched and unworthy that the happiness of Heaven must necessarily be composed of
distinct ingredients from the happiness of Earth ?
God made it too.

That something will yet remain to be superadded—
something entirely new—in that future existence, I
can well believe.   Though God will be—can be—no
nearer to us there than here—yet as our perceptions
of his presence will be clearer, and our insight into
his nature incalculably deeper, it may be that at length

—when the course of those endless gradations of progress through which our spiritual faculties will attain
their full development, we shall have begun to know
Him with something of the same cognizance with
which we know our fellow-creatures here—we shall
learn so to love Him, that that love will absorb into
itself all the other constituents of the Beatific Life.
But I can conceive of this only as the result of the
most ultimate and Seraphic knowledge: to expect it
soon, or to affect it here, seems to me equally irrational
and insincere.

It is unreasonable to expect so entire a change in
the character of the Soul, by the mere event of death,
as would entitle it, or enable it to enter at once on
the enjoyment of supreme felicity. With the shuffling
off this mortal coil, we may indeed hope to lay down
at once and for ever all those temptations with which
in this life the senses beset the soul, all that physical
weakness which has clogged and bounded the exertions
of the intellect, all that obscurity with which our
material nature has too often clouded our moral vision.
But that the Spirit which has been angry, narrow, or
infirm *here*, should suddenly become large, strong, and
placid *there*, is a miracle which the analogies of God's
workings give us no ground to anticipate. We believe
that according to the goal which each soul has
reached on earth, will be its starting-point in Heaven
—that, through long ages of self-elaborating effort, it
must win its way up nourer and nearer to the Throne

of God—and that occupation can never fail, nor
interest ever flag, even through everlasting being;
for, infinite as may be its duration, will it not be sur-
passed by the infinitude of the created .universe?
When we reflect that during a life of seventy years,
the wisest of the sons of men, though aided by all the
knowledge that preceding generations have bequeathed
to them, can penetrate only an insignificant portion of
the wonders of this little earth, we need not fear that
Eternity will exhaust the contemplations of him to
whom will lie open, not only the systems and firmaments we read of and can dimly see, but that larger,
remoter, more illimitable universe which we cannot
even dream of here.

"But the punishments of the next World?" we
hear it asked. Well! is our imagination so poor and
barren that we can conceive of no adequate and ample
ones, without having recourse to the figures of the
worm that dieth not, and the fire that is not quenched?
Must not a future world in itself—the condition of
" spiritual corporeity" alone—bring with it dreadful
retribution to the wicked, the selfish, and the weak?
In the mere fact of their *cleared perceptions*, in the
realization of their low position, in seeing themselves
at length as they really are, in feeling that all their
work *is yet to do*, in beholding all those they loved
and venerated far before them, away from them, fading
in the bright distance, may lie, must lie, a torture, a
purifying fire, in comparison with which the representa-

tions of Dante and Milton shrivel into tameness and
inadequacy. To the base, the sensual, the hard, who
have no notion of a mental torment, translate these, if
you will, by the image of a quenchless flame and a
sulphurous lake ; but seek not to embody such coarse
and earthly conceptions in the theology of better
natures.

TURNBULL AND SPEARS, PRINTERS EDINBURGH.

9 783337 167578